Excel University:
Featuring Excel 2013 for Windows Microsoft Excel Training for CPAs and Accounting Professionals

VOLUME 4

A walk-through of the Excel® features, functions, and techniques that improve the productivity of accountants.

During his live CPE training sessions, Jeff Lenning, CPA CITP, has shown thousands of CPAs and accounting professionals across the country how to use Excel more effectively and leverage its power to improve efficiency and reduce the time it takes to complete job tasks. This series of books is a comprehensive collection of the features, functions, and techniques that directly benefit accountants working in industry, public practice, consulting, and the nonprofit sector. Each book in the Excel University series includes narrative, screenshots, Excel practice files, and video content. This series uses a hands-on approach to learning and provides practice files and exercises that demonstrate the practical application of the items presented in each chapter.

JEFF LENNING CPA
EXCEL UNIVERSITY, INC.

Excel University—Volume 4
By: Jeff Lenning, CPA CITP
Version: 2.0

About the Author

In his live CPE training sessions, Jeff Lenning, CPA CITP, has shown thousands of CPAs and accounting professionals across the country how to use Excel to streamline their work and become more efficient. His Excel articles have been featured in several publications, including the *Journal of Accountancy* and *California CPA Magazine*. Jeff graduated from the University of Southern California.

EXCEL UNIVERSITY RESOURCES

EXCEL UNIVERSITY WEBSITE

✓ *excel-university.com*

EXCEL UNIVERSITY VIDEO LIBRARY

✓ *excel-university.com / videos*

EXCEL UNIVERSITY DOWNLOAD LIBRARY

✓ *excel-university.com / downloads*

EXCEL UNIVERSITY BLOG

✓ *excel-university.com / blog*

INTERACTIVE ONLINE TRAINING VERSION OF THIS VOLUME

✓ *excel-university.com / training*

Contents at a Glance

Table of Contents

OPENING INFORMATION

Excel is my favorite computer application of all time.
My goal is to help you maximize its power.

Chapter 1: Overview

WELCOME BACK!

I'm so glad you've decided to continue on to the next volume in the Excel University series. In Volume 1 we covered the foundations of Excel, in Volume 2 we learned about formula-based reports, and in Volume 3 we took a close look at PivotTables. Now, in Volume 4, we explore numerous features, functions, and techniques that will help you build reliable workpapers in Excel.

We've built many reports together and discovered how to use Excel to streamline reporting tasks. In this volume, we focus on Excel's features for making workpapers more efficient and bulletproof. I use the term *workpaper* broadly to describe the kinds of workbooks that we build to calculate numbers, analyze data, prepare journal entries, track information, and so on. These workbooks take various forms and are known by names such as schedule, journal, worksheet, reconciliation, statement, working paper, ledger, analysis, spreadsheet, register, and log.

For our purposes here, a workpaper is a document primarily intended for our own use, while a report is primarily intended to deliver information to others. Sometimes an Excel workbook can serve both as a workpaper and a report, helping us compute values and communicate the results with others. For now we'll stick with the simple idea that a workpaper is primarily designed for internal use, while a report is primarily designed for external use.

This volume is presented in four parts: Features, Functions, Techniques, and Applications. We get warmed up by exploring several handy Excel features. Then we add some functions to our toolbox so that we can pick the right one for the task at hand. Next we implement techniques that combine many of the features and functions explored during the Excel University series so far. Finally, we apply our Excel skills to several common accounting tasks and build some really fun, technical workbooks.

The things you'll learn in this volume will help streamline your work so you'll be more productive and get your work done faster!

BOOK CONVENTIONS

Let's quickly review the conventions used throughout the Excel University series.

REFERENCES

The following references are used in the series:

 **XREF**—a cross-reference to a related or complementary item

NOTE—a general note about the item being presented

KB—the keyboard shortcut or shortcuts used to perform the task

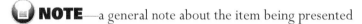 **PRACTICE**—a reference to the exercise workbook and worksheet

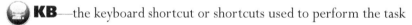 **VIDEO**—a reference to the related video content

STYLE CONVENTIONS

Formulas are presented in monospaced font, as follows:

```
=SUM(A1:A10)
```

Any additional information about the formula or function is explained immediately after the formula.

FORMULA EVALUATION SEQUENCES

Formula evaluation sequences illustrate the logical steps of a formula. The idea is that the same formula is repeated on many lines, with a portion of the formula evaluated on each line. I underline a portion of the formula in question, show the evaluated result on the next line, and so on. For example, assuming *A1* has a stored value of 100 and *B1* has a stored value of 150, a sample formula evaluation sequence would show as follows:

```
=IF(A1=B1,"OK",B1-A1)

=IF(FALSE,"OK",B1-A1)

=IF(FALSE,"OK",150-100)

=IF(FALSE,"OK",50)

=50
```

 NOTE

Evaluation sequences are for illustration purposes and are not necessarily the same steps used by Excel's calculation engine.

CHAPTER STRUCTURE

In general, the chapters that follow contain these sections:

- Set Up—provides an overview and highlights the benefits and uses
- How To—details how to implement the feature or function
- Examples—suggests hands-on exercises that illustrate an application of the feature or function

CORRECTIONS AND SUGGESTIONS

If you have any suggestions or find any errors, please let me know by sending a note to info@excel-university.com.

EXCEL CONVENTIONS

Throughout this text, I refer to navigation through the Ribbon user interface (UI) as follows:

- Ribbon Tab Name > Button Name

EXCEL VERSIONS

The screenshots in this volume were captured with Microsoft Excel 2013 for Windows. Not all features and functions discussed in this text are available in older versions of Excel. Additionally, some items presented in this text may not be available in Excel running on other platforms, such as Mac, tablet, or web.

HOW TO MAKE THE MOST

To make the most of our time together and maximize the benefits of working through the Excel University series, you'll want to be sure to download the sample Excel files and reference the Video Library as needed. Let's briefly dig into the details.

WORKBOOK DOWNLOAD

In my opinion, the best way to learn Excel is through hands-on experience, and I have provided sample Excel workbooks you can use to gain that experience. Each workbook has a worksheet named *Start Here*, which lists each exercise. The exercise sheets are incomplete. You will complete the exercises by writing a formula or using a feature. These workbooks aren't provided as a reference—rather, they are designed for you to gain firsthand experience working with Excel. The exercises attempt to demonstrate the application of each feature and function in a relevant and practical way. You can download the workbooks from the following URL:

www.excel-university.com/downloads

Answers Version

You'll notice that there are essentially two versions of each workbook:

- The exercise version is referenced by name in this text and provides space to write the formulas and otherwise complete various exercises included in the workbook.

- The answers version is denoted with *_answers* appended to the workbook name and contains the completed exercises.

Extra Credit

Some exercise workbooks have Extra Credit worksheets. The sheets named Exercise are demonstrated in this text, while the Extra Credit worksheets carry the feature beyond what is presented, providing additional examples and illustrations. The answers for the Extra Credit exercises are included in the answers version of each workbook.

VIDEO LIBRARY

While I did my best to write narrative text that thoroughly explains each topic, sometimes a video can be more effective. The Excel University Video Library provides solutions to all exercises in video format and can be referenced as you work through the book at the following URL:

www.excel-university/videos

MY FAVORITES

As you progress through this volume, it may be helpful to list the items that are the most relevant to you and that you want to implement into your workbooks. Feel free to make notes of those items in the My Favorites table that follows.

MY FAVORITES

As you work through the content of this book, use this table to note features or functions you want to remember to practice and implement in your workbooks.

Page	Topic

Chapter 2: Selected Shortcuts

SET UP

I hope you've been using the shortcuts we discussed in the previous volumes. If so, your muscles have memorized them, and they are now second nature.

In this volume, we discuss the following shortcuts:

1. Insert current date and time with Ctrl+; and Ctrl+:

2. Copy cell above with Ctrl+' and Ctrl+"

3. Scroll right and left with Alt+PageDown and Alt+PageUp

4. Cycle through workbooks with Ctrl+Tab and Ctrl+Shift+Tab

5. Create your own shortcut in the QAT (Quick Access Toolbar)

Let's see how these shortcuts work.

HOW TO

First let's take a quick look at each shortcut and then jump into the exercises.

CTRL+; AND CTRL+:

Ctrl+; will insert the current date into the active cell, and Ctrl+: (or Ctrl+Shift+;) will insert the current time.

 XREF

> These shortcuts enter stored values, not formulas, and as such won't change over time. If you would like the values to update, consider writing a formula that uses the TODAY or NOW functions discussed in Chapter 13.

CTRL+' AND CTRL+"

Both Ctrl+' and Ctrl+" copy the cell above, but there is a subtle difference. When the cell above contains a formula, Ctrl+' will insert a copy of the formula, whereas Ctrl+" (or Ctrl+Shift+') will insert a copy of the formula result as a stored value. If the cell above contains a stored value, then they effectively accomplish the same thing, copying the value from the cell above.

ALT+PAGEDOWN AND ALT+PAGEUP

We know that the PageUp and PageDown keys move us vertically up and down a worksheet. If we use the Alt key with them, then we move left and right instead. Alt+PageDown moves right, and Alt+PageUp moves left.

CTRL+TAB AND CTRL+SHIFT+TAB

We previously discussed how to cycle through worksheets with Ctrl+PageUp and Ctrl+PageDown, and now we discuss how to cycle through open workbooks.

We navigate through open workbooks with Ctrl+Tab and Ctrl+Shift+Tab. When there are a couple of workbooks open, these commands work great. When there are several workbooks open, you may prefer to view a list with the following Ribbon command:

- View > Switch Windows

 KB

> The keyboard equivalent is Alt+W, W.

The Switch Windows command causes Excel to display an ordered list of open workbooks, and you can navigate directly to a desired workbook by selecting it from the list with your mouse or the corresponding Alt key shortcut.

 NOTE

There is a technical difference between shortcut keys and access keys. Shortcut keys, often used with Ctrl, allow us to perform a common action without having to navigate through Excel's UI, while access keys, often used with Alt, help us navigate through Excel's UI. This means that shortcut keys are typically consistent through Excel versions, whereas access keys may vary depending on the Excel version. For simplicity, we use the term *shortcuts* here to refer to both shortcut and access keys.

QAT

What happens when a command you use frequently has a keyboard shortcut sequence that is lengthy or difficult to remember? Or worse, what if it has no keyboard shortcut at all? That's where the Quick Access Toolbar (QAT) can help. The QAT lets us store our favorite commands. We can quickly execute QAT commands by clicking an icon with our mouse or by using the corresponding Alt shortcut. You can view the Alt shortcut key by pressing the Alt key. You'll notice that the first QAT icon is automatically assigned Alt+1, the second icon is Alt+2, and so on.

We can place a copy of an existing Ribbon icon into the QAT by right-clicking the Ribbon icon and selecting *Add to Quick Access Toolbar*.

Not every Excel command appears in the Ribbon. Wait, what? Yes, it is true. I like to think of these as little hidden commands just waiting to be discovered. When you discover a command you'd like to use frequently, you can add it to the QAT.

To do so, open the Excel Options dialog by clicking the drop-down on the right side of the QAT and selecting *More Commands*, or you can use the following command:

- File > Options

When *Quick Access Toolbar* is selected in the left pane of the Excel Options dialog, you can add or remove QAT commands. When *Customize Ribbon* is selected, you can add, edit, and delete Ribbon tabs, groups, and icons. There are several categories of commands to choose from, including *Popular Commands* and *Commands Not in the Ribbon*. Commands Not in the Ribbon? Yep...those are the Excel commands that don't have a corresponding Ribbon icon by default. They are the little hidden commands you can add to the Ribbon or QAT as desired.

Let's crack open the exercise workbook and practice.

 XREF

For a comprehensive list of shortcuts covered in the Excel University series to date, please refer to the Shortcut Reference near the end of this book.

EXAMPLES

Let's practice with a few hands-on exercises.

 **PRACTICE**

To work along, please refer to *Selected Shortcuts.xlsx*.

 VIDEO

To watch the solutions video, please visit the Excel University Video Library.

EXERCISE 1—INSERT DATE AND TIME

In this exercise, we'll use our keyboard to enter the current date and time.

 **PRACTICE**

To work along, please refer to the Exercise 1 worksheet.

We need to enter the current date into the input cell, so we use the handy Ctrl+; shortcut. We also need to enter the current time into the next input cell, so we use the Ctrl+: shortcut. Done!

EXERCISE 2—COPY CELL ABOVE

In this exercise, we'll use our keyboard to copy the value from the cell above.

 **PRACTICE**

To work along, please refer to the Exercise 2 worksheet.

We need to add a new transaction to the table. The new transaction happens to be for the same account as the last transaction. So we use the keyboard shortcut Ctrl+' to copy the account from the cell above the new transaction. We enter the transaction amount of 100. And…done.

EXERCISE 3—HORIZONTAL SCROLL

In this exercise, we'll use our keyboard to scroll right and left in our worksheet.

 **PRACTICE**

To work along, please refer to the Exercise 3 worksheet.

Our worksheet contains numerous columns, and they don't all fit on one screen. To scroll one screen right, we use the Alt+PageDown shortcut. We scroll one screen left with Alt+PageUp. Easy enough.

EXERCISE 4—NEXT WORKBOOK

In this exercise, we'll use our keyboard to cycle through open workbooks.

 **PRACTICE**

To work along, please refer to the Exercise 4 worksheet.

Begin by opening several random workbooks. Now view a list of the open workbooks by using the following Ribbon command or its keyboard equivalent:

• View > Switch Windows

 NOTE

Since the order of the list is reverse chronological, the most recently opened workbook is at the top of the list.

To switch the active workbook, press Ctrl+Tab. Pressing Ctrl+Tab again continues to the next workbook in the list. Using Ctrl+Shift+Tab will switch to the previous workbook in the list.

EXERCISE 5—QAT

In this exercise, we'll add commands to the QAT.

 **PRACTICE**

To work along, please refer to the Exercise 5 worksheet.

First let's add an existing Ribbon command to the QAT. We frequently use the Increase Indent command rather than using leading spaces or new columns.

 XREF

The Indent command is discussed in Volume 2, Chapter 14.

We right-click the Increase Indent icon and select *Add to Quick Access Toolbar*. Now we can activate the command clicking the QAT icon with our mouse or by using the automatically assigned Alt key shortcut.

Next let's add a command that isn't found in the Ribbon. Occasionally as I'm working, I like to execute the Advanced Document Properties command to open the Properties dialog box. Although there is not a built-in Ribbon command for this, we can get to it by clicking File > Info > Properties > Advanced Properties, or we can use the following keyboard sequence:

- Alt+F, I, Q, S, Down Arrow, Enter

Since we would like to open this dialog more easily, we'll set up a QAT button. Using the QAT pull-down, we select *More Commands*. In the Excel Options dialog, from the *Choose commands from* drop-down, we select *Commands Not in the Ribbon*. We select *Advanced Document Properties* from the list and click the Add button. We can now execute the Advanced Document Properties command quickly with the mouse or keyboard.

CHAPTER CONCLUSION

These additional keyboard shortcuts will help you keep your hands on your keyboard to improve your speed.

FEATURES

Let's examine several handy Excel features.

Chapter 3: Sorting and Filtering

SET UP

In this part, we explore several Excel features that can be useful as we prepare workbooks. We discuss some basic items like sorting, filtering, and outlining, and we take a peek behind their seeming simplicity to discover how robust and helpful these features really are. We uncover a few subtle details about formatting and printing. We talk about Excel's built-in protection options and look at how hyperlinks can make our workpapers easy to navigate.

In this chapter we examine Excel's sorting and filtering capabilities. When we have a worksheet that stores a lot of transactions, Excel's sorting and filtering tools help us quickly get to the desired transactions. For example, we may want to quickly find the total of a group of transactions or copy and paste them into another sheet or table. Sorting and filtering are basic features, and there is a good chance you are already familiar with them. But we'll cover a few interesting details that will let you take full advantage of these features.

Before we get to the specifics, I want to be sure we are on the same page concerning the difference between sorting and filtering. These terms are closely related and sometimes used interchangeably in casual discussions; however, they are distinct features.

Sorting controls the order in which transactions are presented. When we define the sort order, Excel moves and rearranges cell values as needed to produce the desired sort. During a sort operation, Excel doesn't update formulas that reference the range or cells being sorted. This is one reason we prefer lookup functions to direct cell references.

XREF

Preferring lookups to direct cell references is discussed in Volume 1, Chapter 16.

Filtering displays a subset of the transactions based on one or more conditions. When we define the filter, Excel hides worksheet rows as needed to display the desired transactions. Filtering does not cause Excel to move cell values. Sorting defines the order of the transactions, while filtering controls which transactions are displayed.

HOW TO

As with many features of Excel, sorting and filtering work best with flat data. The built-in Sort and Filter commands assume that there is a header row with column labels. If your data doesn't have a header row, you can explicitly select the range of cells to sort or filter if needed.

 XREF

Flat data is discussed in Volume 3, Chapter 24.

SORTING

Sorting is fairly straightforward. If you select a single cell, Excel will sort the current region (the range of cells adjacent or diagonal to the active cell) based on the column that contains the active cell. If you select a range of cells, Excel will sort by the column containing the active cell and apply the sort to the selected range only.

 KB

You can move the active cell within the selected range with Ctrl+. or Tab or Shift+Tab.

To sort, select the desired cell or range and then use either of the following Ribbon commands:

- Home > Sort & Filter > Sort A to Z (Sort Z to A)

- Data > Sort AZ (Sort ZA)

NOTE

The Sort button labels change to reflect the data type of the active cell. For example, the ascending Sort button label is *Sort A to Z* when the active cell contains a text string, but it changes to *Sort Oldest to Newest* when the active cell contains a date.

You can also apply multiple sorts to a single range. For example, maybe you'd like to sort first by region, and then sort within each region by rep. Use either of the following commands to open the Sort dialog and define such a sort:

- Home > Filter & Sort > Custom Sort

- Data > Sort

In the resulting Sort dialog, you can add multiple sort columns (levels), and the sort is executed accordingly. Check the *My data has headers* checkbox if your columns have a header row. Plus, you can click the Options button to change the default orientation from sorting top to bottom to sorting left to right.

 KB

Use Alt+H, S, U to open the Sort dialog box.

In addition to the Ribbon icons, you can right-click a cell to define the sort.

When our data is stored in a table, we can sort and filter with the drop-down controls in the table's header row. And when our data is stored in an ordinary range instead of a table, we can manually add the drop-down controls by using the Filter feature.

FILTERING

The Filter feature has been in Excel a long time. However, there have been numerous enhancements made during the last several versions of Excel that are worth noting.

First the basics. Designed to operate on a region of data that contains column labels, the Filter feature creates little drop-down buttons in the header row that we can use to sort and filter the data. These little buttons are often referred to as Sort and Filter controls, Column Header icons, Drop-Downs, Sort buttons, Filter buttons, and Down arrows. You probably recognize them because these little drop-downs are the same ones that automatically appeared when we used the Table feature.

XREF

Tables are discussed in Volume 1, Chapter 8.

When we store data in tables, we don't need to manually turn on the filter controls. If we store data in an ordinary range instead of a table, it is pretty easy to add these controls to the range. Simply select any cell within the range and use the following command icon:

- Data > Filter

Your ordinary data range will now contain sort and filter controls in the header row.

 KB

Use Alt+A, T or Ctrl+Shift+L to toggle the controls on and off.

When you select a Filter option from a drop-down, Excel displays the desired rows by hiding any rows not meeting the condition. You can remove the controls by clicking the following command icon again:

- Data > Filter

 NOTE

You can toggle the filter controls on and off in a table with this command as well.

You can clear the active filter, but leave the controls on the header row with the following command:

- Data > Clear

You can reapply the current filter if new data is added to the range with this command:

- Data > Reapply

You can open the Advanced Filter dialog by clicking the following icon:

- Data > Advanced

Now that we've covered the basics, let's explore several interesting details and enhancements, namely:

- SUBTOTAL
- Data types

- Color

- AutoFilter

We'll walk through them one at a time.

SUBTOTAL

Let's begin by revisiting the SUBTOTAL function discussed long ago. Do you remember it? Here's a hint: the SUBTOTAL function excludes other SUBTOTAL functions in the range. In addition to excluding other SUBTOTAL functions, it also excludes rows hidden by a filter. So when we set up the drop-down controls discussed above and use them to apply a filter, the SUBTOTAL function includes the visible rows only. This is the same behavior as a table's total row. When we convert an ordinary range to a table and turn on the Total Row, the total excludes hidden rows. In fact, if you turn on a table's Total Row and inspect the formula, you'll see that the formula bar contains the SUBTOTAL function.

 XREF

SUBTOTAL is discussed in Volume 1, Chapter 11.

 KB

If a range has an active filter applied, Alt+= inserts the SUBTOTAL function rather than the SUM function.

Data Types

It is interesting to note that the filter controls recognize the data type of each column and provide relevant options. For example, a Filter button on a column of numbers will include numeric filter options such as *Greater Than*, *Less Than*, and *Between*. A Filter button on a text column will include choices such as *Begins With*, *EndsWith*, and *Contains*. And a Filter button on a date column will include date-related choices such as *January* or *This Year*.

Color

The drop-down controls provide the ability to sort and filter by font and fill color. This works for manually and conditionally formatted cells. When you apply an icon set with the Conditional Formatting feature, you can also filter by icon. This means you can define the filter logic using conditional formatting and then apply the filter based on the resulting cell formats or icons.

 XREF

Conditional formatting is discussed in Volume 1, Chapter 10.

Let's say you want to filter a range to show only the duplicates. When you look at the filter options in the drop-down, do you see a choice for duplicate values? Unfortunately, you do not—but no problem. You can filter to show duplicate values by highlighting duplicates with conditional formatting and then applying a filter based on the resulting color. Nice!

 NOTE

On a related note, the Advanced Filter dialog has a checkbox to show unique records only.

You can also use this technique as a quick way to obtain a total based on color. Since functions primarily operate on stored values, not displayed values, it is difficult to tell a SUM function to include cells based on the formatting. However, you could obtain the total by filtering for the desired color and then using a SUBTOTAL function to add up the visible cells.

AutoFilter

In addition to the standard filter icons discussed above, Excel also contains the AutoFilter command—but it is hidden by default. This command may be useful if you do a lot of filtering because it enables you to immediately apply a filter based on the active cell value, which is often referred to as *filter by selection*. Basically, you select a cell that contains the desired filter value and then select the AutoFilter command. Excel will display the filter controls and apply a filter based on the active cell value in a single step.

You can add the AutoFilter icon to the QAT or the Ribbon by using the Excel Options dialog box. Since we already discussed the steps for adding a command to the QAT, we won't rehash the details here. The command is named AutoFilter, and you can find it quickly in the Commands Not in the Ribbon category.

 XREF

Adding a command to the QAT is discussed in detail in Chapter 2.

Okay, it's time to practice.

EXAMPLES

Please work through the following exercises.

 **PRACTICE**

To work along, please refer to *Sorting and Filtering.xlsx.*

 VIDEO

To watch the solutions video, please visit the Excel University Video Library.

EXERCISE 1—BASICS

Let's warm up with the basics.

 **PRACTICE**

To work along, please refer to the Exercise 1 worksheet.

From our accounting system, we've exported transactions for all departments. We'd like to view the corporate department transactions only. When we use the Filter command, we notice that the filter controls appear in the header row as expected. We select the department drop-down and uncheck all but the *Corporate* department. Bam! Excel displays the corporate transactions and hides the other rows. Easy enough. Let's clear the filter and try this another way.

This time we'll use the search field. In the Department drop-down, we slowly type *corporate* into the search field. As we type each letter, the department list is filtered accordingly. When *corporate* is the only remaining department in the list, we just hit Enter and we've got it.

 KB

Similar to Data Validation drop-down lists, you can activate Filter drop-down controls with Alt+Down Arrow. Once activated, navigate filter options with Arrow keys or use the corresponding Alt shortcut (letter e for the search box). Space checks and clears filter items.

With the filter applied, let's add a new transaction. We enter the following values for the new transaction: *4630, 5051, Small office equipment, 301, Sales, 12/31/2017, 200.* We note that the transaction is for the sales department, not the corporate department. We use the Reapply command, and Excel hides the new transaction row as expected.

EXERCISE 2—DATA TYPES

In this exercise, we'll apply filters based on the data type.

 **PRACTICE**

To work along, please refer to the Exercise 2 worksheet.

We've exported some transactions from our accounting system, and we want to analyze and review them. First we want to view the January transactions. We expand the date column's filter control. Since the column contains dates, Excel provides date-related choices. Excel has automatically grouped the filter checkboxes by month and year, rather than listing one checkbox for each unique date in the column. The drop-down includes a Date Filters option that contains choices such as *This Month, Last Quarter*, and *Next Year*. We select *January* from the drop-down, and now only the January transactions are displayed.

Next we want to see all transactions greater than $2,000. We clear the current date filter and expand the *Amount* column's filter control. Since this column contains numbers, Excel provides relevant options. The drop-down includes a Number Filters option, which contains choices such as *Greater Than, Less Than*, and *Between*. We select *Greater Than* and enter *2,000* into the resulting Custom AutoFilter dialog. Perfect. Now the corresponding transactions are displayed.

Finally, we want to view the transactions for meals and entertainment. We clear the current filter and expand the *Account* column's filter control. Since this column contains text values, Excel provides relevant options. The drop-down includes a Text Filters option, which includes choices such as *Begins With, Ends With*, and *Contains*. We select *Begins With* and enter *M&E* into the resulting Custom AutoFilter dialog. Now we can see the meals and entertainment transactions.

 NOTE

There are additional choices in the Custom AutoFilter dialog box that aren't in the filter control, such as *Does Not Begin With* and *Does Not End With*. Sometimes these additional options come in handy.

Being able to quickly view a subset of transactions is convenient. But let's say we need to copy the subset and paste it into another worksheet. Will all rows be copied or just the visible rows? We examine this issue in the next exercise.

EXERCISE 3—PASTE SELECTED ROWS

In this exercise, we'll paste a subset of exported data into a table.

 **PRACTICE**

To work along, please refer to the Exercise 3 worksheet.

We've exported transactions from our accounting system and need to paste a subset into our reporting workbook's data table. We need the Q4 transactions for the *Internet* and *Telephone* accounts. If the logic that defined the subset was simple, such as the Q4 dates alone, we could sort the range and copy the group of desired rows. However, our logic also includes nonsequential accounts, so we are precluded from using a sort to group the desired transactions. The good news is that we can use filters.

We filter the range and show the October, November, and December transactions. We then use the Account drop-down and select the *Internet* and *Telephone* accounts. Now only the desired rows are visible. We select the resulting range and do a standard copy. We flip to the data table on the **E3 Data** sheet and do a standard paste to append the transactions to the table. We note only the visible rows are included.

 NOTE

If all rows were included rather than just the visible rows, select the range of filtered transactions, and then select *Go To Special, Visible Cells Only* before doing the copy.

EXERCISE 4—REPORT FILTER

In this exercise, we'll filter a report.

 **PRACTICE**

To work along, please refer to the Exercise 4 worksheet.

The data is stored in a table on the **E4 Data** worksheet. We use our friend SUMIFS to populate the **Exercise 4** report. We notice that two items have zero amounts. For presentation purposes, we want to hide zero-dollar rows. So we simply expand the *Amount* filter control and uncheck the zero item and we are done. Or are we? Well, this is a recurring-use workbook, so we want to ensure it will continue working as we go forward. So let's see what happens when we update the workbook.

Let's flip to the **E4 Data** sheet and change the value of the *CG231* transaction from 1,000 to 2,000. We flip back to the report and confirm that *CG231* still appears in the report. We expect it to be displayed because it is a nonzero value and because we haven't reapplied the filter. So we use the Reapply command. Wow—to our surprise the *CG231* row disappears from the report! Why? When we applied the filter, we didn't tell Excel to hide zero values; we actually told Excel to display the checked report values. Since 2,000 wasn't in the original drop-down list, Excel hides the row.

Fortunately, it is pretty easy to communicate our true intent to Excel. Let's begin by clearing the previous filter. Now, rather than using the checkboxes to define the filter, we expand the *Amount* filter control and select the *Number* filter option. We select *Does Not Equal* and Excel displays the Custom AutoFilter dialog. We enter 0 and hit OK. Now the filter knows to show nonzero values. Just to confirm, we change the *CG231* transaction value from 2,000 to 1,000 and then choose *Reapply*. Yes! The report still displays the *CG231* row as desired.

EXERCISE 5—MULTICOLUMN SORT

In this exercise, we'll sort transactions based on multiple columns.

 **PRACTICE**

To work along, please refer to the Exercise 5 worksheet.

We need to sort the transactions by region, and within each region, by rep, and within each rep, by item. We select any cell in the range, and then open the Sort dialog by selecting the following command:

• Data > Sort

We select *Region* for our first sort level. We click the *Add Level* button and select the *Rep* column. We click the *Add Level* button again and select *Item*. Now we click OK and confirm the transactions are sorted in the desired order.

EXERCISE 6—CONDITIONAL FORMATTING

In this exercise, we'll filter based on conditional formatting.

 **PRACTICE**

To work along, please refer to the Exercise 6 worksheet.

Management wants to monitor slow-moving inventory items and asks us to prepare a monthly report to help. We compute inventory turnover for all items. We want management to easily identify the bottom third of our inventory items, and since this is Excel, there are a few options at our disposal.

We could sort the list in descending order and allow management to scan down the report to see the slow items. But our list is long, and we prefer that our report include only the items of concern, the slowest third. We could sort the list and then copy the slow items and paste them into a new sheet, but that introduces additional manual steps. We want to minimize or eliminate manual steps whenever possible.

So we decide to use a filter to show the bottom third. One way to identify the bottom third is to create a new calculated column. The formula could determine whether each item belongs in the top, middle, or bottom third. We could then filter the report based on the new column. But we like to work with the data as it comes, and that means we prefer to avoid such helper columns whenever possible.

Fortunately, we are familiar with a feature that can automatically place our items into top, middle, and bottom thirds. Do you remember what it is? Yes, conditional formatting. We select the *Turnover* column and apply *Conditional Formatting* to the range. We select *Icon Sets* and select the *3 Symbols (Circled)* option. Now we have green icons identifying the top third, yellow icons for the middle third, and red icons for the bottom third. Now we just need to filter the list. We expand the *Turnover* filter control, select *Filter by Color*, and select the red icon. Now the bottom third is shown. Hey—that was fun!

EXERCISE 7—DUPLICATES

In this exercise, we'll filter to show duplicates.

 **PRACTICE**

To work along, please refer to the Exercise 7 worksheet.

We have a list of checks, and we need to identify any transactions with duplicate check numbers. We could sort the list and manually scan for duplicates, but that could be tedious. We want something faster.

Although there is not a built-in option to filter for duplicates, we can use a two-step process involving conditional formatting. First we select the *CkNum* column and apply *Conditional Formatting* to highlight duplicate values. Next we filter by the color of the *CkNum* column. Now it is easy for us to spot the duplicates.

EXERCISE 8—AUTOFILTER

In this exercise, we'll filter by selection.

 **PRACTICE**

> To work along, please refer to the Exercise 8 worksheet.

The exported data includes transactions for all items. We want to view only item *AB101* transactions. Since we filter often, we've added the AutoFilter button to the QAT, as discussed above. We select any cell that contains our desired value, *AB101*, and click the AutoFilter icon. Wow, that was fast!

EXERCISE 9—WITH SUBTOTAL

In this exercise, we'll use the SUBTOTAL function with a filter.

 **PRACTICE**

> To work along, please refer to the Exercise 9 worksheet.

Our worksheet contains a bunch of transactions. To compute the total, we use the SUM function. We note that the total is 11,146. Next we filter the range to display transactions for the *West* region. Interestingly, the SUM function continues to return the total of all transactions: 11,146. The SUM function includes hidden and visible rows. But what if we wanted the total to include only the visible rows? We can do that with the SUBTOTAL function because it excludes rows hidden by a filter. You will recall that we discussed that SUBTOTAL characteristic a while ago, and now we'll apply it. Let's clear the filter and display all transactions.

Let's use the SUBTOTAL function to compute the total. As expected, it also returns a value of 11,146. Once again we filter the range to display the transactions for the *West* region. Nice! The total updates to 3,949. The SUBTOTAL function includes the visible rows only.

CHAPTER CONCLUSION

We've seen how Excel's sorting and filtering capabilities help us quickly grab the transactions we need. Although these are fairly basic features of Excel, they can be really helpful.

Chapter 4: Outlining

SET UP

Let me ask you a question. How do you hide rows? Many Excel users hide rows by clicking the Hide command or by changing the row height to zero. If you've used either of these options, you've probably noticed it's hard to tell hidden rows exist. And once you recognize there are hidden rows in a worksheet, it takes a couple of clicks to unhide them. To increase your productivity, you may want to use the Outline feature instead.

With the Outline feature, Excel users can organize rows and columns by placing them into logical groups, or outline levels. An outline can contain a single level or multiple levels with nested groups. Outline groups can be easily expanded or collapsed as desired. In practice, it is often more efficient to use an outline to hide rows than the Hide command or setting the row height to zero. You see, the Outline feature places a visual indicator (a button) next to the group, making it obvious that hidden rows exist, and it takes only a single click to unhide the rows in the group.

HOW TO

It is super easy to use the Outline feature. We'll walk through the steps to outline rows, but the same steps work for columns as well. We'll cover the following items:

- Outline groups

- Multiple outline levels

- Auto Outline

- Subtotal feature
- SUBTOTAL function

Let's begin with the basics.

OUTLINE GROUPS

To outline rows, simply select one or more rows and then the following Ribbon icon:

- Data > Group

 KB

> Selecting the desired rows and then Shift+Alt+Right (or Alt+A, G, G) will group, and Shift+Alt+Left (or Alt+A, U, U) will ungroup.

The selected rows are now contained in an Outline group. You can show/hide the grouped rows by clicking the new +/- toggle button that just showed up to the left of the row labels.

 KB

> Selecting any cell within the group and then Alt+A, H (or Shift+Mouse Scroll Wheel Down) will hide, while Alt+A, J (or Shift+Mouse Scroll Wheel Up) will show.

If your worksheet contains multiple Outline groups, you can show/hide all groups at once by clicking the corresponding Outline Level button—for example, the little *1* and *2* buttons that just showed up to the left of the column labels.

 KB

> To toggle the display of Outline buttons, use Ctrl+8.

To remove an Outline group, select all of the rows in the outline and then the following Ribbon icon:

- Data > Ungroup

You can also remove all outlines for the entire worksheet with the following Ribbon icon:

- Data > Ungroup > Clear Outline

In addition to creating multiple Outline groups in a flat structure, you can create multiple Outline levels.

MULTIPLE OUTLINE LEVELS

You can create multiple Outline levels, or nested groups, to create a hierarchy. To do so, create an Outline group, and then select rows that either enclose or are within the original group and create the next group. For example, if we wanted to outline a balance sheet, we could start by grouping all assets. We select all rows from the first item, such as Cash, to the last item, such as Total Assets, and group them, creating an outer group. Then we select all Fixed Assets rows and group them, creating an inner group. Each Outline group gets a +/- button, and each Outline level gets an Outline Level button to the left of the column headers.

 NOTE

If you try to set up two Outline groups that are adjacent to each other, with no rows or columns in between, you'll notice that Excel automatically combines them into a single group. If needed, you can split the single combined group into two adjacent groups by selecting the row in the location where you want the split, and then use the Ungroup command.

AUTO OUTLINE

In practice, I often define Outline groups manually, as discussed above. But if the data range includes subtotals that define the desired groups, you can ask Excel to automatically create the outlines with the Auto Outline command.

To use this feature, select any cell in the range and then the following Ribbon icon:

- Data > Group > Auto Outline

Excel will attempt to read the data structure based on the formulas that generate the subtotals and grand total, and it will insert the outline levels accordingly.

 NOTE

You can tell Excel if your subtotals are above or below the data and other details in the Settings dialog, which can be opened by clicking the Outline Launcher icon in the lower-right corner of the Outline Ribbon group.

SUBTOTAL FEATURE

We previously discussed the SUBTOTAL function; now it is time to explore the Subtotal feature.

 XREF

The SUBTOTAL function is discussed in Volume 1, Chapter 11.

When flat data is sorted by the desired column or columns, Excel can insert both the outline and subtotal rows automatically. After sorting your data as desired, select a cell within the range and then the following Ribbon icon:

• Data > Subtotal

This will open the Subtotal dialog box as shown in Figure 1.

Figure 1

The dialog has several options. In the *At each change in* field, we select which column we want Excel to analyze. The column selected here must be sorted for Excel to properly insert the subtotal rows. As it scans down the range, Excel inserts a new subtotal row each time the value changes in the specified column.

The *Use function* dialog field tells Excel which type of math you'd like to use in the subtotal row formulas. You can choose from a variety of aggregate functions, such as Sum, Average, Count, Min, and Max. This essentially defines the first argument of the SUBTOTAL function, where 9 is sum, 1 is average, and so on.

The *Add subtotal to* field allows you to identify which column or columns should store the subtotal formulas. This selection is independent of the *At each change in* column so that you can have Excel analyze one column, such as a region column, and add subtotals to another, such as an amount column.

Since you can apply the Subtotal feature multiple times on a single range, the *Replace current subtotals* checkbox allows you to tell Excel whether you want to replace any current subtotal rows or add new ones. For example, if your range has region and rep columns, you can run the Subtotal command first on the outer group, region, and then again for the inner group, rep.

The *Page break between groups* checkbox is useful if you want to print the report and have separate pages for each Outline group.

The *Summary below data* checkbox tells Excel if the subtotal rows should be inserted below or above the data they summarize.

The *Remove All* button tells Excel to remove all subtotal rows and clear the outline.

As handy as the Subtotal feature is, it violates a couple of our guiding principles for building recurring-use workbooks. For one thing, it combines the data and the report, but we prefer to split the data from the report so that we can paste-and-go each period. Also, it introduces a manual step into a recurring process. As you know, we try to eliminate manual steps. Thus, although this feature could help with a quick one-time analysis, for a recurring task, I'd probably store the data in a table and compute summary values with a PivotTable instead.

SUBTOTAL FUNCTION

In this chapter and the previous, we've discussed various methods for hiding rows, including filtering, outlining, the Hide command, and setting the row height to zero. It's a good time to visit an old friend—SUBTOTAL.

Recall the first argument of the SUBTOTAL function defines the math to apply to the range—for example, 9 and 109 are the codes for sum. Both codes exclude other SUBTOTAL functions, and the difference between them lies in hidden rows. Code 109 excludes hidden rows, regardless of how they were hidden, whereas 9 excludes only rows hidden by a filter. Which one is better to use? They each have their place depending on what we are trying to accomplish.

Let's say we outline a balance sheet that uses SUBTOTAL functions to compute the Fixed Assets Subtotal and Total Assets. We want Total Assets to be the same whether the user shows or hides the Fixed Assets Outline group. Which code would we use? We would use 9 because we want the total to include the Fixed Asset rows, even if hidden by the outline. If we used 109, the hidden Fixed Assets values would be excluded from the total.

Here's one more situation to consider. Let's say we prepare an interactive analysis with a bunch of outlines that create groups of departments. We want to allow the user to click on the Outline buttons to control which department groups to include in the grand total. We want the total to include only the visible departments. Which code would we use? We would use 109 because we want the total to exclude any hidden rows. If we used 9, then our total would include the values in the rows hidden by the outline.

It may be helpful to see this difference in action inside an Excel worksheet, so let's head into the exercises now.

EXAMPLES

It's time to crack open the Excel workbook and work through a few exercises.

 **PRACTICE**

To work along, please refer to *Outlining.xlsx.*

 VIDEO

To watch the solutions video, please visit the Excel University Video Library.

EXERCISE 1—HIDE A ROW

In this exercise, we'll hide a worksheet row.

 **PRACTICE**

To work along, please refer to the Exercise 1 worksheet.

We open the workbook and notice that the worksheet contains a report. We note the report total and see that the report does not seem to foot. The report values are 100, 200, and 300, and we expect the report total to be 600. However, it is only 500. We figure there must be an error in the Total formula. We inspect it and are surprised when we confirm that it correctly includes all report values.

So why does the report's SUM function return 500 instead of the expected 600? After a while, we happen to notice that one of the worksheet rows is hidden! When we unhide it, Excel reveals the missing value, the AR Reserve of -100. Argh! Since the row was hidden manually, it was hard to tell it existed. This caused us to waste a bunch of time, and as you know, we don't like wasting such a precious resource.

Instead of hiding the worksheet row manually, we'll hide it using the Outline feature. That way, it will be easy to see that a hidden row exists. Plus we can quickly show or hide it with the +/- buttons.

This report correctly includes the hidden row in its total. But what if we want our totals to exclude hidden rows? Can we do that? We can—and we will—in the next exercise.

EXERCISE 2—SUBTOTAL FUNCTION

In this exercise, we'll use the SUBTOTAL function with outline groups.

 **PRACTICE**

To work along, please refer to the Exercise 2 worksheet.

This exercise demonstrates three examples of the SUBTOTAL function. Example 1 is located on the *Exercise 2* worksheet, and Examples 2 and 3 are located on the *E2 Outline* worksheet. They are designed to illustrate when we'd want to set the first argument to 9 or 109, or when it doesn't matter.

We find the first example on the *Exercise 2* worksheet, where we are building an interactive report with a filter. As such, we want the user to be able to apply different filters, and we want the report to provide a subtotal for the visible report rows only. Which code should we use, 9 or 109? Both will return the desired result, so in this case it doesn't matter. Since we are hiding rows with a filter, both 9 and 109 codes exclude them.

On the *E2 Outline* sheet, we find the remaining two reports, which use the Outline feature. We are again building an interactive report, but instead of hiding rows with a filter, we are hiding rows with an Outline group. Just as before, we want the report's total to reflect the visible rows only and exclude any hidden rows. So should we use Code 9 or 109? We need to use 109. Since we are hiding rows with an Outline group, Code 109 will properly exclude them, while Code 9 would incorrectly include them.

In the third example, we are again building an interactive report, but this time we want the hidden rows to be included in the subtotals. We want to allow the user to show or hide the detail rows as desired, and the report totals should stay the same as the user interacts with the report. So, which code should we use? We need to use Code 9 in this case. Since we are hiding rows with an Outline group, Code 9 will properly include them, while 109 would incorrectly exclude them.

Hopefully these illustrations will help you determine which code to use for the first argument of the SUBTOTAL function.

EXERCISE 3—COLUMNS

In this exercise, we'll make it easy to view two variations of the same worksheet.

 **PRACTICE**

To work along, please refer to the Exercise 3 worksheet.

Our worksheet contains a list of items. As we work with the data, we need to be able to access all columns. However, only selected columns are needed when we print the worksheet for management. We need two versions of the same worksheet, one for us and one for management. Since this is Excel, there is more than one way to accomplish this. One approach is to create the management report with a PivotTable. The PivotTable would include only the selected columns. In practice, that would be my preferred approach for a recurring-use workbook because it splits the data from the report and makes it easy to maintain over time. However, if this were a one-time project and we just wanted something simple, another option would be to use Outline groups.

We would simply group the columns that need to be hidden. That way we can show all columns when we are working with the data, and then we can hide selected columns for management with a single click. We create individual Outline groups for columns *E:K*, *M:N*, *P:Q*, and *S:V*. Now, when we are working in the worksheet, we can show all columns by clicking the Outline Level 2 button. Before we deliver or print the worksheet for management, we simply click the Outline Level 1 button to instantly hide the outlined columns.

This is a convenient technique to use when certain people need access to only selected columns, while we need access to all columns. It is like creating two versions of the same worksheet.

EXERCISE 4—MULTILEVEL OUTLINE

In this exercise, we'll build a multilevel outline.

 **PRACTICE**

To work along, please refer to the Exercise 4 worksheet.

We have an extract from our accounting system, and we want to analyze the data. After sorting the data by Region and Rep, and manually inserting the subtotals, we are ready to create Outline groups.

Since we want the subtotal for each Rep to remain visible, we create an Outline group for each Rep excluding the subtotal rows. We notice that we have two Outline Level buttons, 1 and 2, that we can use to show/hide Rep rows as desired.

Now we move to the Region outlines. Since we want each Region subtotal to remain visible, we create an Outline group for each region excluding the subtotal rows. Now we have Outline buttons for levels 1, 2, and 3.

To finish up, we select all of the data rows, excluding the *Grand Total*, and create a final Outline group. Now we have four Outline levels. We can click the Outline Level buttons to show the level of detailed desired.

Our interactive worksheet is cool, but it took a long time to create the outlines. In the next exercise, we'll delegate that task to Excel.

EXERCISE 5—AUTO OUTLINE

In this exercise, we'll ask Excel to automatically create the Outline groups.

 **PRACTICE**

To work along, please refer to the Exercise 5 worksheet.

We prepare the same extract as the previous exercise by sorting by Region and Rep and inserting the desired subtotals. This time, rather than manually defining the Outline groups, we'll ask Excel to do it for us. We select any cell in the range, and then use the Auto Outline command. Bam—outlines are done!

That was fun, but in the next exercise, we'll even delegate the task of creating the subtotals to Excel.

EXERCISE 6—SUBTOTAL FEATURE

In this exercise, we'll use the Subtotal feature.

 **PRACTICE**

To work along, please refer to the Exercise 6 worksheet.

Our extract is the same as the previous exercise. This time we'll ask Excel to insert the subtotals and create the outlines. After sorting by Region and by Rep, we are ready. We select any cell in the range, and then select the Subtotal command as follows:

- Data > Subtotal

In the resulting Subtotal dialog box, we tell Excel that at each change in *Region*, we want to use the *Sum* function to add a subtotal to the *Amount* column. We want to replace any existing subtotals and insert the subtotals below the data. We click OK and…bam! We now have subtotals for all regions, along with the related Outline groups. Now that the Region subtotals are done, let's set up the Rep subtotals.

We open the Subtotal dialog again, and this time we tell Excel that at each change in *Rep*, we want to use the *Sum* function to add a subtotal to the *Amount* column and that we do not want to replace the current subtotals. Click OK, and we are good to go.

You have to admit that watching the Subtotal feature in action was pretty fun. Using it for a quick analysis or one-time project is probably just fine, but it does contradict some of our guiding principles. For example, rather than splitting the data from the report, it turns the data into the report. We prefer to work with the data as it comes and eliminate manual steps from our recurring tasks, but this approach requires us to manually sort the data before we even use the Subtotal command, which we have to do twice. Although this approach was fun, how about we use a PivotTable instead? In the next exercise, we'll replace the reports we built in the previous three exercises with a PivotTable.

EXERCISE 7—PIVOTTABLE

In this exercise, we'll create a PivotTable.

 **PRACTICE**

To work along, please refer to the Exercise 7 worksheet.

Rather than use the Subtotal feature to summarize our extracted data, we'll use a PivotTable. The data is stored in a table named ***tbl_e7***. We create the following PivotTable report:

- PT: ROWS: Region, Rep, Item; VALUES: Sum(Amount)

With the basic report structured defined, we finish it up with a few cosmetic touches. We change the report layout to tabular, repeat item labels, remove row headers, and format the value field. Beautiful!

 NOTE

Since we created many PivotTables in Volume 3, only summary instructions are provided above.

Our PivotTable is similar to the report we generated in the previous exercise, and we can show/hide Rep and Region details as well. This approach makes our workbook easy to update and maintain over time, and it falls in line with the principles we established way back in Volume 1.

CHAPTER CONCLUSION

Typically, hiding rows or columns with the Outline feature is preferred to hiding them manually because it is easy to see that the worksheet contains hidden rows or columns. Plus it is fast and easy to unhide them with the Outline buttons.

Chapter 5: Formatting

SET UP

Have you ever seen a worksheet that includes a little blank column between each data column? If you've ever exported a QuickBooks report to Excel, you're probably familiar with this layout. Many Excel users employ this technique manually as well. Typically, these little columns are placed in between the data columns for formatting purposes, often so that the underline in the header row will show little gaps between data columns instead of being displayed as one continuous underline. Without the empty columns, a bottom cell border applied to the header row would span the entire width of the header.

Modifying a worksheet to include these empty formatting columns seems innocent enough, but let's reflect on this technique for a moment. Consider the formula-based report we built at the end of Volume 2. We split the data from the report and used the SUMIFS function to compute the report values for 12 monthly columns. Would inserting an empty column between each of the monthly columns allow us to adhere to the design principles and organizational ideas discussed throughout the series? Unfortunately, no. For example, these empty columns would mess up our consistent date header formulas. Plus they would preclude us from using Ctrl+Right to jump to the end of the report (because it would jump only to the next monthly column).

Basically, the blank columns used for formatting purposes can hurt our productivity. We want to use little blank columns to get the desired format, but we shouldn't use them because they'll slow us down. So what are we supposed to do? Are we stuck? No, not at all. The solution lies in the formatting. A simple cell format can provide the little underline gaps without unnecessary empty columns. This isn't the first time we've observed how our formatting choices can impact productivity. We previously examined how using the Indent command, rather than leading spaces or new columns, allows us to use consistent formulas and improve our productivity.

XREF

The Indent command is discussed in Volume 2, Chapter 14.

Excel's formatting capabilities are vast, and providing a comprehensive review could fill an entire book. So I've handpicked some of the more interesting items to include in this chapter.

HOW TO

Before jumping into the details, I want to share my thoughts about formatting. While I love looking at beautifully formatted worksheets and often marvel at the graphic design capabilities of Excel users, I try to minimize the time I spend maintaining formatting, at least when it comes to my recurring-use workbooks. My motto is to keep it simple and stick with the basics; less is more.

I use built-in cell styles and formats rather than create my own combination of border, font, and fill colors. I'm not a graphics person, and I don't really know which colors go together. In fact, I round my colors to the nearest "whole-color."

I also apply formatting at the end, after the workbook structure and layout are done, and after all the formulas are working. I find that if I format the cells right away, while I'm building the workbook, I spend extra time updating the formatting as I go. I can get the same formatting done in less time if I simply wait till the end.

All right, enough of my personal theory. Let's get into the details. The formatting discussion is organized into the following sections:

- Cell formatting

- Date/Time formatting

- Row and column formatting

Our journey begins with cell formatting, which is something you've been doing for a long time, I'm sure. But there are some interesting items in this chapter, so I hope you don't skip it.

CELL FORMATTING

We already know that the difference between a cell's displayed value and its stored or calculated value is the formatting. Surprisingly, these values can appear quite different owing to the wide assortment of formats available in Excel.

To organize our exploration, we'll take a tour through the Format Cells dialog box, as shown in Figure 2. Some of the formatting options available in the dialog have Ribbon icons, which provide an easy way to apply the desired format. Many dialog options don't have a Ribbon icon, and some of them are worth investigating.

You can open the dialog with the following Ribbon command:

- Home > Format > Format Cells

 KB

Ctrl+1 and Alt+H, O, E opens the Format Cells dialog.

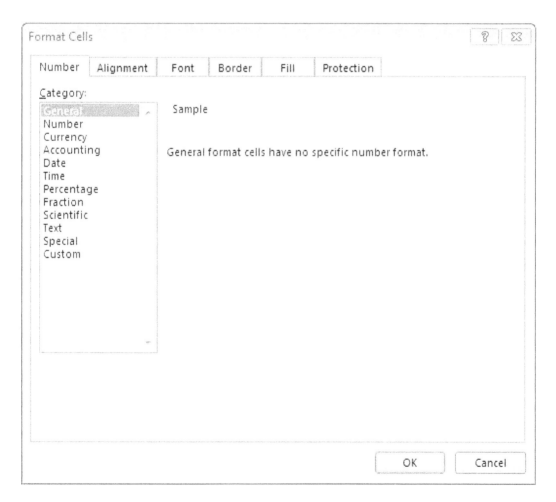

Figure 2

Inside the Format Cells dialog box, you'll notice six tabs: *Number, Alignment, Font, Border, Fill,* and *Protection.* Let's quickly visit each tab.

Number Tab. The Number tab allows us to format the cell value, and Excel provides numerous built-in options organized by category. Although most categories and related formatting options are straightforward, we should briefly look *at Currency, Accounting,* and *Custom.*

The main difference between *Currency* and *Accounting* is the placement of the currency symbol. With the Currency format, the symbol is placed immediately before the first digit in each cell. With the Accounting format, the symbols are lined up within the column of numbers. Additionally, the Accounting format provides a bit of padding to the right of the number so that when parentheses are used for negative numbers the decimals will line up as well. In formal financial statements, it is customary to display a currency symbol on the first and last report rows. This can be accomplished by applying an Accounting format with the currency symbol to the first and last rows and then the Accounting format without the currency symbol to the other report rows.

 KB

Alt+H, K applies Accounting without a symbol and Alt+H, A, N, Enter applies Accounting with the symbol. Ctrl+$ applies Currency and Ctrl+% applies Percentage.

The Custom format category allows us to define a desired format by entering various codes into the dialog's *Type* field. I believe the quickest way to get started is by showing samples of the displayed values for selected codes.

We'll start with a few codes that help format numeric values. Assuming the stored value is 1000.5, the following format codes would produce these displayed values:

- # displays 1001

- #,### displays 1,001

- #,###.00 displays 1,000.50

- #,###, displays 1

You can also include text strings in the format codes. Assuming the stored value is 1000, the following format codes would produce the displayed values below:

- #,### "Dollars" displays 1,000 Dollars

- #, "K" displays 1 K

Excel allows us to individually define how positive, negative, zero, and text values should be displayed. To do so, we simply create format codes for each type and separate them with semicolons. The order of these segments is as follows:

Positive Number; Negative Number; Zero Value; Text String

For example, if we want to tell Excel to display positive numbers with a comma separator and negative numbers with parentheses, we could use the following code:

- #,###;(#,###)

In the above code, we didn't explicitly define the format for zero or text values. If we wanted to tell Excel to represent zero values with a dash, we could update our custom format code as follows:

- #,###;(#,###);-

If we also want to explicitly tell Excel to display a text value as entered, we could update our code to this:

- #,###;(#,###);-;@

If we insert a semicolon into the format code, Excel assumes we are going to provide a format for the value type that follows. If we don't provide a value, it will be excluded from display. For example, we could tell Excel not to display a cell value with the following code:

- ;;;

Here's a question for you. Is it possible for us to display a negative stored value as a positive displayed value? Yes, we could do this by using the following code:

- #,###;#,###

In addition to the basic format codes above, there are a few additional codes that are interesting:

- Underscore (_) displays a space
- Asterisk (*) repeats the character that follows
- Square brackets [] enclose colors and conditions

For example, if we wanted negative numbers to be displayed in parentheses with a red font, we could use the following format:

- #,###;[Red](#,###)

Essentially, value formats are described by these codes, and it is interesting to note that selecting a built-in format from a category in the Format Cells dialog box and then clicking the Custom category will cause Excel to display the corresponding format code. For example, if you select the Accounting category, specify no decimals, and then click the Custom category, you'll see the corresponding format code used. You can use these as a starting point and tweak them as desired.

Alignment Tab. The Alignment tab allows us to control how and where within the cell the value is displayed. In practice, the settings I use most are Horizontal, Wrap Text, and Vertical.

Before we proceed, I want to ask you a question. When you have a cell value that needs to be centered over multiple cells, how do you do it? If there are an odd number of columns to span, perhaps you enter the value into the middle column and then center the value. But what do you do when there are an even number of columns? Many Excel users click the tempting little Merge and Center Ribbon icon to center a value across multiple cells. This actually merges the selected cells, creating one big cell. This seemingly innocent formatting choice could create unexpected issues and make it more difficult to select columns, filter, sort, and format. Once again we discover that our formatting choices can impact our productivity. Realizing the Merge and Center command can decrease our productivity, what do we do? The answer is right here on this tab, in the Horizontal drop-down, and it is called *Center Across Selection*. To apply it, you simply select the value cell and the desired cells to the right and then use the Center Across Selection option. This will center the value across the selected cells without merging them. This approach will make your workbook easier to maintain over time.

 XREF

We first used Center Across Selection in Volume 3, Chapter 2.

The Wrap Text checkbox tells Excel to automatically increase the row height to accommodate the text stored in the cell. It will make the cell operate more like a word processor because the text will wrap down to a new line when it reaches the end of the cell. This is a useful option to display text that is wider than the column.

 NOTE

The Wrap Text option automatically provides line breaks, but if you need to force a line break at a specific point, you can do so with Alt+Enter.

The Vertical drop-down provides formatting options for vertical cell alignment. This can be useful when you wrap text in multiple columns and cells have a varying number of lines—for example, when some of the cells have one line of text and others have two or three lines. When this happens, Excel vertically aligns the text at the bottom of each cell. If you prefer to have a different vertical alignment, such as at the top of the cell, you can use the Vertical drop-down.

 NOTE

If you wrap text and then change the column width, Excel won't automatically resize the row height. You can tell Excel to resize the row height by selecting the cell, pressing F2, and then Enter.

 XREF

This tab allows you to set the indent level to a specific value. Indentation is discussed in Volume 2, Chapter 14.

Font Tab. The Font tab is fairly straightforward, but there is one thing to be aware of.

At the beginning of this chapter, we talked about the empty little columns often placed between data columns for formatting purposes. These little blank columns are frequently inserted so that the header row underline shows little gaps instead of a continuous underline. Take a moment to examine the Underline drop-down and you'll notice it contains options for Single Accounting and Double Accounting. These are similar to the standard single and double underline, except when the cell contains a text string or when the cell is formatted with an accounting number format.

When the cell contains a text string, the Accounting underlines span almost the entire width of the cell rather than underlining just the text string. This is how you can format a header row to display little gaps between columns without introducing empty columns. Yay!

When an Accounting Number format is applied to a cell that contains a number or a text string, the Accounting underlines span the width of the column (except for little side gaps). If you have an eye for detail, you may notice that the gap widths are different between a cell that is formatted with an Accounting Number format and one that isn't. So, if you want all of the underlines in the column to line up, be sure to apply an Accounting format to all of the cells, even column headers that contain text strings.

 NOTE

If your column header contains a numeric value, such as the year 2017, you can have the Accounting underlines work as expected by converting the data type to a text string. If you are using formulas to create dynamic headers, you can wrap a TEXT function around the formula. If you are using stored values, you can precede the stored value with an apostrophe, such as '2017. Preceding a number with an apostrophe causes Excel to store it as a text string.

XREF

Dynamic headers are discussed in Volume 2, Chapter 21. The TEXT function is discussed in Volume 2, Chapter 7.

Now here is an interesting note. If you apply an Accounting Number format first and then click the standard underline Ribbon icon, Excel actually applies an Accounting underline instead of the standard underline.

 NOTE

If you are using a skinny row, you'll notice that an Accounting underline isn't displayed when applied to an empty cell. You can cause the underline to appear by entering a space, a formula or function that creates a space, or a reference to a named constant that is a space.

 XREF

Skinny rows are discussed in Volume 1, Chapter 12.

The workbooks I use in practice don't have strict formatting requirements. Thus, I most often use cell borders instead of underlines because they typically require less effort and maintenance. However, when a report has precise formatting requirements, the Accounting underlines can help.

 NOTE

The elements on the Font tab, such as Bold and Size, can be applied to an entire cell or to selected text within a cell. This can be useful if you want to bold a single word in a text string, for example.

Border Tab. The Border tab allows us to format the cell borders. In practice, I typically format cell borders using the Ribbon instead. However, when defining custom conditional formatting and cell styles, we'll use this dialog, so we should review the steps. First, we select the line style and color. Then we click the desired presets or Border icons to apply the selected line style and color. If we subsequently modify the style or color, we'll need to click the desired Border icons once again to apply the changes.

Fill Tab. The Fill tab allows us to format the cell fill. You basically pick a color along with any fill effects or patterns. In practice, I don't use this tab often, except with conditional formatting.

Protection Tab. The Protection tab contains options useful when protecting a worksheet. We'll cover worksheet protection in a subsequent chapter.

XREF

Worksheet protection is discussed in Chapter 7.

 NOTE

When it comes to formatted cells and copy/paste, you can use Paste Special Values to paste the values without any cell formatting or hit F2 to enter edit mode and then paste. This will paste the selected text cleanly. Similarly, if you want to copy just the cell text, without all of the cell attributes, hit F2, select the cell contents, and then copy.

Now that our tour of the Format Cells dialog is complete, let's revisit the custom format codes we used on the Number tab and explore date and time formatting.

DATE/TIME FORMATTING

We understand that Excel stores dates as serial numbers that increment one for each day. For example, the stored value 42735 represents the date December 31, 2016, and 42736 represents January 1, 2017. Now, let's expand our understanding.

 XREF

Date serial numbers are discussed in Volume 2, Chapter 16.

The date data type is more accurately described as a date/time data type, where the date is stored on the left side of the decimal point and the time is stored on the right. For example, 42736.5 represents noon on January 1, 2017. The decimal value represents the time expressed as a fraction of a day. For example, .5 is half of a day or noon, and .75 represents 6:00 p.m.

Since Excel stores dates and times in this way, we have great flexibility when it comes to formatting. Depending on the format, we can opt to display the date part only, the time part only, or both the date and time. Let's start with the date codes. Assuming the stored value represents January 1, 2017, the following format codes would produce the displayed values below.

- m displays 1

- mm displays 01

- mmm displays Jan

- mmmm displays January

- d displays 1

- dd displays 01

- ddd displays Sun

- dddd displays Sunday

- yy displays 17

- yyyy displays 2017

- mmmm d, yyyy displays January 1, 2017

- ddd m/d/yy displays Sun 1/1/17

Now let's look at some codes that format the time. Assuming a stored value of 0.25, the following format codes would produce the displayed values below.

- h displays 6

- hh displays 06

- h:mm displays 6:00

- hh:mm AM/PM displays 06:00 AM

- hh:mm:ss displays 06:00:00

You can mix and match the date and time formats as desired. Assuming the stored value represents January 1, 2017, at 6:00 a.m., the following format codes would produce the displayed values below:

- m/d/yy h:mm displays 1/1/17 6:00

- mmm d, yyyy h:mm A/P displays Jan 1, 2017 6:00 A

Before proceeding, we need to distinguish between the terms *time* and *duration*. For our discussion, we'll refer to a time as the time of day, such as 6:00 a.m. We'll refer to duration as the amount of elapsed time between a start and end time, such as six hours. Both are represented by the same stored value, 0.25. The displayed value is controlled, of course, by formatting, and there is a special format code we use for duration. Rather than just give the code, I think it will be more helpful, and more interesting, to understand the logic.

To examine the logic, let's use an example of an employee time sheet. Imagine a worksheet that contains five input cells, one for each workday. Let's say an employee works six hours per day, and thus enters

6:00 into each cell. When you sum these cells to determine the total number of hours worked during the week, you expect Excel to display 30:00 hours, but the result is an unexpected 6:00 hours. Why does this happen? Basically, it is because the cell is formatted as a time instead of a duration. Above we noted that .25 is the stored value for 6:00 hours. So .25 times five days is equal to 1.25. We know that the value to the left of the decimal represents the date and the decimal value represents the time. Thus, when a time format such as h:mm is applied, the value is displayed as 6:00. In fact, if you apply a date and time format, such as mmmm d, yyyy h:mm AM/PM, the cell would display January 1, 1900, 6:00 AM. The good news is that we can apply a format to display duration, or elapsed time, rather than the time of day.

Assuming a stored value of 1.25, the following elapsed time format codes would produce the displayed values:

- [hh] displays 30

- [hh]:mm displays 30:00

- [mm] displays 1800

So going forward, when our cell represents a time of day, we'll use a time format such as h:mm. When our cell represents a duration, we'll use an elapsed time format such as [h]:mm.

Finally, we need to know how to convert a duration, such as 6:30, into a decimal value, such as 6.5. This is useful when multiplying hours worked by a pay rate. Let's revisit our weekly time sheet. Our employee worked six hours per day for five days, and the total duration is displayed as 30:00 hours. When we multiply it by an hourly rate such as $10, we expect total pay, formatted as a currency, to be $300. Instead, we see $12.50. Why? Behind the displayed 30:00 hours lies a stored value of 1.25, and, as we've discussed, Excel formulas operate on stored values. We know that 1.25 times $10 is $12.50. Fortunately, the solution is pretty easy.

Let's consider what we know. We know Excel stores days as whole numbers and that one day is equal to 1. The fractional part basically divides one day into 24 hours. So, 12 hours is 12/24 or 0.5 and six hours is 6/24 or 0.25. To convert a duration into hours, we simply multiply it by 24. For example, 24 times 0.25 is six hours. And 24 times 0.5 is 12 hours. For reference, I'll call it out in the text.

To convert a time duration into a decimal value multiply it by 24.

Now that we know how to convert a duration into a decimal value, let's revisit our original issue: applying a pay rate of $10 per hour to the 30:00 hours worked (stored as 1.25). Rather than using a formula that multiplies the duration by the pay rate, such as 1.25*10, we need to multiply the duration by 24 first, such as (1.25*24)*10. This will provide the desired result of $300.

ROW AND COLUMN FORMATTING

The formatting discussed above can be applied to individual cells, ranges, or entire rows or columns. Speaking of rows and columns, we already know how to change the row height manually. During our skinny row discussion, we noted that we can click-and-drag or use the Row Height command.

 XREF

Skinny rows are discussed in Volume 1, Chapter 12.

In addition to changing row heights and column widths manually, we can also ask Excel to size them to automatically fit to the cell contents.

For example, if you have a column filled with data, and you'd like to be able to see the values for all of the cells in the column, you can ask Excel to AutoFit the column width. To do so, select the column and then use the following Ribbon command:

- Home > Format > AutoFit Column Width

 NOTE

If you select a single cell instead of the entire column, Excel will AutoFit the entire column based on the contents of the active cell only.

The same applies to rows, and the related Ribbon command is this:

- Home > Format > AutoFit Row Height

In addition to these commands, you can also double-click the row or column header border. To do so, navigate your mouse up toward the desired column's header (A, B, C, etc.), hover over the border on the right side of the header, and double-click. This causes Excel to AutoFit the column width to display all selected cell values in the column.

In addition to applying the AutoFit command one column at a time, you can select multiple rows or columns and AutoFit them all at the same time. To do this, select all desired columns (or rows), and then double-click the right (bottom) border on any of the selected columns (rows).

 NOTE

Paste Special allows you to paste column widths.

All right, let's do some exercises to practice some of these formatting skills.

EXAMPLES

Time to get to work.

 **PRACTICE**

To work along, please refer to *Formatting.xlsx.*

 VIDEO

To watch the solutions video, please visit the Excel University Video Library.

EXERCISE 1—LITTLE BLANK COLUMNS

In this exercise, we'll examine the efficiency of using little blank columns for formatting purposes.

 **PRACTICE**

To work along, please refer to the Exercise 1 worksheet.

This worksheet includes little blank columns between data columns. They were placed here for formatting purposes, specifically so that there are little gaps in the underlines between columns. Now we just need to finish up the report.

First we need to apply a bottom cell border to the column header cells, excluding the blank columns. We can't select the entire range and apply the border because the blank columns need to remain blank to create the formatting gaps. So we select each cell one by one and apply the bottom cell border. That took a few steps, but we've got it now—great!

Next we need to apply a bottom cell border, excluding the blank columns, on the *Fixed Assets* cells as well. Rather than formatting the cells one at a time as we did for the header row, we'll group-select the desired cells first and then apply the bottom cell border. That wasn't too bad.

XREF

Group-selecting nonadjacent cells is discussed in Volume 1, Chapter 18.

We are almost done. All we need to do now is write a formula that computes Total Assets. Using the SUM function, we write a formula into the first report column. Unfortunately, the little blank columns prevent us from simply filling the formula right. No worries—we know how to copy and paste. We copy and paste the formula into the remaining cells. Sure, it's annoying to have to copy and paste instead of filling right, but that's okay because at least we are done!

Whoops! We remember that we prefer to use a skinny row between our last data row and our formula row. So we insert a new row and change the row height to 4. Drat! Now our formatting is messed up. We remove the bottom cell border from the *Fixed Assets* cells and apply a bottom cell border to the skinny row cells. Again we have to exclude the little blank columns, so we have to format the individual cells instead of the range. Updating the formatting is kind of tedious, but that's okay because now we are done.

Ah, but wait. Our formula needs to include the skinny row. So we update the first Total Assets formula. Rather than once again copy and paste the formula, we decide to fill it right. Argh! Zeros now appear in the little blank columns. Okay, we go cell by cell and delete the formulas in the little blank columns. Hmm...updating this worksheet is a bit frustrating, but we really are done now, right?

Actually, there's one more thing. The skinny row caused us to think about our workbook design principles, and we remember that we prefer to use a SUBTOTAL function rather than a SUM function. So we rewrite the first Total Assets formula. Argh! Now to update the other formulas in the row we can either copy and paste or fill right and then delete the little blank column formulas. Either way we are rather frustrated because this is taking longer than it should. But that's okay because we can save the workbook and print the report.

Finally, we are done. Or are we? Here's the thing. Recurring-use workbooks are, by definition, used on an ongoing basis. We want them to be fast and easy to update and maintain. Our formatting choices impact our productivity, so in the next exercise we'll explore an alternate way to create those little gaps we want.

EXERCISE 2—ACCOUNTING UNDERLINE

In this exercise, we'll achieve the gaps without the little blank columns.

 **PRACTICE**

To work along, please refer to the Exercise 2 worksheet.

This worksheet contains two versions of the same report. In the first version, we were required to leave little gaps between the column underlines. In the second version, the gaps are not required. Let's go ahead and finish them both.

When gaps are required, we can get a productivity boost by creating the gaps with formatting instead of little blank columns. Let's begin with the column headers. We select the entire column header range, and apply a Single Accounting underline using the Format Cells dialog. It worked—we have little gaps!

On closer inspection we notice that the cells with text values include the desired formatting, but the cell with a number doesn't. As noted above, we can easily convert the stored value into a text string by including a leading apostrophe in the stored value. Nice!

Now for the skinny row formatting. We select the range and apply a Single Accounting underline. This time nothing appears. As noted above, we can enter a space into the empty cells to cause Excel to display the underline. Got it.

With the formatting done, let's write the Total Assets formula. We write the formula, and we can easily fill it right. This approach allows us to more quickly update formulas going forward.

When gaps are not required, life is easy. Rather than use little blank columns or formatting tricks, we'll just go with a bottom cell border. Indeed, this is the approach I use most often in practice. To finish the report, we select the column header range and apply a bottom cell border. Then, we select the skinny row cells and apply a bottom cell border. And…done.

EXERCISE 3—CUSTOM FORMATS

In this exercise, we'll practice several custom formats.

 **PRACTICE**

To work along, please refer to the Exercise 3 worksheet.

Custom formats can help us get the displayed value just the way we want. Let's practice by formatting a few dates, numbers, and times.

What you want to do in this worksheet is apply a custom format to achieve the desired format. For example, the first stored value in the worksheet is *43100*. You want to apply a custom format to that cell to achieve the desired format of *Dec*. To do this, open the Format Cells dialog and apply the custom format code "mmm." See how it works? I gave you the first answer. Now see if you can get the others on your own. It will be fun.

Spoiler alert! Stop reading now if you want to practice hands-on before getting the answers. The custom format codes are provided in Figure 3.

Stored Value	Desired Format	Format Code
43100	Dec	mmm
43100	Dec 31, 2017	mmm d, yyyy
250000	250 K	#,###, K
-225	225	#;#
0	-	#;#;-
1.25	6:00	h:mm
1.25	30:00	[hh]:mm

Figure 3

If you enjoyed this, try the Extra Credit exercise, which offers even more fun practice.

EXERCISE 4—WRAP TEXT

In this exercise, we'll wrap text to create paragraphs.

 **PRACTICE**

To work along, please refer to the Exercise 4 worksheet.

This worksheet contains a partial audit opinion letter. Although we could prepare it with Microsoft Word, we'd prefer to stay in Excel. By creating the reporting package with Excel, instead of a combination of Excel and Word, we can use the powerful features and functions of Excel.

We get started on the opinion letter, and things are going fine until we write our first paragraph. We quickly discover that Excel is not a word processor! As we type the paragraph, Excel doesn't wrap text like Word. Instead of automatically creating a new line when you reach the end of a cell, additional text is displayed on the same line. Fortunately, it is easy to tell Excel to wrap text like Word. To do so, we just use the Wrap Text command. Ah yes, much better.

With the formatting complete, we now want to retrieve values from the **E4 Data** sheet—namely, the *Client Name, Address*, and *Year End Date*. To do so, we convert the stored values to formulas and use familiar functions such as CONCATENATE and TEXT.

XREF

CONCATENATE is discussed in Volume 2, Chapter 19, and TEXT is discussed in Volume 2, Chapter 7.

Since we've used CONCATENATE and TEXT before, we won't rehash all the mechanics again here. However, there is an Excel specification to be aware of. Function arguments are limited to 255 characters. Typically, we don't encounter this limit because our function arguments are often short—for example, references such as *A1* or *Table[Column]*. But when using concatenation with paragraphs, we may bump into the 255-maximum-length specification. No problem. All we need to do is break down individual arguments into lengths of 255 or less. The limit applies to each function argument, not to the overall formula length, which has a limit of about 8,000 characters. Once we have our formulas working, we are ready to print or otherwise deliver the reporting package.

 NOTE

When printing, Excel will keep the content of a cell on the same printed page. Thus, you may need to split the cell content into multiple cells for printing purposes.

We are all set. Going forward, we simply update the input cell values as needed, and our formulas instantly pull them into the correct locations within the letter.

 NOTE

You may encounter an unexpected error if you try to write a formula that displays a quotation mark. You can display a quotation mark in a formula by using two quotation marks in a row. Or you can insert a Double Opening Quote and Double Closing Quote by using the Special Characters tab of the Symbol dialog (Insert > Symbol). These special quote marks won't interfere with the formula.

EXERCISE 5—CENTER ACROSS SELECTION

In this exercise, we'll align department headers across Budget and Actual columns.

 **PRACTICE**

To work along, please refer to the Exercise 5 worksheet.

In this report, we have Budget and Actual columns for each department, and we'd like our department headers to be centered over them. To do so, we select the department cell and the cell to the right and then use the *Center Across Selection* option from the Format Cells dialog. Now the cells are centered without being merged.

EXERCISE 6—TIME SHEET

In this exercise, we'll prepare a simple time sheet.

 **PRACTICE**

To work along, please refer to the Exercise 6 worksheet.

Our time sheet tracks the start and stop times for the morning and afternoon work periods. We want Excel to compute the total pay based on the hours worked and the hourly pay rate.

Let's start with the input cells. We want all of the input cells to display a time of day, such as 8:00 a.m. This means we want to apply a Time format. We select the input cells and select the desired Time format, such as a 12-hour Time format that displays a.m./p.m. accordingly. So far, so good.

Now we move to the *Total Hours* column. We notice that the total shows 16:00, but we expect it to be 40 hours for the week since we worked eight hours per day. It appears as though either the formula or Excel is broken. Nobody panic. It's a simple matter of cell formatting. The *Total Hours* column does not represent a time of day; rather, it represents a duration. Thus, we want to apply an elapsed time format. To do so, we select the cells and then apply a Custom format, such as [h]:mm. Now the total displays the expected 40 hours. Whew!

The final task is to compute total pay. We need to apply the hourly pay rate to the number of hours. So we write a formula to populate the *Hours Decimal* column that multiplies the elapsed time by 24. The *Total Pay* column is easy; we simply apply the decimal hours to the pay rate.

CHAPTER CONCLUSION

In this chapter we explored several formatting techniques and options that can help boost our productivity and get our worksheets looking just the way we want.

Chapter 6: Printing

SET UP

If you are like me, you deliver electronic documents far more frequently than paper documents. However, the same settings in Excel that are used to print to paper also determine how worksheets appear when converted to PDF. That is, Excel's print settings are applied when printing to paper or PDF. Fortunately, Excel provides many useful settings that allow us to control how documents are printed, whatever the destination. Although we won't cover them all, I would like to highlight a few of my favorites.

HOW TO

In this chapter we examine the following items:

- Workbook views

- Page layout

- Page setup

- Print preview

Let's get to them.

WORKBOOK VIEWS

It is important to realize that Excel has different options for viewing workbooks. The default view is called *Normal*, but there are other views available. You can change the view with the icons located in the lower-right corner of the Excel window or in the following Ribbon group:

- View > Workbook Views

Let's examine the Page Break Preview and Page Layout views and discuss their related commands.

Page Break Preview

Page Break Preview is a fast way to view and edit the print area and page breaks. Use the following Ribbon icon to check it out:

- View > Page Break Preview

Excel zooms the view to about 60 percent and places blue lines into the display. Solid blue lines identify the print area, and dotted blue lines represent page breaks.

 NOTE

Excel zooms the view to 60 percent, but you can change the magnification level manually with the icons in the View > Zoom Ribbon group, or you can use the Zoom slider or buttons in the lower-right corner of the Excel window.

 KB

Hold down Ctrl and use the mouse wheel to zoom.

The print area, represented by solid blue lines, identifies the range of cells to be printed. You can click-and-drag the blue lines to define the print area as desired. Setting the print area is useful when your sheet includes cells that shouldn't appear when printed. Alternatively, you can select the desired cells and then choose the Set Print Area command from the right-click shortcut menu. You can reset the print area back to the default by right-clicking any cell and then selecting Reset Print Area.

When the print area is larger than a single printed page, Excel displays dotted blue lines to identify the page breaks. You can click-and-drag a page break line as desired. Once you do, the line changes from dotted to solid. You can insert a new page break by selecting a row, column, or cell, and then right-clicking and selecting Insert Page Break. You can reset the page breaks by right-clicking any cell and selecting Reset All Page Breaks.

Speaking of page breaks, two features we've discussed during the series have built-in page break options, the Subtotal feature and the PivotTable feature. In the Subtotal dialog, the *Page Break Between Groups* checkbox causes Excel to automatically insert page breaks between each Subtotal group. To do this with PivotTable row and column fields, use the *Insert Page Break After Each Item* checkbox found in the Field Settings dialog.

Page Layout

The Page Layout workbook view demonstrates how the worksheet will appear when printed, including headers, footers, page breaks, margins, and print headers. Use the following Ribbon icon to check it out:

- View > Page Layout

Once in Page Layout view, you'll see the worksheet displayed in pages rather than a continuous grid of cells. Excel displays any headers and footers. If there are none, the worksheet displays *Click to add header* at the top of each page and *Click to add footer* at the bottom.

Headers and footers are displayed on each printed page. They have three sections (left, center, and right) and support the use of text strings, numbers, images, and elements.

When we click into a header or footer, we get a new Ribbon tab:

- Header & Footer Tools > Design

This tab contains many settings, including built-in header and footer choices and design options. Let's focus on the numerous elements we can place into a header or footer, such as page number and current time. Clicking an element icon inserts a little code into the header/footer, such as *&[Page]* and *&[Time]*. During the print process, Excel converts these little codes into the desired element, such as *1* or *1:00 p.m.* You can mix elements with text as well. For example, a footer could contain *Page &[Page] of &[Pages]*, which would cause Excel to print the current page number and total pages on each page, such as *Page 1 of 10*.

The ampersand (&) character used within a header/footer is reserved by Excel for these elements. If you try to print one in a header, you'll notice it disappears. For example, if you enter *AA & Co* into a header, Excel will display *AA Co* instead. You can force Excel to display an ampersand by using two in a row—for example, *AA && Co* will display *AA & Co*.

Now let's talk about how page numbers work. When you print a single worksheet, the page numbers start at 1 and increment for each printed page. But let's say we need to print more than one worksheet—for example, a balance sheet and an income statement. If we print the sheets one at a time, then the page numbers will start at 1 each time. Although this behavior may be fine in some situations, at times we may need a continuous sequence of page numbers used through all printed reports. That is, we need Excel to start at page number 1 for the balance sheet and page number 2 for the income statement. We already know from a previous discussion that we can group-select worksheets. Remember? And we already know that Excel prints sheets in the order they are located in the workbook. So if we select multiple sheets first, and then print the active sheets, Excel will print them in the order they are stored in the workbook, using continuous page numbers, and the total page count will include the total number of pages for all selected sheets.

Selection groups are discussed in Volume 1, Chapter 18, and print order is discussed in Volume 1, Chapter 15.

If you have the same header/footer to apply to many sheets, group-select them first so that the changes will be made to all selected sheets at once.

Check out the other elements as well. Some are pretty cool, including inserting the file path.

You can insert the file path into a cell using a formula with the CELL function.

In addition to the Page Layout workbook view, Excel also has a Page Layout Ribbon tab with many print-related options.

PAGE LAYOUT RIBBON

Many of the commands available on the Page Layout Ribbon tab are fairly straightforward, such as switching the orientation from portrait to landscape, setting the print area, and changing the page size. Rather than write a comprehensive review of all of them, I'll just cover Scale to Fit and Print Titles.

Scale to Fit

Scale to Fit allows us to squeeze the printed worksheet into a defined number of pages wide and/or high. This is often faster than fussing with page breaks. For example, I'll ask Excel to squeeze all content into one page wide and run for as many pages down as needed. As more content is added to the worksheet over time, Excel will continue to fit it to one page wide and as many high as necessary. To apply this setting, use the following Ribbon control:

- Page Layout > Width > 1 Page

There are other options to explore, such as scaling to a fixed percentage, such as 50 percent.

Print Titles

Print Titles allow us to repeat selected rows or columns on each printed page. Typically, these will include the report's column headers. For example, if you have 12 monthly columns and hundreds of data rows, you can set the header row (with monthly labels) as a print title and Excel will include it on all printed pages. To set print titles, click the following:

- Page Layout > Print Titles

This opens the Page Setup dialog, where you can enter the print titles by using the *Rows to repeat at top* and *Columns to repeat at left* fields. If you want to repeat row *5* on all printed pages, you can select the row with your mouse or enter the row reference *$5:$5* manually.

While we are in the Page Setup dialog box, there are other fun settings to explore. Let's quickly run through a few.

PAGE SETUP

The Page Setup dialog provides numerous print-related settings. The Page Layout Ribbon tab has several Page Setup dialog launcher icons. These are the little icons in the lower-right corner of the Page Setup, Scale to Fit, and Sheet Options Ribbon groups. Each opens to a different tab within the Page Setup dialog.

 KB

Alt P, SP opens the Page Setup dialog.

 NOTE

If you do a lot of printing, you may want to add the Page Setup command to the QAT.

The Page tab of the Page Setup dialog allows you to define orientation and scaling, as well as the first page number to use. This can be useful if you need your page numbers to start at a number other than 1.

The Margins tab allows you to define how much space should appear between the printed content and the edges of the page.

The Header/Footer tab provides similar options to the Header & Footer Tools Ribbon tab discussed previously.

The Sheet tab allows you to set the print area, choose to print titles, and select a variety of other options, including whether to print the gridlines or the row and column headings. Plus you can control how cell comments and errors are displayed.

Comments are discussed in Chapter 15.

Once the desired print settings are applied, it is time to preview the printed document.

PRINT PREVIEW

Print Preview shows us how the printed document will appear. You can open Print Preview with the following Ribbon command:

- File > Print

Ctrl+P and Ctrl+F2 open Print Preview.

In addition to providing a preview of the printed document, this screen includes another option for opening the Page Setup dialog and contains many of the same settings we've explored previously, including orientation and scaling. It also provides a few other options, including selecting the printer and identifying what to print, such as the active sheets, the entire workbook, or just the selected range. Printing the selection can be handy if you want to create several printed reports from a single sheet. If you have several areas within a sheet you want to print separately, you could define a name for each range and then select and print each.

Naming ranges and quickly navigating to them is discussed in Volume 1, Chapter 7.

NOTE

If you have a third-party PDF printer, you can print to PDF by selecting the corresponding printer from Print Preview. You can also use Excel's built-in PDF tool by using the File > Export command.

We've just skimmed the surface of print settings, highlighting a few settings that I've found useful over the years. You may want to explore the Excel Help system for more information.

EXAMPLES

All right, it is time to open the workbook and get to work.

 **PRACTICE**

To work along, please refer to *Printing.xlsx*.

 VIDEO

To watch the solutions video, please visit the Excel University Video Library.

EXERCISE 1—PAGE BREAKS

In this exercise, we'll manually set the page breaks.

 **PRACTICE**

To work along, please refer to the Exercise 1 worksheet.

We've built a quarterly report. If we try to print it in portrait orientation with 8.5" x 11" dimensions, Excel automatically places a vertical page break between the *Q4* and *Total* columns, effectively placing the *Total* column on a separate printed page. Since we want the *Total* column to appear on the same page as the quarterly columns, we need to adjust the page break.

Fortunately, it is easy to manually adjust page breaks when necessary. We switch to the Page Break Preview workbook view, and then click-and-drag the vertical dotted blue page break lines to the right side of the *Total* column. We take a look at the Print Preview and confirm the *Total* column now appears on the same page as the quarterly columns.

Manually setting page breaks like this for one-time reports may work fine, but doing so to maintain recurring-use workbooks can be tedious, especially when column widths are adjusted or new columns are added. In the next exercise, we'll ask Excel to automatically fit the columns.

EXERCISE 2—SCALING

In this exercise, we'll fit all columns on one page.

 **PRACTICE**

To work along, please refer to the Exercise 2 worksheet.

We have the same report as the previous exercise. Instead of manually adjusting the page break, we'll keep the *Total* column with the quarterly columns with print scaling.

To scale the document to fit one page wide, we set the Ribbon's Width field to 1 page, or use the corresponding *Fit to* field in the Page Setup dialog. We take a look at the Print Preview and confirm everything looks good.

This is a great option for recurring-use workbooks because even as column widths are adjusted or new columns are added, Excel will continue to fit the report to one page wide and use as many pages high as needed.

EXERCISE 3—PRINT TITLES

In this exercise, we'll create print titles that repeat on each page.

 **PRACTICE**

To work along, please refer to the Exercise 3 worksheet.

Same report as before. We set the scaling to 1 page wide so that all columns appear together. When we look at the Print Preview, we notice our report is one page wide and two pages high. When we preview the second page, we notice that the report's column headers are not displayed. The column headers would help our reader, so let's set the print titles.

We click the Print Titles Ribbon icon to open the Page Setup dialog box. In the *Rows to repeat at top* field, we select the worksheet row that contains the headers—namely, row *13*. Excel enters the correct row reference, *$13:$13*, and we close the dialog. We take a look at the Print Preview and confirm that each page includes the report's column headers.

EXERCISE 4—HEADER/FOOTER

In this exercise, we'll set up a print header and footer.

 **PRACTICE**

To work along, please refer to the Exercise 4 worksheet.

Okay, same report as before. This time though, we want to include a header to display the date and time, as well as a footer to display the file path and page number, and we want to exclude the instructions from being printed. Let's knock out the easy stuff first. We scale to print one page wide and set row *13* as the print title.

Now let's create the header. We switch to the Page Layout workbook view. We click the top of the worksheet to add a header. We insert the Current Date and Current Time into the right header region. We confirm Excel inserts the codes *&[Date]&[Time]* as expected. We enter a space between these codes so they don't run together.

Next, the footer. We scroll down to the bottom of the sheet to add a footer. We click into the left footer area, and then select the File Path icon. Excel inserts the *&[Path]&[File]* codes, which will display both the path and file name. Next we click into the right footer area and the Select the Page Number icon. Excel inserts the *&[Page]* code.

With the headers and footers complete, let's switch back to Normal workbook view. This will make setting the print area a bit easier. Currently our printed report will include the instructions found in the cells above the report. Since we want to exclude them, we'll set the print area by selecting the report range *B13:G62* and using the Set Print Area command. We take a look at the Print Preview and confirm everything looks good!

CHAPTER CONCLUSION

In this chapter we examined several print-related options that enable us to get our documents formatted for delivery.

Chapter 7: Protecting

SET UP

By thinking about ways future users could break our workbooks, we can anticipate risks and address them up front. This practice enables us to build bulletproof workbooks that work reliably over time. You'll recall that we discussed this principle early on in the series.

 XREF

Workbook design principles are discussed in Volume 1, Chapter 19.

Sometimes addressing these types of risks is as simple as using data validation to control what a user can type into a cell. There are times, though, when we need more. For example, we may want to allow the user to enter values into the input cells but protect the other cells. Perhaps we want to protect all the cells on an entire sheet or prevent the user from deleting sheets. Fortunately, there are many levels of protection offered by Excel. Let's check them out.

HOW TO

This chapter discusses three levels of Excel protection:

- Protecting the cells with Worksheet Protection

- Protecting the sheets with Workbook Protection

- Protecting the workbook with File Encryption

As you can see, each feature addresses a different area of the workbook. The features are independent and can therefore be applied individually or in different combinations depending on your needs. Let's take them one at a time.

WORKSHEET PROTECTION

Worksheet Protection protects the cells. We need to first understand that every cell, in every worksheet, in every workbook, by default is locked. Wait, what? Yes, locked. Now, here is the key. The locked attribute isn't enforced until you turn on Worksheet Protection. And that is the important part, so I'll call it out for reference.

> *The locked attribute isn't enforced until you turn on Worksheet Protection.*

As you can see, there are actually two topics here: locking a cell and protecting a worksheet. Plus we'll want to let the user know which cells are locked and unlocked. We'll cover each of these topics, starting with locking a cell.

Locking a Cell

You can view and set the locked status by selecting the cell and then using the following Ribbon icon:

- Home > Format > Lock Cell

In practice, I most often view and set the locked status from within the Format Cells dialog box. The last tab in the Format Cells dialog box is the Protection tab, and it has two checkboxes, Locked and Hidden. *Locked* means a user is not allowed to type a value into the cell, and *Hidden* prevents the cell value or formula from being displayed in the formula bar.

Here is a fun test that you can try right now. Create a new workbook. Then select any cell on any sheet. Now see whether the cell is locked. It is, right? That is because every cell is locked by default. Now try to type a value into the cell. You are able to do this even though the cell is locked. You can type a value into the cell because the locked attribute isn't enforced until you turn on Worksheet Protection.

In practice, then, you'll want to first unlock the input cells and then turn on Worksheet Protection.

Turning on Worksheet Protection

You can open the Protect Sheet dialog with the following Ribbon icon:

- Home > Format > Protect Sheet

You can also use the following Ribbon icon:

- Review > Protect Sheet

 KB

Alt+R, P, S toggles worksheet protection on and off.

The Protect Sheet dialog box provides numerous options, as shown in Figure 4.

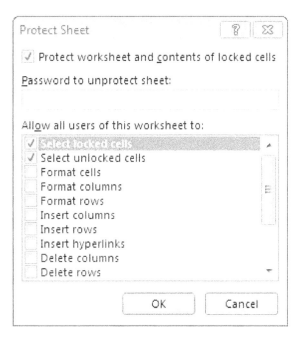

Figure 4

You can set an optional password that would be required to unprotect the worksheet. The *Allow all users of this worksheet to* checkboxes define what a user can do while the sheet is protected. The first two options,

Select locked cells and *Select unlocked cells*, are checked by default, meaning the user can select any cell in the worksheet. If you want to confine a user to navigating through unlocked (input) cells only, uncheck the *Select locked cells* checkbox. There are many other things that we can allow the user to do while the worksheet is protected, such as formatting cells and inserting rows. Feel free to explore the remaining checkboxes in the list using Excel's built-in Help system as needed.

To unprotect a protected sheet, use the following Ribbon icon:

- Review > Unprotect Sheet

If the worksheet was protected with an optional password, Excel will ask for it.

So far, we know that we first unlock the input cells and then turn on Worksheet Protection. This will enable the user to enter values into the unlocked cells only. But how will the user know which cells are unlocked? Well, that leads us back to a discussion we had long ago about highlighting input cells. Let's revisit and refine this discussion.

Highlighting Input Cells

As you know, we can highlight input cells for the user by applying the Input cell style.

 XREF

Highlighting input cells is discussed in Volume 1, Chapter 14.

By modifying the default Input cell style, we can convince Excel to automatically unlock the cell when we apply it. This way, both unlocking and highlighting are accomplished in a single step.

To do this, we right-click the following Ribbon icon:

- Home > Cell Styles > Input

We select *Modify* from the resulting shortcut menu to open the Style dialog box shown in Figure 5.

Figure 5

This dialog allows us to define which formatting elements are included with the style. By default the Input cell style includes Font, Border, and Fill formatting. When we apply the Input cell style, we replace the cell's existing Font, Border, and Fill formatting with those defined by the style. Any existing Number, Alignment, and Protection formatting is preserved, unaltered when we apply the style. We use the checkboxes in the Style dialog to tell Excel which formatting elements to apply.

Each checkbox relates to a tab in the Format Cells dialog. As you can see, there is one checkbox for each tab: Number, Alignment, Font, Border, Fill, and Protection. We click the Format button to open the Format Cells dialog and define the formatting for the style. The selections we make in the Format Cells dialog for the style are only included in the style definition when the corresponding checkbox is checked in the Style dialog. With that background out of the way, let's turn our attention back to the task at hand: telling Excel to unlock the cell when we apply the Input style.

We start by clicking the Style dialog's Format button. This reveals the Format Cells dialog. We clear the Locked checkbox on the Protection tab and click OK. This returns us to the Style dialog, where we confirm the Protection checkbox is checked and click OK. Now when we apply the style to highlight input cells, they will also be unlocked. When we turn on Worksheet Protection, the user can enter values into these cells. This approach allows us to format and unlock input cells in a single step.

 NOTE

Sometimes cells that had the style applied prior to the modification are not automatically updated. When this happens, you can reapply the style to those cells.

 NOTE

Style customizations are stored within the workbook. If you have cells styles in one workbook that you'd like to import into another, use the Cell Styles > Merge Styles command.

WORKBOOK PROTECTION

Workbook Protection protects the sheets. For example, this feature allows us to prevent a user from adding, renaming, or deleting worksheets. You can open the Protect Structure and Windows dialog with the following Ribbon icon:

- Review > Protect Workbook

 KB

Alt+R, P, W activates the Protect Workbook command.

The Structure checkbox is selected by default and it prevents a user from adding, deleting, renaming, moving, copying, hiding, and unhiding worksheets. You can enter an optional password that would be required to unprotect the workbook. Click OK to protect the workbook.

 NOTE

The Protect Structure and Windows dialog includes a Windows checkbox that prevented users from modifying workbook Windows in older versions of Excel. This checkbox is disabled in Excel 2010+ and remains in the dialog for backward compatibility.

To unprotect the workbook, use the following Ribbon icon:

- Review > Protect Workbook

If an optional password was established, Excel will ask for it.

FILE ENCRYPTION

File Encryption protects the workbook by requiring the user to enter a password to gain access to the workbook.

To encrypt a workbook with a password, use the following command:

- File > Info > Protect Workbook > Encrypt with Password

In the resulting Encrypt Document dialog, enter the desired password and then confirm it. Once the workbook is saved and closed, Excel will ask for the password to open the file.

 NOTE

Although the encryption level depends on various factors, including the version of Excel, network group policy settings, and the file format, Excel documents are generally encrypted with AES-128. Group policy may allow IT administrators to bypass this file encryption.

The Save As dialog box also provides access to the File Encryption feature. You can select Tools > General Options to open the General Options dialog. This dialog allows you to set a password to open the file (accomplishing the same thing we did above), as well as set a password to modify the file.

Now let's open Excel to practice.

EXAMPLES

We'll practice by completing several exercises.

 **PRACTICE**

To work along, please refer to *Protecting.xlsx*.

 VIDEO

To watch the solutions video, please visit the Excel University Video Library.

EXERCISE 1—WORKSHEET PROTECTION

In this exercise, we'll use worksheet protection to protect the cells.

 **PRACTICE**

To work along, please refer to the Exercise 1 worksheet.

This worksheet contains a basic travel expense reimbursement request form. We would like our employees to enter values into the *Amount* cells but not be able to modify any other cells, including the formula that computes the total.

Let's begin by checking out the locked status of the *Amount* cells. We select any *Amount* cell. We open the Format Cells dialog and confirm the cell is locked. Yet Excel still allows us to enter a value into the cell because the locked attribute isn't enforced until we turn on worksheet protection. After turning on worksheet protection, we confirm that Excel now prevents us from changing the cell value. Our objective is to allow users to enter amounts, so we'll make a few modifications to the worksheet.

We first unprotect the sheet. Then we select the *Amount* cells and unlock them by clearing the checkbox in the Format Cells dialog. With the *Amount* cells unlocked, we now apply Worksheet Protection. We confirm we can enter amounts as desired, and when we try to enter something into any of the locked cells, we receive the expected error alert.

Before we save, we notice our worksheet looks a little funny because we didn't highlight the input cells. We could adjust this by applying a cell format or a cell style to the input cells. We would first unlock the input cells and then highlight them. Rather than unlocking cells and highlighting them in a two-step process, in the next exercise, we highlight them and unlock them in a single step.

EXERCISE 2—INPUT CELL STYLE

In this exercise, we'll modify the standard Input cell style.

 **PRACTICE**

To work along, please refer to the Exercise 2 worksheet.

This worksheet helps us compute commission for each sales representative. We select the rep from the drop-down, and the formulas update the sales for the selected rep and compute the related commission. We spent time getting the formulas set up just right, so we'd like to address the risk of a user breaking them. We'll apply Worksheet Protection, but we also want to identify the input cell. Rather than thinking about unlocking input cells and then identifying unlocked cells as two separate tasks, we'll think about them as one.

Let's modify the Input cell style's definition so that when applied, the cell is unlocked. We right-click the Input cell style and select Modify. We click the Format button and uncheck the Locked checkbox in the resulting Format Cells dialog. We click OK to close the Format Cells dialog and confirm that the Protection checkbox in the Style dialog is checked. We click OK to close the Style dialog box.

 NOTE

If you try to modify a cell style while the workbook contains a protected worksheet, you may receive an error alert. If so, remove worksheet protection from all worksheets and try again.

Now let's test it out. We apply the Input cell style to the Rep input cell and turn on worksheet protection. We confirm that we are able to select a rep from the drop-down and that we are not able to modify any other cells. It worked!

We like this approach because, going forward, all we need to do is apply the Input cell style to other input cells, and they will automatically be unlocked.

EXERCISE 3—WORKBOOK PROTECTION

In this exercise, we'll apply Workbook and Worksheet Protection.

 **PRACTICE**

To work along, please refer to the Exercise 3 worksheet.

This worksheet computes sales for the selected region. We want to allow the user to select a region from the drop-down. We want to prevent the user from modifying any other cells, and we'll use Worksheet Protection to accomplish that. Additionally, we store values used to create the sales report on an admin sheet, which we name *E3 Admin*. To keep the workbook clean, we'll hide the admin sheet. We want to prevent the user from unhiding the admin worksheet, and we'll use Workbook Protection to accomplish that. Let's get to it.

 XREF

Hiding a worksheet is discussed in Volume 1, Chapter 13.

First we hide the admin sheet. To prevent the user from unhiding it, we protect the workbook by clicking the Protect Workbook command. We test it by trying to unhide a worksheet. Since we can't, we determine the workbook protection is complete and we move to worksheet protection.

 NOTE

Formulas can retrieve values from hidden sheets. The user can also retrieve values from hidden sheets by setting up simple formulas in a visible sheet.

The Region drop-down is the input cell. We want to highlight it and unlock it. Since we modified the workbook's Input cell style in the previous exercise, we don't need to modify it again now. We can simply apply the Input cell style and protect the worksheet. We confirm that we are now able to update the Region cell and not the other cells.

EXERCISE 4—FILE ENCRYPTION

In this exercise, we'll encrypt a workbook and require a password to open it.

 **PRACTICE**

To work along, please refer to the Exercise 4 worksheet.

We begin by creating a new workbook. We encrypt it with a password by selecting the following command:

- File > Info > Protect Workbook > Encrypt with Password

In the resulting Encrypt Document dialog, we enter the desired password and then confirm it. We save and close the workbook. Now for the big test. We open the workbook and confirm a password is required to open it. Perfect!

CHAPTER CONCLUSION

In this chapter we discussed three Excel protection levels. Worksheet Protection protects the cells, Workbook Protection protects the sheets, and File Encryption protects the workbook.

Chapter 8: Hyperlink Feature

SET UP

Do you remember a long time ago when workpapers were made with—you know—paper? Oh yeah, and columnar paper—that was awesome! When I prepared workpapers with actual paper, I didn't like updating them because I'd have to erase totals and recalculate them. Not only was it a lot of work, I'd have little eraser shavings all over the place. But there were a few things I really liked about using paper. I liked that I could easily use a red pencil to index and cross-reference workpapers and tick and tie numbers. Once my workpapers were organized, I could file them in a metal filing cabinet. And the following year when I needed to grab the prior year's workpapers, I could simply retrieve them from the file room. Every single workpaper was neatly labeled, indexed, and organized.

Today we use digital workpapers, often in the form of Excel workbooks. How do you keep your digital workpapers organized? Do you store them in network folders? If so, do you ever have trouble locating the files? For example, let's say you are looking for an Excel file that was used to reconcile the bank statement. You can't remember if you saved it to your network or to your laptop. Eventually, after browsing around the network, you find the right folder. But when you open it, you find multiple copies of the file, such as Bank Rec.xlsx, Bank Rec 2.xlsx, and Bank Rec Updated.xlsx, and you're not sure which is the final version. Argh! If this example resonates with you, I have good news. Excel's Hyperlink feature can help us stay organized.

Hyperlinks help us organize related electronic documents.

Instead of using a red pencil, we can use hyperlinks to cross-reference and organize the digital files that relate to a specific project. For example, you can easily navigate through all the files related to a monthly financial reporting package, a biweekly payroll, an audit, a tax return, or the quarterly financials with hyperlinks.

Excel hyperlinks can link to digital files regardless of file type. We can create Excel hyperlinks not only to a project's Excel files but also to, say, the related PDF source documents, Word documents, CSV files, or a PowerPoint presentation. All the files involved in the project, regardless of file type, can be organized with Excel hyperlinks.

HOW TO

Let's clarify what a hyperlink does and doesn't do. A hyperlink helps a user navigate to a specific destination. It doesn't retrieve values from the destination. Excel hyperlinks are similar to the hyperlinks you encounter in your web browser. Clicking a hyperlink simply navigates you to the destination. An Excel hyperlink is flexible, and the destination can be many things, including a cell, a range, a named range, a worksheet, a workbook, a web page, a PDF file, a Word file, a network folder, and more. When the destination is not an Excel file or reference, the application associated with the file type is used. For example, if an Excel hyperlink refers to a Word document, the document is opened inside of Microsoft Word, and if the destination is a web page, then the default browser is used to open to the page.

 XREF

File type extensions and associated applications are discussed in Volume 3, Chapter 23.

It is important to understand that a hyperlink created with the Hyperlink feature is static. It does not exchange values with the destination file. It doesn't retrieve or update cell values. It is a static link that provides quick access to the destination. Excel doesn't continuously monitor external hyperlink destinations and update them if a file is moved or deleted. If a destination is not available when the hyperlink is clicked, the user receives an error alert.

Let's walk through the following ways to use the Hyperlink feature:

- Managing hyperlinks
- Getting back
- Images and shapes
- Applications

Let's dig into the mechanics now.

MANAGING HYPERLINKS

To use hyperlinks in our workbooks, we need to know how to add, edit, and delete them.

Add a Hyperlink

A hyperlink has two components: the destination and the friendly text. The *friendly text* is the clickable text displayed in the cell, and the *destination* is a reference to the target file or location.

Adding a hyperlink is easy. We select the desired cell and click the following Ribbon icon:

- Insert > Hyperlink

Ctrl+K opens the Hyperlink dialog.

This reveals the Insert Hyperlink dialog as shown in Figure 6.

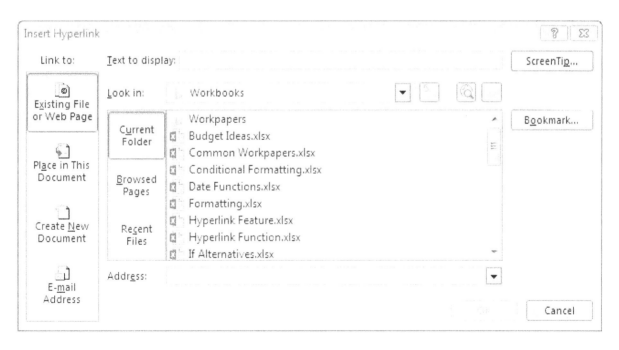

Figure 6

Let's take a quick tour through the Insert Hyperlink dialog. You enter the friendly text in the *Text to display* field. If the active cell is blank, this field will be empty, and you can type in the desired friendly text. If the active cell contains a value, it will be used as the friendly text.

You enter the destination into the *Address* field. You can type, paste, or browse to enter the reference to the target location. For example, if you want the hyperlink to open the Excel file Formatting.xlsx stored in the root of your C drive, the address would be C:\Formatting.xlsx. If you want the hyperlink to open Google's home page with the default web browser, the address would be http://www.google.com.

 NOTE

To view the destination file, the user needs to have access to the target location.

The *ScreenTip* button allows you to customize the pop-up that appears when a user hovers over the hyperlink. By default the destination is displayed, but you can enter something else if desired.

The *Link to* buttons provide four types of destinations:

- Existing File or Web Page—creates an external link to another file or URL, such as an Excel workbook, a PDF file, or a web page

- Place in This Document—creates an internal link to a range within the workbook

- Create New Document—creates a new file and a corresponding link to it

- E-mail Address—creates a link that will initiate a new email message with the specified email address and subject in the user's default mail program

There are a few other buttons in the dialog. The *Bookmark* button is useful when you want to navigate to a specific worksheet or range within another workbook. After selecting the destination workbook, click the *Bookmark* button to reveal the sheets and named ranges. The little Browse the Web icon launches a web browser, making it easy to navigate to the desired page and then copy and paste the URL into the *Address* field.

Once the hyperlink is inserted, single-clicking it will navigate to the destination.

 NOTE

In addition to inserting a hyperlink into your worksheet, you can also embed existing documents such as PDF files into your workbook. This makes a copy of the file and saves it inside the workbook. Use the Insert > Object command and navigate to the desired file by clicking the Browse button on the Create from File tab. Check the *Display as Icon* box to generate an icon in the Excel file that the user can double-click to open the associated application.

Edit a Hyperlink

To edit a link, right-click the link and select Edit Hyperlink, or use the following Ribbon icon:

- Insert > Hyperlink

The Edit Hyperlink dialog will be displayed, and you can make the desired changes.

 NOTE

Once a cell contains a hyperlink, it may appear as if you are unable to edit the cell value (because clicking the cell with the mouse navigates to the hyperlink destination). You can select the cell to edit it by using your Arrow keys or by holding the mouse down until the pointer turns to a plus.

Delete a Hyperlink

To delete a hyperlink, right-click the link and select Remove Hyperlink, or use the following Ribbon icon:

- Insert > Hyperlink

Then click the Remove Link button in the Edit Hyperlink dialog.

GETTING BACK

After navigating to the destination by clicking a hyperlink, you may want a way to get back to the original file other than by manually navigating or closing the destination file. There are several options.

If the destination is another Excel location, you could create a return link that points back to the original file. For example, if you have a collection of related documents all hyperlinked from an index worksheet, you could set up return links in the various destination files that point back to the index.

 NOTE

Other document types support hyperlinks as well, including Office documents such as Word and PowerPoint.

Another option is to add the Back command icon to your QAT. After navigating with a hyperlink, clicking the Back button returns you to the previous location.

XREF

Adding commands to the QAT is discussed in Chapter 2.

 NOTE

You can also add the Forward command icon to the QAT.

The Go To dialog also tries to track previous locations allowing you to navigate back. Simply open the Go To dialog and press Enter.

 KB

The Go To dialog can be opened with F5 or Ctrl+G.

Although in practice the Back button and Go To dialog work fairly well, they can get confused occasionally. When navigation between files needs to be reliable for users, creating return links in the destination files is a solid option.

IMAGES AND SHAPES

In addition to creating hyperlinks that display clickable text, we can create a hyperlink using numerous other Excel objects, such as images and shapes. To do so, right-click the object and select Hyperlink, or click the object and then the following Ribbon icon:

- Insert > Hyperlink

Excel displays the standard Hyperlink dialog and allows you to specify the destination.

 XREF

Inserting shapes and images is discussed in Volume 3, Chapter 26.

This capability provides many fun options for incorporating hyperlinks into your workbooks.

APPLICATIONS

There are many ways to apply the Hyperlink feature. Here are just a few ideas.

- Workpaper index—organizes the digital files related to a project

- Worksheet index—navigates within large workbooks that have many worksheets

- Cross-referencing—references values to the related workpapers or supporting documents

- Digital reporting—creates a report index to make it easy for users to access digital reports

Workpaper Index

You can create a workbook that contains external hyperlinks to the related project files. It provides quick access for you, your manager, or your staff.

Worksheet Index

Have you ever worked in a workbook that contains a lot of sheets? Navigating to the right sheet can take a while. A worksheet index contains internal hyperlinks to the worksheets within the workbook, helping you navigate within the workbook more quickly.

 XREF

An index worksheet is discussed in Volume 1, Chapter 15.

Cross-Referencing

You can use hyperlinks to cross-reference values to the related workpapers, lead schedules, source files, or other supporting documents.

Digital Reporting

When we deliver digital reports to others, we can create a convenient report index using Excel hyperlinks. This is a nice alternative to emailing report attachments to all users each period. After opening the report index workbook, the user sees a list of available reports. The user can open any desired report simply by clicking the corresponding hyperlink.

NOTE

If you don't want the report users having access to your source files, you can save a reporting copy of them to a network drive providing users with read-only permission. If the reports don't need to be interactive, you can use Excel's Save As command to convert the Excel reports to a static file type such as PDF or HTML.

The report index can be organized in a variety of ways—for example, in monthly or quarterly sections. It is easy to maintain an ongoing archive of reports as well. You can copy the previous period's links— for example, January—and paste it into a new section, February. Then you can edit the hyperlink destinations so they point to the correct current period reports. This makes it easy for users to gain access to historical reports.

If you want to make the report index clean, remove gridlines and the worksheet row and column headers with the following Ribbon checkboxes:

- View > Gridlines

- View > Headings

 NOTE

The Gridlines and Headings checkboxes apply to the active worksheet. The Formula Bar checkbox applies to the Excel application, not the active worksheet.

Well, enough talk. Let's get to work.

EXAMPLES

We'll experiment with hyperlinks in the following exercises.

 **PRACTICE**

To work along, please refer to *Hyperlink Feature.xlsx*.

 VIDEO

To watch the solutions video, please visit the Excel University Video Library.

EXERCISE 1—WORKPAPER INDEX

In this exercise, we'll create a simple workpaper index.

 **PRACTICE**

To work along, please refer to the Exercise 1 worksheet.

We want to use hyperlinks to organize our digital workpapers to facilitate a review by our manager and next year's staff. We decide to create an index that includes a list of the workpapers and related hyperlinks. After entering the workpaper names, we are ready to create the hyperlinks.

The first hyperlink will navigate to the trial balance workbook. We select the cell and then use the Hyperlink feature to create a hyperlink to the *Workpapers\Trial Balance.xlsx* workbook. Excel automatically updates the font color and underlines the text. Time to test it out. We click the new hyperlink and confirm that Excel opens the destination workbook. We close the trial balance workbook and are ready to set up the next link.

Next we hyperlink the cash reconciliation workpaper to the *Workpapers\Cash Recon.xlsx* workbook. We click the link and confirm Excel takes us to the destination workbook. We close the workbook and are ready for our final link.

We create the AR reserve analysis hyperlink to the *Workpapers\AR Reserve.xlsx* workbook, test the link, and we are good to go.

EXERCISE 2—BANK RECONCILIATION

In this exercise, we'll create hyperlinks for our bank reconciliation.

 **PRACTICE**

To work along, please refer to the Exercise 2 worksheet.

The worksheet contains a basic bank reconciliation. We want to make it easy for the user to navigate to the sources of our numbers.

We begin with the balance per bank amount. We select the *Amount* cell and then create a hyperlink to the *Workpapers\Bank Statement.pdf* file. We test the link, and we confirm that our computer's default PDF application opens the file. We close the bank statement and are ready for our next link.

We select the cell containing the *Outstanding checks* amount and create a hyperlink to the **E2 Outstanding** worksheet. We test the link and confirm it takes us to the intended worksheet. We head back to the **Exercise 2** worksheet and are ready for our last link.

We select the cell containing the *Deposits in transit* amount. For this link, rather than navigating to cell **A1** of the **E2 Deposits** worksheet, we want to navigate to the total cell named **deposits_total**. We create the link by selecting the name **deposits_total,** rather than the worksheet name, in the Insert Hyperlink dialog. We test the link and confirm that it works as expected.

 NOTE

> When you link to a worksheet name or A1-style cell reference, the hyperlink will not be updated if you change the sheet name. When you link to a named reference, the link will continue to work if the sheet name is changed.

EXERCISE 3—REFERENCES

In this exercise, we'll create links to a few reference documents.

 **PRACTICE**

> To work along, please refer to the Exercise 3 worksheet.

The *Chart of Accounts* link will navigate to the chart of accounts, which is stored on the **Accounts** worksheet within the **Lists.xlsx** workbook. We select the cell and click the Hyperlink command. Within the Insert Hyperlink dialog, select the **Workpapers\Lists.xlsx** workbook, and then use the Bookmark button to select the **Accounts** worksheet.

The *Department List* link will take the user to the department list, which we'll reference via its name, **dept_list**. Within the Insert Hyperlink dialog, we select the **Workpapers\Lists.xlsx** workbook and use the Bookmark button to select the **dept_list** name.

Now, here's a question for you. If we didn't want to set up a link for each individual file, could we set up a link to the folder instead? Yes! Let's do that. The third link we'll set up will take the user to the **Workpapers** folder. In the Insert Hyperlink dialog, we select the **Workpapers** folder. We test the link to confirm…yes—it works!

CHAPTER CONCLUSION

In this chapter we used the Hyperlink feature to help us stay organized and make it easy to navigate to related documents. In addition to powerful features, Excel also contains powerful functions. In this part we discussed several Excel features, and now it is time to transition our discussion to Excel functions. In fact, we'll begin the next part by examining how to create hyperlinks without using the Hyperlink feature.

FUNCTIONS

Additional functions offer more tools and options.

Chapter 9: HYPERLINK Function

SET UP

In this part we examine several additional functions. As you know, we want to avoid overreliance on familiar tools. We want to expand our options so we can pick the right one for the job. In this chapter we begin our exploration with the HYPERLINK function, which is an alternative to the Hyperlink feature.

We like to anticipate ways our workbooks can break and address the related risks up front. When we were working with the Hyperlink feature in Chapter 8, we noted that Excel doesn't continuously monitor external hyperlink files. That means Excel won't rewrite or update an external hyperlink if the destination file is moved. If a destination file is not available at the location specified in the hyperlink, Excel displays an error alert.

In addition to the Hyperlink feature, we can use the HYPERLINK function to create hyperlinks. The HYPERLINK function provides flexibility and makes it easy for us to update file paths when we move files.

HOW TO

When we use the Hyperlink feature, we specify the destination and friendly text manually, using the Insert Hyperlink dialog box. In contrast, when we use the HYPERLINK function, we define the destination and friendly text with function arguments. This provides flexibility because we can define the arguments using standard formula syntax and include functions, cell references, names, and other supported expressions and operators. We can use this function to help us quickly set up hyperlinks and make subsequent updates. And at the same time, we make our recurring-use workbooks fast and easy to maintain.

In this chapter we talk about the following items:

- Arguments

- Full versus partial paths

- Concatenation

- Consistent formulas

- Bookmarks

First we'll examine the function's arguments.

ARGUMENTS

The HYPERLINK function has two arguments, as follows:

=HYPERLINK(link_location,[friendly_name])

Where:

- **link_location** is the destination expressed as a text string

- **[friendly_name]** is the optional friendly text (displays **link_location** if omitted)

To create a hyperlink that opens a file stored in the same folder as our workbook, we can set the **link_location** argument to the file name, such as "Bank Statement.pdf." Since this argument contains the file name only, Excel assumes the file is stored in the same folder as the workbook that contains the hyperlink. This type of partial (relative) path is different from a full (absolute) path, such as "C:\My Documents\ Bank Statement.pdf." Let's examine full and partial paths in more detail.

FULL VERSUS PARTIAL PATHS

Why is the difference between full (absolute) and partial (relative) paths important to note? Because the path determines what happens when the files are moved. For example, let's say we were in the field working on our laptop, and we created a workpaper index workbook. In this workbook we set up various hyperlinks to related project files stored in the same folder on our laptop's C drive. When we get back to the office, we move the project folder, which contains the index workbook and the linked files, to a network drive. If the hyperlinks store full paths, they will break because they continue to reference the C drive. However, if the hyperlinks use partial paths that contain the file names only, they will continue to work because the references are relative to the active workbook, wherever it may be.

The HYPERLINK function is flexible. In addition to creating relative file references, such as "Bank Statement.pdf," we can also define the destination with its full path, such as "C:\My Documents\Bank Statement.pdf." Since we just established that absolute paths prevent us from moving files around, why would we ever want to use the full path? Well, this is where it gets interesting.

CONCATENATION

We can use things like functions and operators to help define the destination argument. Do you remember concatenation? We used it previously to create a text string by combining values.

 XREF

Concatenation is discussed in Volume 2, Chapter 19.

We can use concatenation to help define the full path to the file. For example, if we store the base path "C:\My Documents\" in cell *A1,* we could set up the following function.

```
=HYPERLINK(A1&"Bank Statement.pdf","Bank Statement")
```

Where:

- **A1&"Bank Statement.pdf"** uses the concatenation operator to join the base path in *A1* with the file name

- **"Bank Statement"** is the friendly text

 NOTE

Be sure that you include the trailing slash after the base path so that when combined it creates a valid file path.

Let's say that while in the field, you store the base path to the files in cell *A1.* When you return to the office and copy the files to the corporate network, you can simply change the value in *A1* as needed. For example, you can change the base path in *A1* from "C:\My Documents\" (used in the field) to "P:\Clients\ABC\" (back in the office). As you can imagine, this idea opens up many options for defining hyperlink destinations.

CONSISTENT FORMULAS

As you know, we like using consistent formulas that can be filled down. The problem with the formula above is that it can't be filled down because we've defined the file name "Bank Statement.pdf" and the friendly name "Bank Statement" as text strings. But if we store the file name and friendly name in cells, our function can use the corresponding cell references instead of text strings, and we can fill the formula down. For example, if the base path was stored in *A1*, the file name in *B10*, and the friendly text in *C10*, we could use the following formula in *D10* to generate the desired hyperlink:

```
=HYPERLINK($A$1&B10,C10)
```

Where:

- **$A$1&B10** uses the concatenation operator to join the base path with the file name

- **C10** is the friendly text

This formula can be filled down through the range as desired. After the links are working, we could clean up the display for the user by hiding the file name and friendly name columns with the Outline feature.

 XREF

The Outline feature is discussed in Chapter 4.

BOOKMARKS

In addition to linking to other workbooks, we can link to a specific worksheet cell within a workbook. The syntax for Excel hyperlinks is similar to web hyperlinks. Both use a hashtag (#) to indicate an internal location within a file or page, commonly called a bookmark. You can create a link to a bookmark using both the Hyperlink feature and the HYPERLINK function. When using the Hyperlink feature, you click the Bookmark button in the Insert Hyperlink dialog. When using the HYPERLINK function, you include the hashtag in the argument.

Let's say we wanted to create a hyperlink to cell *A1* on the worksheet named *Worksheet Name* in the workbook named *Workbook.xlsx*. The following function would do the trick:

```
=HYPERLINK("Workbook.xlsx#'Worksheet Name'!A1")
```

You'll notice the sheet name is enclosed in single quotes and is separated from the cell reference with an exclamation mark. This syntax may seem familiar since we've discussed it before.

XREF

External reference to workbooks, worksheets, and cells is discussed in Volume 1, Chapter 3.

As you know, we try to anticipate ways our workbooks can break. We know that Excel does not continuously monitor hyperlink destinations and thus won't update the link if a workbook or worksheet name changes. Although we would need to make an update to reference a new workbook name, we can easily address the risk of a worksheet name change.

Whether we create the hyperlink with the feature or function, the link will break when the referenced worksheet name changes. We've addressed a similar issue before. Previously we used a name instead of a traditional A1-style reference to improve an external formula reference. We can use a similar approach here and link to a name.

 XREF

Creating and using a name for external formula references is discussed in Volume 1, Chapter 7.

To reference a name, simply use the name in the bookmark. For example, to hyperlink to the named reference *My_Name* in the workbook named ***Workbook.xlsx***, we could use the following formula:

```
=HYPERLINK("Workbook.xlsx#My_Name")
```

We can also reference a name stored within the same workbook as the hyperlink. We just bookmark the name. For example, to create a hyperlink to the name *My_Name* that is in the same workbook as the hyperlink, we could use the following formula:

```
=HYPERLINK("#My_Name")
```

Fortunately, using a name also covers us if the desired destination cell moves around when new worksheet rows or columns are inserted. This technique also opens up another possibility. You can write a formula that retrieves a value from another cell and creates a hyperlink to that cell. You create a name to the desired cell, and then you can reference the name in both function arguments, as follows:

```
=HYPERLINK("#My_Name",My_Name)
```

This formula will retrieve the value from the *My_Name* cell and create a hyperlink to the *My_Name* cell.

All right, think you got this? Great, let's talk through a few frequently asked questions and then jump into the exercises.

FREQUENTLY ASKED QUESTIONS

Here are some common questions about Excel hyperlinks.

Can I use a base path with the Hyperlink feature?

In addition to storing a base path in a cell and using it with the HYPERLINK function, we can also use the built-in hyperlink base property. Excel prepends the hyperlink base path to partial path destinations such as "MyWorkbook.xlsx." A workbook's base path can be viewed and edited using the Advanced Properties command (File > Info > Properties > Advanced Properties). The default base path is undefined. When the base path is undefined (empty), partial links are relative to the workbook containing the hyperlink. If you set a base path to, say, "C:\My Documents\," then this path is prepended to partial path destinations. The base path property is applied to partial path links created with the Hyperlink feature and the HYPERLINK function. Any full path destinations override the base path value.

Should I use the Hyperlink feature or the HYPERLINK function?

In short, it is personal preference. In practice, there are a few factors to consider when deciding between the feature and the function. If this is a recurring-use workbook with lots of links, you probably want the function. On the other hand, if this is a small one-time project with few links, you may want to consider the feature instead. If your Excel file contains numerous base paths, and you want to be able to move them independently, you want the function. However, if all links point to the same base path, then the feature should work just fine. If you want to be able to change the base path by updating a cell value instead of a dialog box value, you want to use the function. If the links need to be dynamic—for example, automatically matching text labels—you want the function, but if the links will be static, consider the feature.

How can I create a relative path to a subfolder?

Partial paths can direct Excel to look down into a subfolder or up a directory as well. To look down into a subfolder, include the folder name, such as "subfolder name\file.pdf," and to look up a directory, include two dots, such as "..\file.pdf."

When do I use absolute (full) or relative (partial) paths?

When the destination files are in fixed locations that won't change, an absolute path works well because the links will work regardless of the location of the workbook containing the hyperlinks. When the hyperlink workbook and linked files will move around together, and maintain the same position relative to one another, relative paths without a hyperlink base work well. When the destination files may move independently of the hyperlink workbook, relative paths with a hyperlink base will work well.

Can the Hyperlink feature create full and partial path references?

Yes. In the Insert Hyperlink dialog, define the desired destination along with either its full or partial path using the address field.

How does linking to a name with HYPERLINK work?

To link to a name that has a workbook scope, simply use the bookmark hashtag with the name, such as #My_Name, and exclude the sheet name. If the name has a worksheet scope, include the sheet name, such as #Sheet1!My_Name.

Named range scope is discussed in Volume 3, Chapter 21.

Can I hyperlink to a specific location within another file, regardless of file type?

An Excel hyperlink can link to a specific location within some, but not all, file types. For example, in addition to linking to a specific cell within an Excel file, we can also link to a bookmark in a Word file. Within Word, create the bookmark first (use the Insert > Bookmark Word command) and then create the Excel hyperlink using the bookmark hashtag, such as WordFile.docx#My_Bookmark. Linking to a specific page in a PDF file may work with or without a macro, but there are several environmental dependencies, including Excel version, operating system, registry settings, file location, and the PDF application. To create hyperlinks to specific locations within other files types, please visit Excel Help, the help files for the related application, and perhaps Google as needed.

EXAMPLES

Now let's practice using the HYPERLINK function to create hyperlinks.

To work along, please refer to *Hyperlink Function.xlsx.*

To watch the solutions video, please visit the Excel University Video Library.

EXERCISE 1—INDEX

In this exercise, we'll get warmed up with the HYPERLINK function.

 **PRACTICE**

To work along, please refer to the Exercise 1 worksheet.

We are at a client site working on our laptop, and we want to build a workpaper index. We need to ensure that if we move all the project files, including the workpaper index, to another location, such as our corporate network, all the links will continue to work.

Our first link is to the trial balance workbook. To create the hyperlink, we write the following formula that uses a relative path to the file:

```
=HYPERLINK("Workpapers\Trial Balance.xlsx","Trial Balance")
```

Where:

- **"Workpapers\Trial Balance.xlsx"** is the hyperlink location
- **"Trial Balance"** is the friendly name

We test the resulting hyperlink by clicking it. We confirm that the trial balance workbook opens as expected. We use similar formulas to create hyperlinks to the cash reconciliation and the AR reserve analysis workbooks.

Since the hyperlinks were created with partial paths, they are relative to the index workbook. That means that when we return to the office and move all of the project files to the network, the links will continue to work.

EXERCISE 2—BASE PATH

In this exercise, we'll store the base path in an input cell.

 **PRACTICE**

To work along, please refer to the Exercise 2 worksheet.

We'll create hyperlinks to various project files. We want to be able to update the hyperlink base path so that we can move the location of the referenced files independently of the workbook that contains the links. We'll store the base path in an input cell and use concatenation to join it to the file name. We enter the base path *Workpapers* into an input cell and name the input cell *base_path*.

With our base path set up, we begin on the first hyperlink. We want to create a link to cell *A1* on the sheet named *Accounts* in the *Lists.xlsx* workbook. To do so, we write the following formula:

```
=HYPERLINK(base_path&"Lists.xlsx#Accounts!A1","Chart of
Accounts")
```

Where:

- **base_path&"Lists.xlsx#Accounts!A1"** is the destination
- **"Chart of Accounts"** is the friendly name

We click the resulting hyperlink and confirm the desired location is opened as expected.

The next link will be to a named reference, *dept_list*, in the *Lists.xlsx* workbook. Thus, we set up the following formula:

```
=HYPERLINK(base_path&"Lists.xlsx#dept_list","Department
List")
```

Where:

- **base_path&"Lists.xlsx#dept_list"** is the destination
- **"Department List"** is the friendly name

We click the resulting hyperlink and confirm the desired location opens as expected.

Finally, we want to create a hyperlink that opens the *Workpapers* folder. We write the following formula:

```
=HYPERLINK(base_path,"Workpapers")
```

Where:

- **base_path** is the destination
- **"Workpapers"** is the friendly name

We click the resulting hyperlink and confirm that the file browser pops up and shows the folder contents as expected. Yay!

EXERCISE 3—CONSISTENT FORMULAS

In this exercise, we'll create several hyperlinks using consistent formulas.

 **PRACTICE**

To work along, please refer to the Exercise 3 worksheet.

Instead of writing the file name and friendly name in each unique hyperlink formula, let's store these names in cells so that we can write a formula and fill it down. We begin our preparations by storing the base path *Workpapers* in a cell on the *E3 Start Here* sheet and naming the cell *path*. On the *Exercise 3* worksheet, we enter the file names in Column *B* and the friendly names in Column *C*. With our stored values entered, we can now write our formula.

We write the following formula into cell *D14*:

```
=HYPERLINK(path&B14,C14)
```

Where:

- **path&B14** is the destination

- **C14** is the friendly name

We fill the formula down and test the links to confirm they navigate to the expected files. To clean up the worksheet, we use the Outline feature to hide Columns *B* and *C*. We select Columns *B* and *C* and use the following Ribbon command:

- Data > Group

We hide the columns, and our worksheet looks good!

CHAPTER CONCLUSION

In this chapter we used the HYPERLINK function to create hyperlinks. Knowing how and when to use the HYPERLINK function gives us flexibility and improves the efficiency of our recurring-use workbooks.

Chapter 10: IF Alternatives

SET UP

Although the IF function is popular and used all the time, there are some clever alternatives that can simplify our formulas and make our workbooks cleaner and easier to maintain over time. Since we previously discussed the details of the IF function, let's proceed to the alternatives.

 XREF

The IF function is discussed in Volume 2, Chapter 10.

Do you remember an IF function alternative that we discussed previously in this series? Think back to our Error Check Worksheet. Instead of using IF functions to generate the Boolean test results, we used comparison formulas. For example, to see whether the value in *A1* equals zero, we could have used the following formula:

```
=IF(A1=0,TRUE,FALSE)
```

Instead of using the IF function, we used the following comparison formula:

```
=A1=0
```

This is one example of an IF alternative.

 XREF

Comparison formulas are discussed in Volume 2, Chapter 25.

In this chapter we discuss several additional alternatives, including MIN, MAX, AND, OR, NOT, and CHOOSE. Before we jump into the technical details of these functions, let me address a question that is undoubtedly on your mind. Your question probably sounds something like this: "Why would we spend time discussing alternatives to the IF function? I already know the IF function and feel comfortable using it." Early in Volume 2, we had a little discussion about Maslow's hammer. We talked about the efficiency gains that can be achieved by picking the right tool instead of relying on a familiar one. Here again my goal is to equip you with more functions so you can pick the right one for the task at hand. Plus we'll do things with the CHOOSE function that we can't do with the IF function, at least not very easily. For example, if you try to build a formula with several nested IF functions, the formula can get confusing pretty quickly. By contrast, the CHOOSE function keeps us organized and allows us to more easily write and maintain the formula. It's time to dig into the details.

HOW TO

We'll discuss the following functions and explore when and how they can be used as alternatives to the IF function:

- MAX—returns the largest number from its arguments

- MIN—returns the smallest number from its arguments

- AND—returns TRUE when all arguments are TRUE

- OR—returns TRUE when one or more arguments is TRUE

- NOT—reverses a Boolean value

- CHOOSE—returns a value based on the specified argument

Let's start off with the easy functions.

MAX

The MAX function returns the largest number from its arguments.

```
=MAX(number1,[number2],…)
```

Where:

- **number1** is the first required argument

- **number2** is an optional argument

- …up to 255 total arguments

The arguments can be expressed in various ways, including cell references, range references, constants, dates, and names. If an argument contains many values, such as a range reference, the function uses the largest value found in the argument. Although MAX has a variety of uses in practice, we focus on one narrow application and use it as an alternative to IF.

Since MAX automatically returns the greater of two arguments, we can use it instead of IF when we are comparing the same values we are returning. For example, let's say we have an Amount column where positive numbers are debits and negative numbers are credits. We want to create a new Debit column next to it. We'll write a formula that compares the amount to zero, and when the amount is greater than zero, we'll return the amount; otherwise, we'll return zero. Assuming the first amount is stored in *A1*, we could accomplish this task with the following formula:

```
=IF(A1>0,A1,0)
```

Notice that the values compared in the first argument of the IF function are also the values returned in the second and third arguments. Since the function essentially returns the greater of the two values, we have the option of using the shorter formula below:

```
=MAX(A1,0)
```

The MAX function returns the greater of *A1* or zero. Thus, it will return the value in *A1* when it is a positive number (a debit) and zero when it is a negative number (a credit). In this case, MAX is an alternative to IF and provides us with an additional approach.

While the benefits of this approach may appear negligible at first, the advantages offered by its simplicity become apparent when used in more sophisticated formulas. As you know, we like to make our recurring-use workbooks efficient to update and maintain. With that idea in mind, consider the IF and MAX functions above. The IF function references cell *A1* twice, while the MAX function references it only once. Before you mock me, stay with me a moment longer. In a simple formula, we'd need to change the *A1* cell reference twice instead of once. Big deal, right? But what if the update isn't as simple as changing a cell reference? What if it is something more complicated, such as modifying a complex expression, function, or series of nested functions? We'd prefer to make such a change once instead of twice. When our formulas are complex, considering details such as this makes an impact.

By using the MAX function instead of the IF function in the example above, we eliminated the duplicate reference to *A1*. Removing the duplicate reference made our formula shorter, cleaner, and easier to maintain. In fact, we can generalize this idea as follows:

Remove or minimize duplication within formulas.

As we work through the upcoming chapters and exercises, we'll have a chance to experience the benefits of this type of simplicity. Enough theory—let's move ahead to the next IF alternative.

MIN

As expected, the MIN function returns the smallest value from its arguments:

```
=MIN(number1,[number2], …)
```

Where:

- **number1** is a required argument
- **number2** is optional
- **…**up to 255 total arguments

We can use the MIN function as an alternative to IF. Continuing the example above, we now want to build a Credit column. When the amount is less than zero, we want to return the amount, otherwise, zero. We could use the following IF function:

```
=IF(A1<0,A1,0)
```

But since the IF function essentially returns the lesser of the two values, we can use MIN instead:

```
=MIN(A1,0)
```

We have removed the duplicate *A1* reference, and our formula is a bit easier to maintain.

Let's take the next logical step. Let's say we want our Credit column formula to flip the sign and return a positive number. We could do this by modifying our IF function as follows:

```
=IF(A1<0,-A1,0)
```

As a result of this change, it may seem that we are precluded from using the MIN function because the values compared aren't the exact values being returned. That is, *A1* is the value compared but *-A1* is the value returned. We learned many rules back in algebra class, and we know that expressions written in one form can often be rewritten in another form. Applying these ideas to our Excel formula, we can rewrite it as follows:

```
=-IF(A1<0,A1,0)
```

In this form, the duplication of *A1* jumps out. We can eliminate the duplication with the following alternative:

```
=-MIN(A1,0)
```

In addition to MAX and MIN, there are other IF alternatives. Excel has numerous functions in the Logical category, and we'll take a look at three of them: AND, OR, and NOT.

AND

We first explored the AND function when building error checking worksheets, and now we'll use it to both enhance and replace the IF function. Recall that the AND function returns TRUE when all of its arguments are TRUE; otherwise, it returns FALSE.

 XREF

The AND function is discussed in Volume 2, Chapter 25.

Let's begin by using the AND function to enhance the IF function. Since the IF function has a single *logical_test* argument, it stands to reason that it can test only one condition. When we need to test multiple conditions, we could use nested IF functions. For example, if we need to see whether the values in *A1* and *B1* are both equal to zero, we could use two IF functions and have each one test a single condition, as follows:

```
=IF(A1=0,IF(B1=0,TRUE,FALSE),FALSE)
```

Since the AND function returns TRUE when all of its arguments are TRUE, we can use it here to perform both tests and simplify our formula, as follows:

```
=IF(AND(A1=0,B1=0),TRUE,FALSE)
```

In addition to enhancing the IF function, the AND function can replace it when we just need to return TRUE or FALSE. Since the formula above returns TRUE or FALSE, we could replace it with the following:

```
=AND(A1=0,B1=0)
```

This IF alternative is more concise and easier to maintain going forward.

For our next trick, recall that Excel's calculation engine treats FALSE as 0 and TRUE as 1. We can use this information and multiply the result of an AND function to another value. For example, consider the following formula logic. If the values in *A1* and *B1* are equal to zero, return the value in *C1*; otherwise, return zero. We could accomplish this task with the following formula:

```
=IF(AND(A1=0,B1=0),C1,0)
```

Or, we could use the following alternative instead:

```
=AND(A1=0,B1=0)*C1
```

While the motivation for such a simplification may not be apparent right now, we'll appreciate this technique when we have to build a monthly subscription formula in an upcoming exercise.

OR

The OR function is similar to the AND function, except that only one of its arguments needs to be TRUE for the function to return TRUE. We can use it to simplify our formulas.

Let's say we have a worksheet that tracks orders and the status of each order. An order status could be Received, Pending, Shipped, or Canceled. For our purposes, an order is considered complete when its status is either Shipped or Canceled. We want to write a formula that returns TRUE when the order is complete. One approach is to use nested IF functions, as follows:

```
=IF(A1="Shipped",TRUE,IF(A1="Canceled",TRUE,FALSE))
```

Alternatively, we can use the OR function to perform the tests as shown in the following formula:

```
=IF(OR(A1="Shipped",A1="Canceled"),TRUE,FALSE)
```

Or we could do away with the IF function altogether and use the following formula instead:

```
=OR(A1="Shipped",A1="Canceled")
```

While all three formulas produce the same result, my favorite is the last one because it is short and concise.

NOT

The NOT function changes a Boolean value from TRUE to FALSE or from FALSE to TRUE. This can help us reverse the result when desired. For example, we can update the formula above to display FALSE when the order status is Shipped or Canceled by wrapping a NOT function around it, as follows:

```
=NOT(OR(A1="Shipped",A1="Canceled"))
```

As you can see, the NOT function simply flips a Boolean value.

CHOOSE

So far, the example formulas in this chapter have included up to two IF functions. Have you ever tried to nest more than two IF functions? If so, you know that the formula gets really complicated really fast. Fortunately, the CHOOSE function can provide an organized alternative to nested IF functions.

The CHOOSE function returns the specified value argument:

```
=CHOOSE(index_num,value1,[value2], …)
```

Where:

- **index_num** is the value argument to return
- **value1** will be returned if index_num is equal to 1
- **[value2]** will be returned if index_num is equal to 2
- **…**up to 254 total value arguments

Let's say our order-tracking worksheet stores status codes instead of labels, where Code 1 represents Received, 2 is Pending, 3 is Shipped, and 4 is Canceled. We want to create a Status Label column and plan to write a formula that returns the proper label for the given code. Assuming that the code is stored in *A1*, we could use the following formula:

```
=IF(A1=1,"Received",IF(A1=2,"Pending",IF(A1=3,"Shipped",
IF(A1=4,"Canceled",""))))
```

There are four IF functions in the formula above. Since the CHOOSE function returns the corresponding value argument, we could use this shorter alternative:

```
=CHOOSE(A1,"Received","Pending","Shipped","Canceled")
```

The CHOOSE function helps us stay organized and makes the formula easier to understand and maintain over time.

I used this warm-up example because it was easy to visualize. In practice, we would probably approach this type of label translation task with lookups instead of a CHOOSE function. For example, we'd create a table, store the codes in the first column and the labels in the second column, and then use a lookup function such as VLOOKUP to return the label based on the code. Now that we are warmed up, it is time to have some fun.

You see, the CHOOSE function supports many kinds of arguments, including text strings, cell references, functions, and expressions. Given the variety of Excel arguments we can create, this opens up many possibilities. Consider the SUBTOTAL function. As you recall, we tell it what type of math to apply to the range using its first argument.

SUBTOTAL is discussed in Volume 1, Chapter 11.

The value of the first SUBTOTAL argument determines which summary function is applied. Essentially, we pick a function from a list of options, such as Sum, Count, and Average. Similarly, the value of the first CHOOSE argument determines which of the remaining arguments is evaluated. Each value argument represents an option.

Let's say our worksheet stores data in *A1:A10*. We could create various options within a CHOOSE function, such as Sum, Count, and Average. We would use the first argument to select the desired option. For example, the following formula would sum the range:

```
=CHOOSE(1,SUM(A1:A10),COUNT(A1:A10),AVERAGE(A1:A10))
```

So far, so good? Good, because this is where our discussion gets interesting. We can allow a user to pick from a list of options, and depending on the selection, our CHOOSE function will evaluate the corresponding argument. Rather than provide the user with a list of integer options, such as 1, 2, and 3, we'd like to provide the user a list of descriptive labels, such as Sum, Count, and Average. The problem is that the first CHOOSE argument is expecting an integer value, not a text string. I'm not sure if you recall, but we solved a similar challenge before. Even though the third argument of the VLOOKUP function expects an integer value, we wanted to use a column label instead. Do you remember which function came to our rescue? Yes, it was the MATCH function. We used the MATCH function to convert a column label into an integer value.

The MATCH function is discussed in Volume 2, Chapter 6.

The same idea can help here. Recall that the MATCH function returns the relative position of a list item. We can use the MATCH function as the first argument of the CHOOSE function to translate a text label into an integer value based on its list position. If we store the descriptive labels in a range of cells, we can create a drop-down based on the range. When the user makes a selection from the drop-down, the MATCH function can determine whether it was the first, second, or third option. This position is used in the first CHOOSE argument. Here's the updated version of our formula, with the argument details removed for simplicity:

```
=CHOOSE(MATCH(…),SUM(…),COUNT(…),AVERAGE(…))
```

Don't worry; I've prepared some exercises that help illustrate this technique and how all the moving parts fit together.

The cool part about this technique is that we aren't limited to basic math functions such as Sum, Count, and Average. Since our options are defined with function arguments, essentially our only limit is our imagination.

EXAMPLES

Please work along and complete the exercises below to get a better understanding of how these functions work.

 **PRACTICE**

To work along, please refer to *If Alternatives.xlsx.*

 VIDEO

To watch the solutions video, please visit the Excel University Video Library.

EXERCISE 1—COMMISSION

In this exercise, we'll revisit a previous worksheet and solve it in a new way.

 **PRACTICE**

To work along, please refer to the Exercise 1 worksheet.

When we initially discussed the IF function in Volume 2, we had a commission exercise. We'll compute the same commissions again now, but this time we'll use an alternative to the IF function.

Our compensation plan pays commission on sales in excess of quota. When sales fall short of the quota, zero commission is paid. The commission rate is stored in a cell named **rate**. Since the excess for the first rep is computed in cell **E17**, the following formula computes the correct commission amount:

```
=MAX(E17*rate,0)
```

Where:

- **E17*rate** is the excess times the rate

- **0** is returned if greater than the first argument

We push the formula down, and yes—it works!

EXERCISE 2—DEBIT AND CREDIT COLUMNS

In this exercise, we'll use the MAX and MIN functions instead of the IF function.

 **PRACTICE**

To work along, please refer to the Exercise 2 worksheet.

We've exported a trial balance, and it contains accounts and amounts. The *Amount* column displays debits with positive numbers and credits with negative numbers. We want to split the *Amount* column into separate *Debit* and *Credit* columns. We could use the IF function. For example, since the first amount is stored in **C12**, we could do something like this for the Debit column:

```
=IF(C12>0,C12,0)
```

But we can simplify our formula and eliminate duplication by using the MAX function as follows:

```
=MAX(C12,0)
```

We can compute the Credit column in a similar way with the MIN function:

```
=MIN(C12,0)
```

Since we actually want to flip the sign from a negative amount to a positive value, we update our formula like this:

```
=-MIN(C12,0)
```

We push both formulas down and notice that the amount values flow into the debit and credit columns as expected.

EXERCISE 3—SUBSCRIPTION REVENUE

In this exercise, we'll compute subscription revenue.

 **PRACTICE**

To work along, please refer to the Exercise 3 worksheet.

Our company sells subscriptions. At the time of purchase, customers may opt to prepay for a 6-, 9-, or 12-month term. Since our company collects the cash at the time of purchase, but hasn't yet earned it, we have to recognize revenue over the subscription term. Our worksheet contains the basic contract information, such as the monthly amount, the term, and the start and end dates. We need to write a formula that we can fill down and right through the monthly columns to compute the amount earned.

For the first contract, the monthly amount is stored in *C18*, the contract start date is stored in *E18*, and the end date is stored in *F18*. The monthly column headers begin in *G17*. Our formula should determine if the column header date (*G17*) falls between the contract start (*E18*) and end (*F18*) dates. If so, the formula should return the monthly amount; otherwise, it should return zero. We write the following formula as an alternative to using the IF function:

```
=AND(G$17>=$E18,G$17<=$F18)*$C18
```

Where:

- **AND(G$17>=$E18,G$17<=$F18)** returns TRUE (or 1) when both arguments are TRUE and FALSE (or 0) otherwise

- **Where:**

    ○ **G$17>=$E18** returns TRUE if the column header is greater than or equal to the start date

    ○ **G$17<=$F18** returns TRUE if the column header is less than or equal to the end date

- **$C18** is the monthly amount

Since we took care to set up the proper cell reference styles, we fill the formula down for all contract rows and right through all monthly columns and are happy that the formula works as expected.

EXERCISE 4—CLOSED ORDERS

In this exercise, we'll use the OR function to identify closed orders.

 **PRACTICE**

To work along, please refer to the Exercise 4 worksheet.

Our worksheet contains a list of orders. Each order has a status of Received, Pending, Complete, or Canceled. We don't have any additional work on orders with a status of Complete or Canceled. We refer to these orders as closed. We want to write a formula that returns TRUE when an order is closed, and FALSE otherwise.

Since the status of our first order is stored in *C12*, we write the following formula:

```
=OR(C12="Complete",C12="Canceled")
```

Where:

- **C12="Complete"** is TRUE if C12 is equal to Complete

- **C12="Canceled"** is TRUE if C12 is equal to Canceled

We fill the formula down and confirm it returns TRUE for closed orders and FALSE for others as expected.

EXERCISE 5—OPEN ORDERS

In this exercise, we'll use the NOT function to flip the result of the formula used in the previous exercise.

 **PRACTICE**

To work along, please refer to the Exercise 5 worksheet.

Once again, the worksheet contains a list of orders. The formula we used previously returned TRUE when the order was closed. This time we want the opposite result. We want to display FALSE for closed orders. We can easily modify the formula used in the previous exercise. We simply reverse the result by wrapping a NOT function around it as follows:

```
=NOT(OR(C12="Complete",C12="Canceled"))
```

Where:

- **C12="Complete"** is TRUE if C12 is equal to Complete

- **C12="Canceled"** is TRUE if C12 is equal to Canceled

We fill the formula down and note that it returns TRUE when the order is not closed and FALSE when it is closed, as expected.

 NOTE

This exercise was designed to illustrate how the NOT function reverses the value. An alternative way to approach this task is to write a formula that determines whether the status is equal to Pending or Received.

EXERCISE 6—STATUS

In this exercise, we'll begin our journey with the CHOOSE function and get warmed up.

 **PRACTICE**

To work along, please refer to the Exercise 6 worksheet.

Our worksheet contains a list of orders. Each order has a *Status ID* of 1, 2, 3, or 4. We need to write a formula that translates the ID into the corresponding status name, Received, Pending, Complete, and Canceled, respectively. One way to do this is to use the CHOOSE function. Since the ID for the first order is stored in *C14*, we use this formula:

```
=CHOOSE(C14,"Received","Pending","Complete","Canceled")
```

Where:

- **C14** contains the ID

- **"Received"** is returned if the ID is 1

- **"Pending"** is returned if the ID is 2

- **"Complete"** is returned if the ID is 3

- **"Canceled"** is returned if the ID is 4

We fill the formula down for all orders and note that it returns the expected results. Now that we are warmed up, let's take the next step with the CHOOSE function.

 NOTE

This approach was designed as an easy first step with the CHOOSE function for training purposes. In practice, we would probably prefer to store the status ID and name values in a table and use a VLOOKUP function.

EXERCISE 7—FUNCTION CODE

In this exercise, we'll take the next step in our CHOOSE journey and control the math.

 **PRACTICE**

To work along, please refer to the Exercise 7 worksheet.

Our worksheet contains order transactions. We want to allow the user to identify an aggregate function by entering a code into a cell. Based on the user's choice, we want our formula to return the corresponding result. When the user enters 1, our formula should return the sum. Code 2 represents the count, 3 the average, 4 the maximum value, and 5 the minimum value.

Since the user enters the code into input cell **C14** and the order amounts are stored in **C20:C27**, we write the following formula:

```
=CHOOSE(C14,SUM(C20:C27),COUNT(C20:C27),AVERAGE(C20:C27),
MAX(C20:C27),MIN(C20:C27))
```

Where:

- **C14** is the function code input cell

- **SUM(C20:C27)** is returned if the function code is 1

- **COUNT(C20:C27)** is returned if the function code is 2

- **AVERAGE(C20:C27)** is returned if the function code is 3

- **MAX(C20:C27)** is returned if the function code is 4

- **MIN(C20:C27)** is returned if the function code is 5

We confirm the formula returns the expected result by testing all of the codes.

Now, here's a question for you. Could the user break our workbook? Yes, by entering a value that our formula is not designed to evaluate, such as 6 or above, negative numbers, 0, or decimal values. Another problem is that the codes are arbitrary and difficult to remember. We strive to make workbooks bulletproof and easy to maintain. So rather than asking the user to enter a code, in the next exercise we allow them to make a selection from a drop-down menu.

EXERCISE 8—FUNCTION NAME

In this exercise, we'll provide a drop-down for the user.

 **PRACTICE**

To work along, please refer to the Exercise 8 worksheet.

In the previous exercise, the user entered an integer value to identify the function. In this exercise, we provide a drop-down list of choices instead. We prepare the workbook by storing the function names Sum, Count, Average, Max, and Min in a table. Then we name the table *tbl_functions* and set up a name *dd_functions* that refers to the table name. We use the name to allow a list with the Data Validation feature. Excellent. Now that we have the drop-down working, it is time to focus on the formula.

 XREF

The detailed steps for creating a table and using it in a Data Validation drop-down are discussed in Volume 1, Chapter 9.

The basic idea is the same as the previous exercise; however, the function input cell now stores a text string, such as Sum or Count, rather than an integer value such as 1 or 2. Since the CHOOSE function requires an integer value, we use the MATCH function to convert the function name into an integer representing its relative position within the drop-down list.

Since the *tbl_functions* table stores the function names, we can use the MATCH function to find the selected function name in this table and return its relative position. When we ask Excel to MATCH the function name *Sum*, it returns 1 since Sum is the first function in the list. When we ask Excel to MATCH *Count*, it returns 2 since it is the second function in the list, and so on.

Since our function input cell is **C9**, our function list is ***tbl_functions***, and our amounts are stored in **C15:C22**, we write the following formula:

```
=CHOOSE(MATCH(C9,tbl_functions,0),SUM(C15:C22),
COUNT(C15:C22),AVERAGE(C15:C22),MAX(C15:C22),MIN(C15:C22))
```

Where:

- **MATCH(C9,tbl_functions,0)** converts the function name to an integer that represents the relative position in the list

- **SUM(C15:C22)** is returned when the MATCH function returns 1

- **COUNT(C15:C22)** is returned when the MATCH function returns 2

- **AVERAGE(C15:C22)** is returned when the MATCH function returns 3

- **MAX(C15:C22)** is returned when the MATCH function returns 4

- **MIN(C15:C22)** is returned when the MATCH function returns 5

When we select various functions from the drop-down, we are delighted that the formula returns the desired result.

To recap, we stored a list of choices in a table. We used the table values to create a drop-down menu. We allowed the user to pick a choice from the drop-down. We used the MATCH function to translate the choice into an integer value. The CHOOSE function used this integer value to determine which argument to evaluate and return. Now that we see how these moving parts work together, let's apply them to something more practical.

EXERCISE 9—PAYMENT

In this exercise, we'll use the CHOOSE function to enable the user to specify the payment period for a loan.

 **PRACTICE**

To work along, please refer to the Exercise 9 worksheet.

The PMT function computes the payment of a loan with given terms. We have already seen the PMT function, but it is time to dig into a few details.

XREF

The PMT function is discussed in Volume 1, Chapter 3.

The function has the following arguments:

```
=PMT(rate,nper,pv,[fv],[type])
```

Where:

- **rate** is the interest rate per period

- **nper** is the total number of payments

- **pv** is the present value

- **[fv]** is the optional future value, 0 if omitted

- **[type]** is the optional payment type where 1 means beginning of period and 0 means end of period, 0 if omitted

Here is the key to working with the PMT function. The resulting payment is for each period specified in the **nper** argument, which must be consistent with the **rate** argument. That is, if **nper** is the number of months, then **rate** must be expressed as a monthly interest rate, and the monthly payment is returned. If **nper** is the number of years, then **rate** must be expressed as an annual interest rate, and the annual payment is returned. So when you are writing the PMT function, you want to check that three items have consistent units: the number of periods, the interest rate, and the payment.

The PMT function works on a cash flow basis. So if the **pv** is a positive number (representing a cash inflow), then the PMT function returns a negative payment value (representing a cash outflow). For this reason, it is common to precede the function with a subtraction operator (-) to flip the sign of the result.

Let's create a loan payment calculator that computes the monthly payment. We want the user to enter the principal amount and the annual interest rate. We'll allow the user to define the loan term by choosing Months, Quarters, or Years from a drop-down and then entering the corresponding number of periods. Our formula should return the monthly payment.

To prepare the workbook, we create a table named **tbl_periods** to store the list of choices, Months, Quarters, and Years. We set up a name **dd_periods** that refers to **tbl_periods**. We use data validation to provide the drop-down in **C12**. To create the label for the number of periods input cell, we use the concatenation formula in **B13** shown below:

```
="Number of "&C12
```

This prompts the user for the number of selected periods, such as Number of Months or Number of Years accordingly.

 XREF

Concatenation is discussed in Volume 2, Chapter 19.

With the initial preparations complete, it is time to write the formula that computes the monthly payment amount. Since the principal amount is stored in *C8*, the annual interest rate in *C9*, the period selection drop-down in *C12*, the period list in the *tbl_periods* table, and the number of periods in *C13*, we write the following formula:

```
=-CHOOSE(MATCH(C12,tbl_periods,0),
PMT(C9/12,C13,C8),PMT(C9/12,C13*3,C8),PMT(C9/12,C13*12,C8))
```

Where:

- **MATCH(C12,tbl_periods,0)** converts the period name into an integer value 1, 2, or 3

- **PMT(C9/12,C13,C8)** is returned when the period is Months and the MATCH function returns 1

- **PMT(C9/12,C13*3,C8)** is returned when the period is Quarters and the MATCH function returns 2

- **PMT(C9/12,C13*12,C8)** is returned when the period is Years and the MATCH function returns 3

Our formula is organized. And look—not a single IF function in sight!

Before we continue, I am curious whether you noticed the duplication in our formula? The PMT function is used three times. Can you eliminate the duplication? You bet! And if you want to practice, there is an Extra Credit exercise waiting for you.

CHAPTER CONCLUSION

In this chapter we explored several alternatives to the IF function. These alternatives can help eliminate or minimize duplication within formulas. In simple formulas or one-time workbooks, the benefits may be negligible, and you may prefer to use the IF function. But by using these alternatives in simple formulas, you'll become comfortable using them in complex formulas in your recurring-use workbooks. You'll boost your productivity because the formulas will be easier to write and maintain going forward.

Chapter 11: Lookup Functions

SET UP

So far during the series, we've explored numerous lookup functions. They've helped us with all sorts of tasks, such as retrieving account names from a chart of accounts, building reports, grouping transactions into fiscal quarters, determining the correct bonus amount, and reconciling a bank statement. By now VLOOKUP, INDEX, MATCH, and GETPIVOTDATA are familiar friends, and we also spent a chapter using SUMIFS to perform lookups. We've had some good times together, but it is time to invite some new friends to the party.

Although the above functions can handle many lookup tasks, occasionally we may need assistance from the following functions:

- OFFSET—returns a range reference given its arguments

- ROW—returns the row number of the reference

- ROWS—returns the number of rows in the reference

- COLUMN—returns the column number of the reference

- COLUMNS—returns the number of columns in the reference

- INDIRECT—returns a valid Excel reference based on a text string

- ADDRESS—returns a cell reference based on its arguments

Let's get into the details now.

HOW TO

Have you ever opened a workbook, *not* made any changes, and felt surprised when Excel asked if you wanted to save your changes before closing the workbook? If you haven't experienced this before, take a moment and open ***Lookup Functions_answers.xlsx*** and immediately close it without making any changes. Excel asks if you want to save your changes, even though none were made. When this happens to you in practice, it is likely that the workbook contains volatile functions. To really understand what a volatile function is and how it works, we take a brief tour inside Excel's calculation engine.

 NOTE

You may also receive the prompt if the workbook was created in a different version of Excel.

We love Excel because it quickly recalculates formulas. We make a change to a cell and—bam!—a millisecond later our formulas display updated results. This all seems to happen automatically, so we don't worry about when and how Excel does it. Indeed, Excel's default calculation option is set to Automatic. If we change the calculation option to Manual, Excel recalculates formulas only when directed. We set the calculation option with the following Ribbon icon:

- Formulas > Calculation Options

When we are ready for Excel to recalculate the workbook, we use the following Ribbon command:

- Formulas > Calculate Now

 KB

The keyboard equivalent is F9.

We can also tell Excel to recalculate just the active worksheet with this Ribbon command:

- Formulas > Calculate Sheet

 KB

The keyboard equivalent is Shift+F9.

These calculation options and commands generally escape our attention because the default setting seems to work just fine. When we update a cell value, Excel just recalculates as needed. But what *exactly* is being recalculated? Is it all workbook formulas? Only the formulas in the active worksheet? Well, here's where our discussion gets interesting.

The recalculation process is optimized for speed. Excel doesn't recalculate every formula every time a cell value is updated. It only recalculates formulas that use, or depend on, that cell. It is fascinating to me how Excel does this. Excel tracks which formulas depend on which cells by creating a dependency tree. When a cell value changes, Excel notes which dependent formulas need recalculation. Cells marked in this way are known as *dirty*. Excel uses the relationships defined in the dependency tree to build a calculation chain that defines the order in which the formula cells should be updated. When a recalculation occurs, Excel recalculates the dirty cells in the order provided by the calculation chain. This system is designed so that Excel only spends time recalculating formulas that need to be updated.

With that background understanding, let's revisit the idea of volatile functions. All the functions discussed in the series so far are nonvolatile and, as such, are recalculated only when dependent values change. In contrast, volatile functions are recomputed each time Excel recalculates, even when their dependent values haven't changed. So even if you haven't changed any cell values, Excel will ask if you want to save changes when you close a workbook that contains a volatile function.

Microsoft recommends using volatile functions sparingly because they can slow down recalculation times. You see, in addition to the volatile functions, Excel also recalculates any dependent formulas. One of the workbook design principles we discussed long ago is efficiency. Our definition of improving efficiency is reducing human effort. Even though volatile functions can increase the time it takes to refresh formulas, we use them when they reduce the time it takes us to prepare or maintain the workbook. But we use them sparingly as Microsoft recommends, and we use nonvolatile alternatives when available.

 XREF

Workbook design principles are discussed in Volume 1, Chapter 19.

So what are the volatile functions? The Microsoft website provides the following list of volatile functions: RAND, NOW, TODAY, OFFSET, INDIRECT, INFO, and CELL. Two of the lookup functions we're discussing in this chapter are volatile: OFFSET and INDIRECT. Let's begin with OFFSET.

OFFSET

The OFFSET function is a volatile function that returns a range reference based on its arguments. This is important to understand, so I'll state it again.

The OFFSET function returns a reference.

It returns a reference, such as **B2:D5**. Here is the syntax for the function:

```
=OFFSET(reference,rows,cols,[height],[width])
```

Where:

- **reference** is the starting point, a cell, range, or name
- **rows** is the number of rows to move the reference down (+) or up (-)
- **cols** is the number of columns to move the reference right (+) or left (-)
- **[height]** is the optional height of the returned range (same height as reference if omitted)
- **[width]** is the optional width of the returned range (same width as reference if omitted)

When I use the OFFSET function and the starting point is a single cell, I think about using the first three arguments to identify the upper-left cell of the return range and the last two arguments to identify the lower-right cell of the range. For example, let's say we wanted to return the range **B2:D5** as shown in Figure 7.

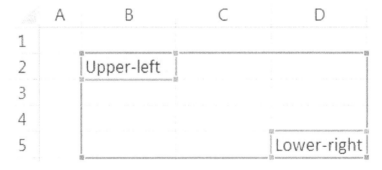

Figure 7

If the starting point was **A1**, we would need to move the starting point down *one* row and right *one* column to identify the upper-left cell of the range, **B2**. To identify the lower-right cell in the range, **D5**, we would need the return range height to be *4* rows and the width to be *3* columns. We can return the range **B2:D5** by using these values as OFFSET arguments, as follows:

```
=OFFSET(A1,1,1,4,3)
```

Where:

- **A1** is the starting point

- **1** moves the starting point down one row

- **1** moves the starting point right one column

- **4** is the return range height, in number of rows

- **3** is the return range width, in number of columns

If the starting point was **B2** instead, we could return the range **B2:D5** with the following argument:

```
=OFFSET(B2,0,0,4,3)
```

Where:

- **B2** is the starting point

- **0** moves the starting point zero rows

- **0** moves the starting point zero columns

- **4** is the return range height, in number of rows

- **3** is the return range width, in number of columns

Remember—OFFSET returns a reference. If the reference is to a single cell, the cell value is returned. If the reference is to a range of many cells, then you'll probably use OFFSET as an argument of another function, such as SUM. This is illustrated in the formula below, where I've removed the argument details for simplicity:

```
=SUM(OFFSET(...))
```

One last note before we move on to the next idea. In addition to the starting point being a single cell, we can also define it other ways, including a range of cells, a named range, or a table name. When the starting point represents a range of cells, we visualize moving the entire starting point range around with the remaining arguments as needed.

Now that we are warmed up with OFFSET, let's revisit the idea of volatile functions. As discussed, we can use volatile functions when they can improve our efficiency, but we use them sparingly and seek alternatives. With that in mind, can you think of another function we've discussed that is capable of returning a range reference? If you said INDEX, good for you!

XREF

Using INDEX to return a range reference is discussed in Volume 3, Chapter 14.

Before we see how we can use INDEX as an alternative to OFFSET, we need to discuss one additional detail. We can use the INDEX function with the range operator (:). We can use it on either side of the range operator to define the desired range. For example, we could create a range reference by using a cell reference on one side of the range operator and an INDEX function on the other, such as A1:INDEX(...). Alternatively, we could use INDEX on both sides, such as INDEX(...):INDEX(...). As you can imagine, this opens up many interesting possibilities.

We can use OFFSET to return a range by identifying the upper-left and lower-right cells. But we can also use INDEX with the range operator to define a range based on the upper-left and lower-right cells. This means that we can often use INDEX as an alternative to the volatile OFFSET function. We practice this in the exercises below.

 NOTE

Even though the INDEX function is not volatile, using it with the range operator causes Excel to update its reference when the workbook is opened.

ROW/ROWS

Since ROW and ROWS are related, we'll discuss them at the same time. In summary, ROW returns the row number of the reference, and ROWS returns the number of rows in the reference.

The ROW function returns the worksheet row number of the reference:

```
=ROW([reference])
```

Where:

- **reference** is the optional reference. Returns the row of the formula cell if omitted.

For example, ROW(A10) returns 10, and ROW() returns the row number of the cell that contains the function.

The ROWS function returns the number of rows in the reference:

```
=ROWS(array)
```

Where:

- **array** is the reference

For example, ROWS(A1:A10) returns 10.

We can apply these functions in a variety of ways, and we'll practice them in the exercises.

COLUMN/COLUMNS

Since COLUMN and COLUMNS work pretty much the same as ROW and ROWS, let's skip the formal explanation. The one thing I do want to mention is that COLUMN returns the column number, such as 5, rather than the column letter, such as E.

INDIRECT

The volatile INDIRECT function creates a valid Excel reference from a text string:

```
=INDIRECT(ref_text,[a1])
```

Where:

- **ref_text** is the text string that represents a valid Excel reference
- **[a1]** is the optional reference style

This function converts a text string into an actual Excel reference. This gives us the ability to define a reference in many flexible ways, including using text strings, cell values, concatenation, and text functions.

Let's say that cell *A1* has a stored value of 100. What would the following formula return?

```
=SUM("A1")
```

Did you say 100? Tempting, I know. But the formula returns #VALUE!, not 100. Although SUM(A1) would return 100, SUM("A1") does not. This is because the A1 argument is a text string, not a valid Excel reference. The INDIRECT function can help here because it can convert a text string into a valid Excel reference. As used below, INDIRECT converts A1 into the corresponding Excel reference and enables our SUM function to work as expected:

```
=SUM(INDIRECT("A1"))
```

In addition to specifying simple cell and range references, we can also incorporate sheet names and table names. Let's say we have a workbook that contains numerous tables. We want to allow the user to pick a table, and we want Excel to add up the values in the selected table. We can use the INDIRECT function to convert a text string, the table name, into a valid Excel reference that can be processed by a SUM function. Assuming that the desired table name is stored in *A1*, the following formula will add up the table values:

```
=SUM(INDIRECT(A1))
```

In the formulas above, we've specified only the first argument, and we've omitted the second optional argument. The second argument allows us to specify which reference style we used in our text string. Wait, what? Excel supports two reference styles. We've used the familiar A1-style throughout the series. It uses letters for columns (A) and numbers for rows (1). Excel also supports the R1C1-style, which uses numbers for rows and columns.

Check this out. You can toggle Excel into R1C1-style now by checking the *R1C1 reference style* checkbox in the Formulas section of the Excel Options dialog. Columns are now labeled with numbers and cell and range references have been updated accordingly. The R1C1 reference style supports relative and absolute references, where relative references are indicated with square brackets ([ ]). For example, R1C1 is the equivalent of $A$1, while R[1]C[1] references the cell that is one row down and one column right of the formula cell. Check out the Excel Help system for more information about the R1C1 reference style.

ADDRESS

The ADDRESS function returns a text string based on the Excel reference defined by its arguments. I think of it as the opposite of the INDIRECT function, which returns an Excel reference based on a text string:

```
=ADDRESS(row_num, column_num, [abs_num], [a1], [sheet_text])
```

Where:

- **row_num** is the row number of the reference

- **column_num** is the column number of the reference

- **[abs_num]** is the optional reference type, 1 or omitted is absolute $A$1, 2 is A$1, 3 is $A1, and 4 is A1

- **[a1]** is the optional reference style, TRUE or omitted is A1-style, and FALSE is R1C1-style.

- **[sheet_text]** is the optional sheet name

For example, if we need a formula that returns a text string representation of $A$1, we could use the following:

```
=ADDRESS(1,1)
```

Being able to create these text string references can come in handy from time to time—for example, when building hyperlinks. If you recall, the HYPERLINK function allows us to set up a link based on a cell reference, and it expects the cell reference to be a text string. We can use the ADDRESS function to create such a text string. Rather than walk through the steps here, I've set up an exercise that demonstrates this application of the ADDRESS function. Let's head into the exercises now.

EXAMPLES

Let's work on a few examples to get comfortable with our new lookup functions.

 **PRACTICE**

To work along, please refer to *Lookup Functions.xlsx*.

 VIDEO

To watch the solutions video, please visit the Excel University Video Library.

EXERCISE 1—COMPARISON

In this exercise, we'll compare OFFSET and INDEX.

 **PRACTICE**

To work along, please refer to the Exercise 1 worksheet.

Our worksheet includes sales data by region with quarterly columns as shown in Figure 8.

	B	C	D	E	F	G
23	Region	Q1	Q2	Q3	Q4	Total
24	Midwest	58,367	38,260	47,374	8,634	152,635
25	Northeast	48,441	134,164	67,347	126,137	376,089
26	Southeast	10,897	54,400	54,616	76,529	196,442
27	Southwest	27,169	48,833	97,331	30,180	203,513
28	West	32,638	90,806	30,563	42,210	196,217
30	Total	177,512	366,463	297,231	283,690	1,124,896

Figure 8

Our goal is to retrieve specified values first using the OFFSET function, and then again with the INDEX function. During this exercise, all OFFSET reference arguments must be *B23*, which represents the upper-left cell in the range. All of our INDEX reference arguments must be *C24:F28*.

Midwest Q1 Value

Let's begin by retrieving the Midwest amount for Q1 with the OFFSET function. The starting point is cell *B23*, and we notice that Midwest is one row down and that Q1 is one column right. Thus, we write this formula:

```
=OFFSET(B23,1,1)
```

Where:

- **B23** is the reference for the starting point

- **1** moves the starting point down one row

- **1** moves the starting point right one column

We confirm the function returns the expected value of 58,367. The OFFSET function enabled us to start at *B23* and then move one row down and one column right.

Now let's do the same thing with the INDEX function. Our reference argument is *C24:F28*, which includes the values in the data range. Midwest data is located in the first row within the reference and Q1 data in the first column, so we use the following formula:

- =INDEX(C24:F28,1,1)

Where:

- **C24:F28** is the reference

- **1** is the first row within the reference

- **1** is the first column within the reference

We confirm the function returns the expected value of 58,367. It is the same value returned by our OFFSET function—excellent! The INDEX function enabled us to start with the data range and then retrieve a value within the range at the intersection of the first row and the first column.

Both of these functions returned the same value. However, since the OFFSET function is volatile, we'd prefer to use the INDEX function.

Northeast Q3 Value

Now let's grab the Q3 value for the Northeast region. The Northeast region is the second row and Q3 is the third column. We use the following formulas:

```
=OFFSET(B23,2,3)
=INDEX(C24:F28,2,3)
```

We confirm they both return the expected result of 67,347. Now that we have retrieved a couple of cell values, let's add up a range reference.

Northeast Q1:A4 Sum

We want to add up the Northeast region's Q1 through Q4 values with the SUM function. We use the OFFSET and INDEX functions to provide the sum range to the SUM function. The Northeast region is in the second row, and the quarters are in the first through fourth columns. We write the following formula:

```
=SUM(OFFSET(B23,2,1,1,4))
```

Where:

- **B23** is the starting point

- **2** moves the starting point down two rows

- **1** moves the starting point right one column

- **1** returns a range one row high

- **4** returns a range four columns wide

The formula returns 376,089 as expected. Now let's try it with the INDEX function:

```
=SUM(INDEX(C24:F28,2,0))
```

Where:

- **C24:F28** is the reference

- **2** is the second row within the reference

- **0** means all columns within the reference

The formula returns 376,089 as expected. Now that we've added all quarterly columns, let's see how we can add a subset.

West Q1:Q2 Sum

Here we want to add up the West region's Q1 and Q2 values. Since the West region is in the fifth row, and Q1 and Q2 are the first and second columns, we can use this formula:

```
=SUM(OFFSET(B23,5,1,1,2))
```

Where:

- **B23** is the starting point

- **5** moves the starting point down five rows

- **1** moves the starting point right one column

- **1** returns a range one row high

- **2** returns a range two columns wide

The formula returns 123,444 as expected.

How do we do this with the INDEX function? We create the sum range with the range operator. We indicate the first cell in the range and use the INDEX function to identify the last cell in the range as follows:

```
=SUM(C28:INDEX(C24:F28,5,2))
```

Where:

- **C28** is the first cell in the sum range

- **INDEX(C24:F28,5,2)** returns a reference to the last cell in the sum range

- **Where:**

- **C24:F28** is the reference

- **5** is the fifth row in the reference

- **2** is the second column in the reference

The formula returns the same amount as the OFFSET function, 123,444.

Now that we've retrieved a range consisting of one row and many columns, let's retrieve a range with one column and many rows.

All Regions Q3 Sum

We want to add up the Q3 column for all regions. Starting with the OFFSET function, we write the following formula:

```
=SUM(OFFSET(B23,1,3,5,1))
```

Where:

- **B23** is the starting point

- **1** moves the starting point down one row

- **3** moves the starting point right three columns

- **5** returns a range five rows high

- **1** returns a range one column wide

We can also accomplish this with the INDEX function and range operator, as follows:

```
=SUM(E24:INDEX(C24:F28,5,3))
```

Where:

- **E24** is the first cell in the sum range

- **INDEX(C24:F28,5,3)** returns a reference to the last cell in the sum range

- **Where:**

  - **C24:F28** is the reference

  - **5** is the fifth row within the reference

  - **3** is the third column within the reference

The formula returns the same values as the OFFSET function: 297,231.

The final task is returning a range that consists of several rows and columns.

All Regions Q3:Q4 Sum

To retrieve the Q3 and Q4 columns for all region rows, we start with the OFFSET function as follows:

```
=SUM(OFFSET(B23,1,3,5,2))
```

Where:

- **B23** is the starting point
- **1** moves the starting point down one row
- **3** moves the starting point right three columns
- **5** returns a range five rows high
- **2** returns a range two columns wide

The formula returns 580,921 as expected.

Now let's try using the INDEX function and the range operator as follows:

```
=SUM(E24:INDEX(C24:F28,5,4))
```

Where:

- **E24** is the first cell in the sum range
- **INDEX(C24:F28,5,4)** returns a reference to the last cell in the sum range
- **Where:**
    - **C24:F28** is the reference
    - **5** is the fifth row in the reference
    - **4** is the fourth column in the reference

We confirm the formula returns the same value as the OFFSET function: 580,921.

I hope you had fun comparing INDEX and OFFSET because we do something similar in the next exercise.

EXERCISE 2—TABLE ROW

In this exercise, we'll retrieve values from a table.

 **PRACTICE**

To work along, please refer to the Exercise 2 worksheet.

Our worksheet has a data table named ***tbl_e2***. Each month we add a row to the table for the current period. We want to write two formulas: one that retrieves the value in the last table row, and one that sums the values in the last three table rows. When new data is added to the table, we want the formulas to continue to work without modification.

Since the total number of rows in the table changes each month, we need to ask the ROWS function for assistance. The ROWS function will return the number of rows in the table, which is essentially the last data row. We will nest the ROWS function inside the OFFSET and INDEX functions. Should be fun.

Let's begin by getting the sales amount from the last data row. We use the OFFSET function as follows:

```
=OFFSET(tbl_e2[#Headers],ROWS(tbl_e2),1,1,1)
```

Where:

- **tbl_e2[#Headers]** is the starting point, the header row of the table
- **ROWS(tbl_e2)** returns the number of data rows in the table and moves the starting point down accordingly
- **1** moves the starting point right one column
- **1** returns a range one row high
- **1** returns a range one column wide

We confirm it returns the sales amount from the last table row. Now let's do the same thing with the INDEX function:

```
=INDEX(tbl_e2,ROWS(tbl_e2),2)
```

Where:

- **tbl_e2** is the reference

- **ROWS(tbl_e2)** is the last row in the reference

- **2** is the second column in the reference

We confirm it returns the sales amount from the last row.

Now let's try summing the last three months, first with OFFSET as follows:

```
=SUM(OFFSET(tbl_e2[#Headers],ROWS(tbl_e2)-2,1,3,1))
```

Where:

- **tbl_e2[#Headers]** is the starting point

- **ROWS(tbl_e2)-2** moves the starting point down to the last row and then up two rows

- **1** moves the starting point right one column

- **3** returns a range three rows high

- **1** returns a range one column wide

We confirm the formula sums the final three sales amounts as expected.

Now let's try again, but this time with INDEX, as follows:

```
=SUM(INDEX(tbl_e2,ROWS(tbl_e2)-2,2)
:INDEX(tbl_e2,ROWS(tbl_e2),2))
```

Where:

- **INDEX(tbl_e2,ROWS(tbl_e2)-2,2)** returns the first cell in the sum range

- **INDEX(tbl_e2,ROWS(tbl_e2),2)** returns the last cell in the sum range

We confirm the formula sums the final three sales amounts as expected. As a final test, we can enter a new table row and confirm that the formulas provide the updated totals—excellent!

EXERCISE 3—TABLE SELECT

In this exercise, we'll allow the user to select the table to sum.

 **PRACTICE**

To work along, please refer to the Exercise 3 worksheet.

Our workbook has several tables, and we want to allow the user to select a table from a drop-down list. Our formula should sum the values in the selected table. The tables are named *E3A*, *E3B*, and *E3C*. We use data validation to create the drop-down list for the input cell and use our table names as the list source.

To sum up the values in the selected table, we use the INDIRECT function to convert the table name in the input cell to a valid Excel reference, and we use the SUM function to add the values. Since the input cell is *C9*, we write the following formula:

```
=SUM(INDIRECT(C9))
```

Where:

- **INDIRECT(C9)** converts the table name stored as a text string into a valid Excel reference

This is great! We can select a different table name and our formula updates the result as expected.

EXERCISE 4—SHEET NAVIGATION

In this exercise, we'll make it easier to navigate within a large worksheet.

 **PRACTICE**

To work along, please refer to the Exercise 4 worksheet.

It is common for big web pages to have a set of hyperlinks up top that allows the user to quickly jump to selected areas on the page. We'd like to do something similar in our big worksheet. We start by setting up the section labels throughout the sheet, in Column *A* of course.

 XREF

Setting up sheet section labels in Column A is discussed in Volume 1, Chapter 16.

After creating a summary of the section labels up near the top of the sheet, it is time to set up the hyperlinks. One option is the Hyperlink feature. We could name each section label cell and then manually create a corresponding hyperlink to each name. However, we don't really like manually repeating a series of steps, especially in recurring-use workbooks. Another option is the HYPERLINK function. We'd like to use consistent formulas here because it would make it easy to add new section labels in the future.

 XREF

The Hyperlink feature is discussed in Chapter 8, and the HYPERLINK function is discussed in Chapter 9.

Here's what we'll do: 1. We'll use the HYPERLINK function to create the links. 2. We'll use the ADDRESS function to provide the HYPERLINK function with the cell address. 3. We'll use the MATCH function to provide the ADDRESS function with the corresponding row of the section label cell. We take this formula one step at a time, starting with the MATCH function.

All of the labels are stored in Column *A*, and our label summary up near the top begins in *B11*. We can ask the MATCH function to find the label text stored in *B11* in the label Column *A*, as follows:

```
=MATCH(B11,A:A,0)
```

Where:

- **B11** is the label text

- **A:A** is the label column

- **0** means exact match

Since the first label is found in *A20*, the MATCH function returns a value of 20.

Now we can use that result inside of the ADDRESS function to create a cell address, as follows:

```
=ADDRESS(MATCH(B11,A:A,0),1)
```

Where:

- **MATCH(B11,A:A,0)** returns 20 for the row number

- **1** represents the first column, Column A

This formula returns the text string *$A$20*—which is excellent because that is the cell that contains our first label. Now all that remains is to create a hyperlink with that destination.

For the hyperlink destination, we use the result of the ADDRESS function. But as discussed previously, we need to begin the internal reference with #, and we can use concatenation to accomplish that. For the friendly label, we could use just about any intuitive or logical label. In our case, we'll use a "v" to indicate a down direction. We put it all together in the following formula:

```
=HYPERLINK("#"&ADDRESS(MATCH(B11,A:A,0),1),"v")
```

Where:

- **"#"&ADDRESS(MATCH(B11,A:A,0),1)** is the destination

- **"v"** is the friendly label

The formula evaluation sequence is as follows:

```
=HYPERLINK("#"&ADDRESS(MATCH(B11,A:A,0),1),"v")

=HYPERLINK("#"&ADDRESS(20,1),"v")

=HYPERLINK("#"&$A$20,"v")

=HYPERLINK("#$A$20","v")
```

We fill this formula down through the summary of section labels to create the hyperlinks that jump to the matching section label cells.

We can easily set return links as well, using the HYPERLINK function. The links help a user return back to the top of the sheet from each of the section labels. We can use the same formula for all of the return links, as follows:

```
=HYPERLINK("#A1","^")
```

Where:

- **"#A1"** is the destination

- **"^"** is the friendly label

We used hyperlinks to simulate a common navigation mechanism that is used on big web pages, and they help navigate our big worksheets as well.

EXERCISE 5—MULTICOLUMN TEXT

In this exercise, we'll revisit two of our favorite functions.

 **PRACTICE**

To work along, please refer to the Exercise 5 worksheet.

Before we jump into the exercise, let's reminisce. Two functions we've used often during this series are VLOOKUP and SUMIFS. We have been using these functions since Volume 2, and it is my guess that you are fairly comfortable with them by now.

We've used both of these heavyweights to perform lookups. In one corner we have VLOOKUP. It has been around for decades and is probably the most popular function. SUMIFS is a relatively new function with impressive capabilities, and it is gaining favor quickly among users. We formally compared these rivals and analyzed their capabilities.

 XREF

VLOOKUP and SUMIFS are compared in Volume 2, Chapter 15.

In our comparison, we saw that the SUMIFS function supports multiple conditions and returns the sum of all matching records. We saw that the VLOOKUP function returns the first related value. We understand which function to use based on the data. Since the SUMIFS function returns the sum, when the value we wish to return is numeric we prefer to use SUMIFS. However, when the value we wish to return is a text string, we use VLOOKUP. With this history in mind, let's jump into the exercise.

The *Exercise 5* worksheet contains the first and last names of selected employees. We need to retrieve related values from our employee extract stored in the *tbl_e5* table on the *E5 Data* worksheet.

Back on the *Exercise 5* sheet, the first value we need to retrieve is the HMO premium amount. We need to decide which function to use in our formula. The HMO premium amount is numeric, so we'll go with SUMIFS. Since the first name is stored in *B11* and the last name is stored in *C11*, we write the following formula to retrieve the HMO premium amount from the table:

```
=SUMIFS(tbl_e5[HMO],tbl_e5[First],B11,tbl_e5[Last],C11)
```

Where:

- **tbl_e5[HMO]** is the sum range

- **tbl_e5[First]** is the first criteria range

- **B11** is the first criteria value

- **tbl_e5[Last]** is the second criteria range

- **C11** is the second criteria value

We fill the formula down—and we are looking good.

The next value we need to retrieve is the city name. We need to decide which of our two rival functions to use. The city name is a text string, so we clearly can't use the SUMIFS function, which returns numeric values only. We need to perform our lookup based on both the first and last name values. Since VLOOKUP is designed to work with a single lookup value and not multiple lookup values, we clearly can't use VLOOKUP. Well, it seems obvious that neither of our two rivals can help. Or can they?

We've thought about these two heavyweights as competitors. In any given formula, we would simply use the one that was best equipped to help. But the truth of the matter is that they can work together. When the data contains a numeric Key column and no duplicates, they can help each other out. A Key column contains a unique numeric identifier for each row—for example, an employee ID. The restriction about duplicate values is that only a single row meets all lookup conditions—for example, multiple employees do not share the same first and last name. Under these conditions, SUMIFS and VLOOKUP can be incredible allies. Let's check it out.

Our employee data table *tbl_e5* contains an employee ID column. We could use SUMIFS to return this ID based on employee first and last names. Then VLOOKUP could use the ID to return the city. If we nest the functions, we eliminate the need for a helper column. Basically, SUMIFS will be the first argument of the VLOOKUP function. Will this work? You bet!

We write the following formula to retrieve the city for the first employee:

```
=VLOOKUP(SUMIFS(tbl_e5[ID],tbl_e5[First],B11,
tbl_e5[Last],C11),tbl_e5,4,0)
```

Where:

- **SUMIFS(tbl_e5[ID],tbl_e5[First],B11,tbl_e5[Last],C11)** returns the ID

- **tbl_e5** is the lookup range

- **4** returns the value from the fourth column, the city

- **0** means exact match

We fill the formula down, and it works. As it turns out, VLOOKUP and SUMIFS can work together as allies! I hope you had fun with that exercise. I know that I sure had fun setting it up.

CHAPTER CONCLUSION

As you know, we prefer lookups to direct cell references. In this chapter we examined several additional lookup functions. We met many new friends and even spent time with a couple of old ones.

Chapter 12: Text Functions

SET UP

We can increase our opportunity for automation when we consider using functions that operate on, and return, text strings. You'll recognize these text functions that we've already discussed:

- CONCATENATE—returns the text string of its combined arguments

- FIND—returns the position number of a matching text string

- LEFT—returns characters from the beginning of a value

- LEN—returns the length of the text string

- MID—returns characters from the middle of a value

- REPT—returns a text string that repeats the specified character a given number of times

- RIGHT—returns characters from the end of a value

- TEXT—returns a text string of the specified value

- VALUE—returns a numeric value of the specified text string

In this chapter we round out our skills by exploring the following functions:

- TRIM—returns a text string with excess spaces removed

- SUBSTITUTE—returns a text string after replacing specified characters

- DOLLAR—returns a text string formatted as a currency

- UPPER—returns a text string with all uppercase text

- LOWER—returns a text string with all lowercase text

- PROPER—returns a text string with proper case text

These text functions can be helpful in data preparation, reporting, and workpapers.

HOW TO

Let's take them one by one, starting with TRIM.

TRIM

The TRIM function removes excess spaces from a text string, such as leading spaces, trailing spaces, or extra spaces between words. We briefly noted it earlier in the series, but we examine the details now.

 XREF

TRIM was noted in Volume 2, Chapter 14.

The syntax is easy:

```
=TRIM(text)
```

Where:

- **text** is the text string

For example, to remove the excess spaces from "Cash " we could use the following formula:

```
=TRIM("Cash  ")
```

We can nest the TRIM function within a lookup function to help work with the data as it comes, and we apply it in this manner when we get to the exercises.

SUBSTITUTE

The SUBSTITUTE function allows us to replace characters in a text string with the characters of our choice.

Here's how it looks:

```
=SUBSTITUTE(text,old_text,new_text,[instance_num])
```

Where:

- **text** is the text string to modify
- **old_text** is the existing character or characters to replace (case sensitive)
- **new_text** is the replacement character or characters
- **[instance_num]** specifies which occurrence of old_text to replace, all instances if omitted

For example, let's say our accounting system exports our accounts with a dash delimiter, such as 100-20-4456. We need to switch the delimiter to a colon, such as 100:20:4456. This is easily accomplished with the following formula:

```
=SUBSTITUTE("100-20-4456","-",":")
```

We have an opportunity to practice this application in our upcoming exercises.

 NOTE

> SUBSITUTE is useful when you know the characters but not their position within the text string. The related REPLACE function is useful when you know the position but not the characters. See Excel Help for more information.

DOLLAR

The DOLLAR function converts a number to text with the currency format. We previously did something similar with the TEXT function, which converts a number into a text string based on the specified formatting code. TEXT supports a wide variety of formatting options, but when you want to return a currency, the DOLLAR function is an easy alternative:

```
=DOLLAR(number,[decimals])
```

Where:

- **number** is the number to convert into a currency string
- **[decimals]** is the number of digits to the right of the decimal to display

We previously used TEXT to return a currency string, but now we can use DOLLAR. For example, instead of using the following formula:

```
=TEXT(A1,"$#,###")
```

We can use this one instead:

```
=DOLLAR(A1,0)
```

In practice, either function will get the job done, so it is simply a matter of personal preference.

UPPER

The UPPER function converts lowercase characters to uppercase:

```
=UPPER(text)
```

Where:

- **text** is the string to convert to upper case

For example, if the state code "ny" is stored in **A1** and you'd like to write a formula that returns an uppercase state code "NY," you could use UPPER as follows:

```
=UPPER(A1)
```

To go the other direction and create lowercase characters, we can use the related LOWER function.

LOWER

The LOWER function converts uppercase letters to lowercase:

```
=LOWER(text)
```

Where:

- **text** is the string to convert to all lowercase letters.

For example, if "JOHN@Gmail.Com" is stored in **A1**, and you'd like to write a formula that returns "john@gmail.com," you could use LOWER as follows:

```
=LOWER(A1)
```

To create proper case, we can use the related PROPER function.

PROPER

The PROPER function converts a text string to proper case, where the first letter in all words are uppercase and remaining letters are lowercase:

=PROPER(text)

Where:

- **text** is the string to convert to proper case

For example, if "excel university" is stored in *A1*, and you'd like to write a formula that returns "Excel University" you could use PROPER as follows:

=PROPER(A1)

Let's practice these text functions by working on a few exercises.

EXAMPLES

It is time to put these text functions to work and find out firsthand how handy they are.

 **PRACTICE**

To work along, please refer to *Text Functions.xlsx.*

 VIDEO

To watch the solutions video, please visit the Excel University Video Library.

EXERCISE 1—SG&A

In this exercise, we'll retrieve values from a data table.

 **PRACTICE**

To work along, please refer to the Exercise 1 worksheet.

Let's revisit a worksheet and solve it in a new way. The report labels in this worksheet were indented by adding leading spaces. As you know, we prefer to indent with the Indent command.

XREF

Indentation is discussed in Volume 2, Chapter 14.

If we were setting this up the first time, or if this were a recurring-use workbook, we would take the time to create proper indents. But this is a one-time project, and we don't want to spend the time manually removing existing spaces from all of the report labels. So we'll get help from the TRIM function.

Since the first report label is stored in **B12**, and the data is stored in the *tbl_e1* table, we write the following formula:

```
=VLOOKUP(TRIM(B12),tbl_e1,2,0)
```

Where:

- **TRIM(B12)** removes the leading spaces from the report label
- **tbl_e1** is the lookup range
- **2** returns the value from the second column
- **0** means exact match

We fill the formula down through the report and confirm it retrieves the values from the data table as expected.

 XREF

If the excess spaces are in the lookup range, rather than the lookup value, consider using wildcards as discussed in Chapter 18.

EXERCISE 2—DELIMITER

In this exercise, we'll switch the delimiter.

 **PRACTICE**

To work along, please refer to the Exercise 2 worksheet.

One of our systems exports accounts with a dash delimiter, but we need to prepare the data for import into another system that requires a colon delimiter. We can easily prepare the data by switching the delimiter with the SUBSTITUTE function.

The accounts were exported with a dash delimiter—for example, 100-20-4456. We need to import them with a colon delimiter—for example, 100:20:4456. Since the first account is stored in *B11*, we write the following formula:

```
=SUBSTITUTE(B11,"-",":")
```

Where:

- **B11** is the account

- **"-"** is the character to find and replace

- **":"** is the replacement character

We fill the formula down and confirm it works as expected.

EXERCISE 3—DOLLAR

In this exercise, we'll revisit a previous exercise.

 **PRACTICE**

To work along, please refer to the Exercise 3 worksheet.

We would like to write a formula that displays the text string, "The cash balance is $57,886." The cash balance is stored in a cell, and we had previously accomplished this concatenation task with the TEXT function. This time, we use the DOLLAR function.

 XREF

We previously completed this task with TEXT in Volume 2, Chapter 19.

Since the cash balance is stored in a cell named *cash_bal,* we write the following formula:

```
= "The cash balance is "&DOLLAR(cash_bal,0)
```

Where:

- **cash_bal** is the cell with the cash balance amount

- **0** means display the amount in whole dollars

Yep, looks like we got it.

EXERCISE 4—HEADER

In this exercise, we'll format a report header.

 **PRACTICE**

To work along, please refer to the Exercise 4 worksheet.

We would like to generate a report header that incorporates the date. When we completed this task previously, it was displayed in title case—for example, "For the Year Ended December 31, 2017." Now we want to display it in upper case—for example, "FOR THE YEAR ENDED DECEMBER 31, 2017."

 XREF

We previously completed a similar task in Volume 2, Chapter 19.

The report date is stored in a cell named *rpt_date*, and the header text is stored in a cell named *rpt_header*. Thus, we use the following formula to create the desired header:

```
=UPPER(rpt_header&TEXT(rpt_date,"mmmm d, yyyy"))
```

Where:

- **rpt_header** is the reference to the header text

- **TEXT(rpt_date, "mmm d, yyyy")** displays the date as desired

In addition, now that we know how to center across a selection, we center the header across the two columns. Nice.

EXERCISE 5—CONTACTS

In this exercise, we'll prepare exported data for import.

 **PRACTICE**

To work along, please refer to the Exercise 5 worksheet.

We've exported a list of contact form submissions from our website and would like to import it into our Customer Relationship Manager (CRM) system. Before we do, we want to try to clean it up a bit. You see, some people have submitted the form with all lowercase names, and we want them in proper case. They've also submitted some state codes in lower case, and we need all state codes in upper case. Plus, they've submitted some email addresses in upper case, and we want them all in lower case. Fortunately, this is pretty easy stuff.

For the columns that need proper case, such as *Name*, *Address*, and *City*, we use the PROPER function, as illustrated below:

```
=PROPER(B11)
```

We need the *State* column in upper case, so we use the UPPER function as shown below:

```
=UPPER(E11)
```

We need the *Email* column in lower case, so we use the LOWER function as shown below:

```
=LOWER(F11)
```

We fill the formulas down and are happy that our data is now much cleaner and ready for import.

CHAPTER CONCLUSION

In this chapter we explored several additional text functions. By understanding these new text functions, along with the ones we already used, and including them in our workbooks, we gain a productivity boost because they help us increase the number of formula cells and decrease the number of input cells.

Chapter 13: Date Functions

SET UP

Dates are often an integral component of our workpapers. For example, pay periods span a specific date range, and the number of workdays in a month typically excludes weekends and holidays. Fortunately, Excel has many helpful functions that operate on, and return, date values. So far during the series, we have explored the following date functions:

- EOMONTH—returns the last day of the month

- DATE—returns a valid Excel date based on its arguments

- MONTH—returns the month of the date

- YEAR—returns the year of the date

- DAY—returns the day of the date

Now let's cover several additional date functions that can be useful in our workbooks:

- DATEVALUE—returns a valid Excel date from a text string that represents a date

- EDATE—returns a date a given number of months before or after the specified date

- WEEKDAY—returns the day of the week, 1 through 7

- TODAY—returns today's date

- NETWORKDAYS—returns the number of workdays between two dates

Let's get to it.

HOW TO

When we import data from other sources, Excel tries its best to interpret the data type and store the values accordingly. Although Excel is pretty good at recognizing dates, sometimes it stores dates as text strings instead of date values. Fortunately, Excel includes a function designed to convert a text string that represents a date into an actual date value. We can use the resulting date value with date functions. Let's check out the DATEVALUE function.

DATEVALUE

The DATEVALUE function is designed to convert a text string that represents a date into a date value:

```
=DATEVALUE(date_text)
```

Where:

- **date_text** is a text string that represents a date

For example, if *A1* stored the text string "5-Dec-2017," we could use the DATEVALUE function to convert it into a valid Excel date as follows:

```
=DATEVALUE(A1)
```

Since Excel is pretty good at recognizing dates, date functions can often operate directly on a text date without conversion. But when you are getting unexpected results because the date is stored as a text string, DATEVALUE can be helpful. In addition, since the DATEVALUE argument is a text string, we can use text functions such as LEFT, RIGHT, SUBSTITUTE, and CONCATENATE to help prepare the original value for use by DATEVALUE.

EDATE

The EDATE function returns a date that is a given number of months after (or before) the starting date:

```
=EDATE(start_date,months)
```

Where:

- **start_date** is the date we want to move

- **months** is the number of months after (before) the start date

This function is handy when you need an end date that falls on the same day of the month as the start date. For example, if the start date of 1/15/2017 was stored in *A1*, the following formula would return 4/15/2017:

```
=EDATE(A1,3)
```

 NOTE

When the EDATE function is asked to roll a date, such as March 31, forward to a month that doesn't have as many days, such as April, it returns the last day of the month instead, such as April 30.

WEEKDAY

The WEEKDAY function returns an integer that represents the day of the week, such as 1 for Sunday and 2 for Monday:

```
=WEEKDAY(serial_number,[return_type])
```

Where:

- **serial_number** is the date

- **[return_type]** determines which integer value corresponds with which weekday, if omitted 1 represents Sunday

For example, if the date stored in *A1* is Sunday 12/31/2017, then the following formula would return the integer that represents Sunday, such as 1:

```
=WEEKDAY(A1)
```

The optional return_type argument allows us to change which integers represent the weekdays. When the value is 1, or omitted, Sunday begins the week and is represented with 1. If 2, Monday begins the week and is represented with 1. The remaining codes are documented in the Excel Help system.

 NOTE

When the return_type argument is omitted, or 1, you can apply custom formatting to the formula cell, such as "ddd," to display the correct weekday.

TODAY

TODAY is a volatile function that returns today's date, and it has no function arguments:

```
=TODAY()
```

 XREF

Volatile functions are discussed in Chapter 11.

You can use TODAY when you want Excel to determine the current date, and you want the value to be updated continuously.

 NOTE

To enter today's date as a stored value that isn't updated, use Ctrl+; instead of creating a calculated value with TODAY.

TODAY is a useful function when determining relative dates—for example, all invoices dated Today, Last Week, or Last Month.

 NOTE

If you need the current time as well as the current date, use the NOW function.

NETWORKDAYS

The NETWORKDAYS function returns the number of workdays between two dates, excluding weekends and optionally holidays:

```
=NETWORKDAYS(start_date,end_date,[holidays])
```

Where:

- **start_date** is the beginning date
- **end_date** is the ending date
- **[holidays]** is an optional list of dates to exclude

For example, to compute the number of weekdays in any given month, we could store the first day of the month in *A1* and the last day of the month in *B1* and use the following formula:

```
=NETWORKDAYS(A1,B1)
```

The number of days returned would exclude Saturdays and Sundays. If you also need to exclude holidays, then you could specify them with the optional third argument. For example, you could store the list of holiday dates in a range and name it *holiday_dates* and then use the following formula:

```
=NETWORKDAYS(A1,B1,holiday_dates)
```

 NOTE

If you need to customize which days are considered weekends, use NETWORKDAYS.INTL.

 NOTE

The related WORKDAY function computes the end date, given a start date and the number of workdays.

EXAMPLES

Let's improve our date math skills with a few hands-on exercises.

 **PRACTICE**

To work along, please refer to *Date Functions.xlsx*.

 VIDEO

To watch the solutions video, please visit the Excel University Video Library.

EXERCISE 1—DATE VALUES

In this exercise, we'll convert text strings into valid dates.

 **PRACTICE**

To work along, please refer to the Exercise 1 worksheet.

We have imported several transactions from another system, and unfortunately, Excel interpreted the dates as text strings. As a result, when we try to add up the values within a specific date range with our friend SUMIFS, the function returns zero. This is because the dates are stored as text strings rather than valid Excel dates. Additionally, we notice that when we try to sort the transactions based on these text date values, the sort is not chronological. Fortunately, Excel provides the DATEVALUE function that converts a date text string into a date value. Since our first date text is in *B21*, we use the following formula:

```
=DATEVALUE(B21)
```

Where:

- **B21** is the text date

When we use SUMIFS and reference the new calculated date column, it works. Plus we can sort on the calculated column and confirm that the resulting sort is in the expected chronological order.

EXERCISE 2—DATE DELIMITER

In this exercise, we'll ask a friend to help us convert date text strings into date values.

 **PRACTICE**

To work along, please refer to the Exercise 2 worksheet.

Here we've imported several transactions from another system. We notice that the dates are delimited with dots, such as 12.31.2017, and as such are stored as text strings instead of date values. When we try to convert them with the DATEVALUE function, it returns an error. Bummer. So what are we supposed to do—convert the dates manually? No, we try to eliminate manual steps from recurring tasks.

Let's think for a moment. The DATEVALUE worked in the previous exercise with text strings such as 12/31/2017, but it doesn't seem to work now with text strings such as 12.31.2017. Do we know of a function that can replace the dots (.) with forward slashes (/)? If you said the SUBSTITUTE function, good for you!

We can use the SUBSITUTE function to change the dots into slashes, and the resulting text string should be recognized by DATEVALUE. Since the first date text is stored in **B11**, we use the following formula:

```
=DATEVALUE(SUBSTITUTE(B11,".","/"))
```

Where:

- **SUBSTITUTE(B11,".","/")** replaces the dots with forward slashes

- **Where:**

    o **B11** is the text string

    o **"."** is the character to replace

    o **"/"** is the replacement character

Yes, it worked! We fill the formula down and notice it properly converts the text strings into date values. Taking the time to work with the data as it comes will pay efficiency dividends in future periods.

EXERCISE 3—CONTRACT DATES

In this exercise, we'll compute contract end dates based on the start dates.

 **PRACTICE**

To work along, please refer to the Exercise 3 worksheet.

We sell support contracts and customers can purchase a 1-, 3-, 6-, or 12-month term. Since the term is based on the number of months, not the number of days, the contract should generally end on the same day of the month as the start date. For example, a 3-month contract purchased on 1/15 should expire on 4/15. The only exception is when a contract is purchased near the end of the month and the expiration month has fewer days. For example, a 1-month contract purchased on 3/31 should expire on 4/30.

Fortunately, we know just the date function that can help—EDATE. Since the first contract date is in **C11** and the number of months is in **D11**, we use the following formula to compute the contract end date:

```
=EDATE(C11,D11)
```

Where:

- **C11** is the start date

- **D11** is the number of months

We push the formula down and verify the formula returns the expected results.

EXERCISE 4—PAY PERIOD

In this exercise, we'll determine the day of the week.

 **PRACTICE**

To work along, please refer to the Exercise 4 worksheet.

In our worksheet, the user enters the first day of the pay period into the input cell. Since our pay periods begin on Monday, we want to ensure that the entered date is a Monday. Since this is Excel, there are a variety of ways to accomplish this task—for example, by using data validation. In this exercise, we'll use the error check idea and compute the weekday of the entered date and compare it to the expected day. Since the pay period input cell is named **pp_begin**, we use the following formula to compute the weekday of the entered date:

```
=WEEKDAY(pp_begin)
```

Where:

- **pp_begin** is the entered date

We simply compare the result to our expected weekday, 2, which represents Monday, and if the difference is zero, then we know the entered pay period date is a Monday. Otherwise, we have an error. If we wanted to, we could apply a custom format, such as "ddd" to display the day name, Mon, instead of the number.

EXERCISE 5—WORKDAYS

In this exercise, we'll determine the number of workdays for each month of the year.

 **PRACTICE**

To work along, please refer to the Exercise 5 worksheet.

Our worksheet contains columns for each month's start and end date. We need to compute the number of workdays in each month. Workdays exclude weekends (Saturday and Sunday) and company holidays. We have created a table named **tbl_holidays** to store the company holidays. The table includes a Date column, which stores the date of each holiday, such as 12/25/2017.

We use Excel's NETWORKDAYS function to compute the number of workdays in each month. Since January's start date is stored in **B22** and its end date in **C22**, we write the following formula:

```
=NETWORKDAYS(B22,C22,tbl_holidays[Date])
```

Where:

- **B22** is the start date

- **C22** is the end date

- **tbl_holidays[Date]** is the list of dates to exclude

We fill the formula down, and we are all set!

CHAPTER CONCLUSION

In this chapter we explored several additional date functions. Date functions can be helpful in our line of work because they are often an integral component of our workbooks.

Chapter 14: Insert Function

SET UP

At this point in the series, we've discussed approximately 50 functions. Wow—that's a lot! We've covered the core functions I use most often in practice, but Excel has well over 450 functions! Since many of them can be quite useful, I want to talk about the steps I use to research them. I hope this chapter enables you to discover and implement useful functions, as well as quickly understand what a function does when you encounter an unfamiliar one in a workbook.

 NOTE

For a list of functions covered in the series, see the Function Reference at the end of this volume.

HOW TO

Excel's Function Library is organized by category. There are a variety of related icons available in the following Ribbon group:

- Formulas > Function Library

Let's start at the left of this Ribbon group. The following Ribbon icon executes the Insert Function command:

- Formulas > Insert Function

KB

Alt+M, F and Shift+F3 execute the Insert Function command.

The little *fx* button to the left of the formula bar also executes the Insert Function command.

When the active cell is empty, or doesn't contain a function, the Insert Function command opens the Insert Function dialog box. However, the Insert Function command opens the Function Arguments dialog instead if Excel is in Ready mode and the active cell contains a function, or if the cursor is within a function in Edit mode. Let's review both of these dialogs.

 XREF

Ready and Edit modes are discussed in Volume 2, Chapter 2.

The Insert Function dialog is shown in Figure 9.

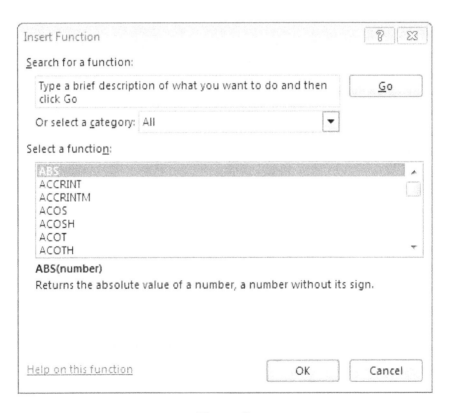

Figure 9

The Insert Function dialog allows you to search and browse through Excel's vast Function Library. Use the search field to search for a function based on name, keyword, or description. Use the category drop-down to browse a filtered function list. Select a function in the list to view a brief description. Click the *Help on this function* hyperlink to view more detail about the selected function.

 KB

You can navigate through the function list by using Arrow and Letter keys on your keyboard.

Once you've located the function you'd like to use, double-click it or select it and press Enter or the OK button to open the Function Arguments dialog, as shown in Figure 10.

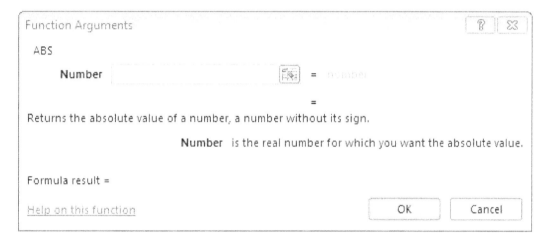

Figure 10

The Function Arguments dialog provides a brief description of the arguments and makes them easy to enter. Required arguments are displayed with bold text and optional arguments are displayed with plain text. You can populate the argument fields by entering values or selecting a cell or range with your mouse. Once the arguments have been defined, you can click OK or hit Enter to insert the function.

Recall that the Function Arguments dialog also opens when you use the Insert Function command while the active cell contains a formula or the cursor is placed within a function. The cool thing is that Excel populates the argument fields with the actual argument values from the formula. This is a quick way to learn about unfamiliar functions you may encounter in workbooks and formulas.

In addition to the Insert Function command, the Function Library Ribbon group provides category icons you can use to research and insert functions. When you click a category icon, a list of related functions appears. Hovering over a function displays a brief description and selecting the function opens the Function Arguments dialog.

All right, time for some practice.

EXAMPLES

Let's discover some more functions.

 PRACTICE

To work along, please refer to *Insert Function.xlsx.*

 VIDEO

To watch the solutions video, please visit the Excel University Video Library.

EXERCISE 1—SUMMARY

In this exercise, we'll browse for functions to compute total interest and total principal.

 **PRACTICE**

To work along, please refer to the Exercise 1 worksheet.

We'd like to enable a user to enter a loan amount, annual interest rate, and number of payments, and we'd like Excel to compute the related monthly payment, total principal, and total interest.

We easily set up the input cells for principal, rate, and number of months, and we are ready to write the formulas. Up first is the monthly payment. We are already familiar with the PMT function, so we can easily use it in a formula to compute the monthly payment. Then we get to the total principal and interest calculations, and we get stuck. We are not sure whether Excel has functions to compute these values, and even if it does, we aren't sure about the arguments. So we open the Insert Function dialog to have a look around.

First we need to compute the total principal paid over the life of the loan. We look in the Financial Functions category and browse through the list of functions. We soon discover the CUMPRINC function. Based on the brief description, it appears this function returns the cumulative principal paid on a loan between two periods. That sounds exactly like what we need. We click OK and use the Function Arguments dialog to understand and define the arguments. We confirm that the formula returns the initial principal amount as expected.

 NOTE

This chapter is designed to allow you to research and implement functions. Rather than show the formula and explain the arguments, I'll ask you to use the Function Arguments dialog as needed.

Now for total interest paid over the life of the loan. We discover the CUMIPMT function and see from its description that it returns the cumulative interest paid between two periods. We use the Function Arguments dialog to understand and define the arguments. After defining the arguments, we click OK and confirm that Excel inserts the formula into the cell.

Now that we have browsed the function list, let's try to search it instead.

EXERCISE 2—PRINCIPAL

In this exercise, we'll search for a function.

 **PRACTICE**

To work along, please refer to the Exercise 2 worksheet.

In the previous exercise, we computed the monthly payment given the principal amount, interest rate, and number of months. In this exercise, we need to compute the principal amount given the interest rate, number of months, and target monthly payment.

After using the PMT, CUMPRINC, and CUMIPMT functions, we understand they have similar arguments. The interest rate argument is *rate*, the number of periods is *nper*, and the present value for the principal amount is *pv*. We have a hunch that if Excel had a function that computed the present value, it may be named *pv*.

So we open the Insert Function dialog and search for our suspected function name. It turns out that Excel has a function named PV, and based on its brief description, it sounds perfect for our worksheet. We open the Function Arguments dialog and define the arguments. Excel computes the principal amount. Just to double-check, we enter this principal amount into the previous exercise worksheet and confirm that the monthly payment values agree.

EXERCISE 3—DEPRECIATION

In this exercise, we'll search for keywords to find depreciation functions.

 **PRACTICE**

To work along, please refer to the Exercise 3 worksheet.

Our worksheet contains a list of our computer equipment and includes the initial cost and salvage value. We would like to compute the depreciation by year for each of these five-year assets. Can Excel compute depreciation? I don't know; let's find out. We open the Insert Function dialog and do a search for depreciation. Wow! Turns out there are several depreciation functions.

Let's start with the SLN function, which, according to its description, returns the straight-line depreciation of an asset. Using the Function Arguments dialog, we enter the cell reference for the cost and salvage arguments. Since we are going to fill the formula down and right, we are careful to use absolute column references and relative row references. We enter 5 for the life argument. Excel inserts the function, we fill the formula down and right, and it seems to work! We compare the total deprecation with the net amount (cost less salvage) for each asset, and we note that the function fully depreciates all assets. Nice! But straight-line depreciation is fairly easy math, and we don't really need a fancy SLN function to do that. So let's try something more interesting. Let's see whether Excel has any accelerated deprecation methods.

We open the Insert Function dialog and do another search for depreciation. This time let's try the SYD function, which, according to its description, returns the sum-of-years' digits depreciation of an asset. We use the Function Arguments dialog to enter the cell references for the cost and salvage arguments, and 5 for the life argument. For the period, we simply reference the Recovery Period column header, and we're careful to use a relative column reference and an absolute row reference. We fill the formula down and right and it seems to work. We double-check the total depreciation and note that Excel has once again fully depreciated the assets—yay!

Now let's see whether Excel can depreciate using the declining balance method. We open the Insert Function dialog, search for depreciation, and notice the DB function, which, according to its description, returns the depreciation of an asset for a specified period using the fixed-declining balance method. Excellent. We define the arguments, fill the formula down and right, and once again note that Excel fully depreciates the assets.

What about double-declining? Let's see. We do another search and notice the DDB function, which, according to its description, returns the depreciation of an asset for a specified period using the double-declining balance method. We populate the function arguments and fill the resulting formula down and right. We check to see that the assets are fully depreciated, and—uh-oh—we have a problem. Excel did not fully depreciate the assets. This isn't because we made a mistake in the formula; it is because of the math inherent in the double-declining balance method. It takes a percentage of the remaining book value each period. So when using the double-declining balance method in our workbooks, we need to switch back to the straight-line method at some point in the recovery period. Fortunately, there is an Excel function that can do that for us automatically. Let's see if we can find it.

We head back to the Insert Function dialog and search for depreciation. We notice the VDB function, which, according to its description, returns the depreciation of an asset for any period using the double-declining method or some other method you specify. We define the arguments and fill the formula throughout the range. Yes—it worked! The total deprecation is equal to the net amount as expected.

EXERCISE 4—QUARTER

In this exercise, we'll use the Insert Function dialog to learn more about a function we encounter in a worksheet.

 **PRACTICE**

To work along, please refer to the Exercise 4 worksheet.

The worksheet computes the calendar quarter of the date entered into the input cell. When we inspect the formula, we see the ROUNDUP function. Since we haven't used this function before, we are not familiar with what it does or how its arguments work.

Fortunately, we know a fast way to learn more about the function. We simply select the cell and then open the Insert Function dialog. Instead of displaying the Insert Function dialog, Excel displays the Function Arguments dialog populated with the ROUNDUP function and related arguments. Based on its brief description, we see the function rounds a number up, away from zero. We see it has two arguments. Since there are three months per quarter, we see that the first argument is the month number divided by three. The second argument is the number of digits, and we see it is set to zero, rounding up to the nearest whole number. This way, dividing months 1, 2, and 3 by 3 yields a value between 0 and 1, all of which round up to return Quarter 1. Months 4, 5, and 6 yield a number between 1 and 2, all of which round up to Quarter 2, and so on. After this research, we now understand how the previous user computed the calendar quarter.

EXERCISE 5—ABSOLUTE VALUE

In this exercise, we'll write a formula that converts negative values into positive values.

 **PRACTICE**

To work along, please refer to the Exercise 5 worksheet.

We exported transactions from our accounting system. Our accounting system exports invoices as positive numbers and credit memos as negative numbers. However, we need to import the data into a reporting system that uses the Type column to distinguish between invoices and credits, and requires that all amounts be imported as positive numbers. So we need to prepare the data for import by creating a calculated column that converts all amounts into positive numbers.

Let's use the Insert Function dialog to find a function that converts negative values to positive values. We figure if such a function existed, it would be in the Math & Trig category. Sure enough, the first function in the category is ABS, which, based on its description, returns the absolute value of a number. We fill the resulting formula down and we look good.

CHAPTER CONCLUSION

In this chapter we practiced how to find new functions and learn what they do. We are now ready to discover the hundreds of Excel functions available to us. Implementing them in our workbooks will help us get more done in less time.

TECHNIQUES

It is time to explore techniques that combine various features and functions.

Chapter 15: Ribbon Review

SET UP

In this part we apply techniques that combine various features and functions discussed throughout the series. We use the things we've learned to build depreciation schedules, create budgets, amortize expenses, compare loans, and even prepare journal entries. The exercises you'll work on throughout this section are super fun!

When planning this series, I considered several factors when determining the order and priority of Excel topics. I prioritized items based on their relevancy to accountants in general. Since accountants work on a wide variety of different tasks, some Excel features are more important to some than others. I tried to generalize.

I also had to figure out how deep to take each topic. I had to determine whether I should simply scratch the surface or dig into the details. For example, should a function get only a short note (NOW), share a chapter with others (LEFT and RIGHT), get its own chapter (SUBTOTAL), be discussed over several chapters (SUMIFS), or be revisited multiple times throughout the series with a new capability or application revealed each time (INDEX)?

I think the items we've covered in detail are the core ingredients you'll use in various combinations to create your incredible workbooks. I believe you'll use them frequently. The items we've covered in less detail aren't less awesome, but they'll probably be used in fewer workbooks.

In this chapter we take a brief tour of the Ribbon. Some commands are good friends that we know well, some are familiar acquaintances, and some are strangers we haven't met yet.

I hope that as we take this tour through the Ribbon, you'll feel happy seeing how many items we've covered during our time together so far, you'll be pleased with how much we've discussed, and you'll be glad to recognize how comfortable you are putting what you've learned to use. I also hope you appreciate the breadth of Excel's capabilities and realize there's much more to Excel than what we've covered. If you see something on our tour that could be useful in your work, please grab some additional information from the Excel Help system.

HOW TO

Let's begin our tour with a background of the Ribbon development. Before the Ribbon, we had menus. We used menus for decades, from the beginning of Office through Office 2003. The developers at Microsoft felt that the number of features and capabilities of Office had outgrown its user interface (UI). So for Office 2007, they wanted to create a new UI that would make the software easier to use, as well as help people focus on the content and work more efficiently. In planning the next UI, they did a ton of research. They analyzed 10,000-plus hours of video and watched people using Office. Plus they used a cool eye-tracking system so they could observe how users located commands. They summarized more than three billion data sessions to determine the most popular commands and command sequences. (Interestingly, the command used most in Excel is Paste.) Their labs had users organize commands into logical groups. Microsoft considered all this data when determining command size, placement, and organization. The end result was a new UI and the Ribbon.

The Ribbon was designed to display commands based on their importance and frequency of use, regardless of screen size. Thus, the Ribbon resizes dynamically as the width of the Excel window changes. Since the Ribbon is so dynamic, rather than talk about each individual command icon, we'll talk about the Ribbon groups, which combine related commands.

 NOTE

To allow you to focus on content, the Ribbon can be collapsed into a single tab strip by double-clicking any tab name.

 KB

Ctrl+F1 expands or collapses the Ribbon tabs.

Let's begin our tour with the Home tab.

HOME

Clipboard: This has commands like Copy and Paste. Be sure to check out the various Paste options and the format painter when applying the same format to other cells. As I mentioned above, the most frequently used Excel command is Paste. You can see Microsoft used this information because Paste is the very first command in the Home tab. You'll also notice a Launcher icon in the lower right corner of this group. Many Ribbon groups have similar launcher icons that reveal related dialogs or panels.

Font: This refers to popular formatting options for fonts and cells. Remember—the Underline command applies an accounting underline when the cell is first formatted with an accounting number format. In designing the new UI, Microsoft wanted users to see the effects of a command rather than command names, when possible, so you'll notice that the Font, Font Size, Cell Fill, and Font Color commands have live preview. When you expand the control and hover over various options, the worksheet provides a preview of the results of the command. This capability is carried out numerous times throughout the Ribbon.

Alignment: This aligns text within cells vertically, horizontally, and diagonally. Don't forget about the Indent buttons! Remember we prefer Center Across Selection to Merge & Center.

Number: This provides popular value formatting options. The Currency icon applies the Accounting number format.

Styles: This is one of our favorite groups! It includes Conditional Formatting, Cell Styles, and the Format as Table icon, which creates a table and formats it in a single step.

Cells: This has commands for inserting, deleting, and formatting cells, rows, columns, and sheets. The Format icon includes a bunch of fun stuff to explore, including a variety of AutoFit, visibility, organization, and protection options.

Editing: The AutoSum command also appears on the Formulas tab, and inserts a SUM (or other aggregate) function and auto-detects the range. This works when you select a single cell as well as multiple cells. Clicking the Down Arrow of this split icon reveals additional aggregate functions such as AVERAGE and MAX. When a range is filtered, this icon inserts the SUBTOTAL function instead of the SUM function.

The Clear icon allows you to clear various attributes. Find & Select offers several tools for locating values, including the ability to replace values. It also has options to open the Go To and Go To Special dialog boxes, plus popular options found within the Go To Special dialog. Most of the Sort & Filter commands are also available on the Data tab.

The Fill command offers options like filling down and right, as well as across worksheets when multiple sheets are selected. It also includes Fill Series, which is actually pretty cool. This is where we can have Excel auto-increment a value. To do so, type a value in a cell, such as 1, and then select that cell as well as the additional empty target cells. Use Fill Series, and then you can define the type of series. This works for dates as well. Additionally, Excel is pretty good at auto-detecting a series. For example, enter 2 into a cell and then 4 into the next cell. Select these two cells and then drag the fill handle down to watch Excel fill the series. This also works to fill custom lists, which can be created in the Excel Options dialog.

 NOTE

PivotTables can also be sorted with custom lists.

 KB

If you drag the fill handle with the right mouse button, Excel will provide numerous Fill options, including Fill Series, Fill Weekdays, and others when you release the button. If you drag the fill handle with the left mouse button while holding down the Ctrl key, Excel modifies the AutoFill behavior based on selection and data type. If you drag the fill handle with the left mouse button while holding down the Shift key, Excel inserts cells or entire rows, depending on the current selection.

 XREF

After reviewing this Ribbon tab, we feel fairly comfortable with its contents and are familiar with many of its commands, including the following: Paste Special (Volume 2, Chapter 7); Indentation (Volume 2, Chapter 14); Conditional Formatting (Volume 1, Chapter 10); Cell Styles (Volume 1, Chapter 14); Tables (Volume 1, Chapter 8); Accounting Underlines (Volume 4, Chapter 5); Protection (Volume 4, Chapter 7); AutoFit (Volume 4, Chapter 5); Tab Color (Volume 1, Chapter 15); Rename Sheets (Volume 1, Chapter 15); Fill (Volume 2, Chapter 2); Sort and Filter (Volume 4, Chapter 3); Go To (Volume 1, Chapter 7); and Go To Special (Volume 3, Chapter 24).

INSERT

Tables: This is another one of our favorite groups because it includes PivotTables and Tables!

Illustrations: This inserts images and shapes into the drawing layer of the worksheet. It also includes SmartArt. Check out the Take a Screenshot icon as well, which is helpful if you need to do a screen grab of a window or region of your monitor.

Add-Ins: Head to the Office store to install Apps for Office written by Microsoft and third-party developers.

Charts, Reports & Sparklines: This includes icons that help summarize and visualize data.

Filters: This has commands useful for filtering data, such as Slicers.

Links: This includes hyperlinks. (Yay!)

Text: This has icons for various text objects, including text boxes and headers and footers.

Symbols: This includes symbols and mathematical equations.

 XREF

We previously encountered many of the commands on this tab, including the following: PivotTables (Volume 3); Tables (Volume 1, Chapter 8); Pictures (Volume 3, Chapter 26); Shapes (Volume 3, Chapter 26); SmartArt (Volume 3, Chapter 26); Slicers (Volume 3, Chapter 19); and Hyperlinks (Volume 4, Chapter 8).

PAGE LAYOUT

Themes: This is a collection of workbook design presets.

Page Setup and Scale to Fit: This has various printing options.

Sheet Options: This includes options to view and print gridlines and row/column headings.

Arrange: This allows for arranging and aligning objects and layers.

 XREF

We previously discussed several print settings and related commands (Volume 4, Chapter 6).

FORMULAS

Function Library: This has commands related to inserting functions into your formulas. AutoSum also appears on the Home tab. The Insert Function icon to open the Insert Function dialog and the category drop-downs provide quick access to functions.

Defined Names: This includes commands related to names. The Define Name command opens the New Name dialog, and the Apply Names command allows you to replace existing A1-style references in your formulas with the corresponding named reference. The Use in Formula command allows you to insert names into your formula. Create from Selection allows you to generate names based on cell values, although, in practice we prefer using Tables and structured table references.

Formula Auditing: This has commands related to helping research and troubleshooting formulas. Trace Precedents highlights the cells referenced by the formula in the active cell. Trace Dependents highlights the formula cells that reference the active cell. Remove Arrows removes the highlighting generated by the Trace commands. Show Formulas toggles the worksheet to display formulas instead of formula results. Error Checking helps locate and troubleshoot built-in error conditions, such as circular references. Evaluate Formula demonstrates each step Excel uses to process the active formula. Watch Window allows you to set up cells to watch as other cells throughout the workbook update.

Calculation: This includes options related to formula recalculation.

 XREF

> We discussed inserting functions and the Function Library (Volume 4, Chapter 14); Names (Volume 1, Chapter 7); and Calculation Options (Volume 4, Chapter 11).

DATA

Get External Data: This is for retrieving data from external sources, such as Microsoft Access or the web.

Connections: This has commands that help manage existing external connections. Refresh All updates the workbook with external data. Connections opens the Workbook Connections dialog used to manage external data connections. Properties is used to manage connection properties. Edit Links is used to manage links to other workbooks. Please note that this does not refer to hyperlinks, but to formulas that retrieve values from other workbooks.

Sort & Filter: This includes options for sorting and filtering data, some of which also appear on the Home tab. The Advanced command opens the Advanced Filter dialog, which allows you to filter or copy filter results, define criteria, and include unique records only (similar to the Remove Duplicates but hides rather than deletes duplicates).

Data Tools: This has various commands related to working with data ranges. Text to Columns splits a single column of data into multiple columns based on a delimiter or fixed width. Flash Fill detects a pattern and fills the pattern down. Remove Duplicates removes duplicate rows within the selected range. Data Validation allows you to control what a user can type into a cell. Consolidate combines multiple ranges of data into a single range based on the selected aggregate functions and labels. What-If Analysis provides options for Scenario Manager, Data Tables, and Goal Seek. Scenario Manager and Data Tables allow you to see the results of a set of predefined input values—for example, viewing the monthly payment for several defined interest rates. Goal Seek operates in the reverse, where you define the desired formula result and it provides the required input cell value—for example, what interest rate is needed to produce a given monthly payment amount.

 NOTE

In addition to the What-If Analysis commands, Excel includes a Solver Add-In, which changes a set of input values subject to defined constraints to compute the optimal value of the formula cell. Excel Add-Ins are managed in the Excel Options dialog.

Outline: This has commands used to manage Outline groups including Group, Ungroup, and Subtotal.

 XREF

We discussed external data (Volume 3, Chapter 22); sorting and filtering (Volume 4, Chapter 3); Text to Columns (Volume 3, Chapter 23); Remove Duplicates (Volume 2, Chapter 3); Data Validation (Volume 1, Chapter 9); and outlining (Volume 4, Chapter 4).

REVIEW

Proofing & Language: This includes spell check, language translation, and other proofreading tools.

Comments: This allows you to create, delete, display, and navigate through cell comments. Additional options regarding comments and how they are displayed are available in the Excel Options dialog. Options for how comments should appear when the worksheet is printed are available in the Sheet tab of the Page Setup dialog.

Changes: This has Worksheet and Workbook Protection, and Workbook Sharing commands.

 NOTE

Excel displays an error message if you try to share a workbook that contains a table.

 XREF

We discussed Worksheet and Workbook Protection in Chapter 7.

VIEW

Workbook Views: This has various options for viewing the workbook. Custom views can be used to save specific display and print settings, making them easy to apply as needed. For example, you could create a custom view that defines the hidden and visible worksheets, filter selections, margins, and headers.

Show: This allows you to show or hide certain worksheet elements, such as gridlines and row or column headings. Gridlines and Headings checkboxes are also available on the Page Layout tab.

Zoom: This includes commands for controlling the Zoom level of the worksheet.

Window: This has commands to help manage various Excel windows, including when you have multiple workbooks open and when you're switching the active workbook.

Macros: These commands help record a new macro and view existing macros.

 XREF

We discussed workbook views (Volume 4, Chapter 6); Zoom (Volume 4, Chapter 6); and Switch Windows (Volume 4, Chapter 2).

In addition to the core tabs discussed above, there are numerous contextual tabs that provide useful commands related to the object you are working on. We've discussed several of these so far, including Table Tools and PivotTable Tools. Although we won't cover these tabs during our Ribbon review, you can view a list of them in the Excel Options dialog by selecting Tool Tabs in the Customize the Ribbon drop-down.

Let's work on a few exercises to practice some of the commands discussed above.

EXAMPLES

Let's crack open the exercise workbook for practice.

 **PRACTICE**

To work along, please refer to *Ribbon Review.xlsx.*

VIDEO

To watch the solutions video, please visit the Excel University Video Library.

EXERCISE 1—APPLY NAMES

In this exercise, we'll use the Apply Names command.

 **PRACTICE**

To work along, please refer to the Exercise 1 worksheet.

Our worksheet uses the PV function to compute the amount that can be borrowed given a target monthly payment, interest rate, and loan term. The formula is already written, and it currently uses A1-style references. Our goal is to name the interest rate input cell, and then have Excel replace any A1-style formula references to it with the new name.

We begin by assigning the name *interest_rate* to the interest rate input cell. We confirm that the PV function still uses the cell reference *C11* instead of the new name. So we tell Excel to replace any reference to *C11* with a reference to *interest_rate* by selecting the following Ribbon command:

- Formulas > Define Name > Apply Names

We select *interest_rate* from the Apply Names dialog and click OK. We inspect the formula and confirm that the name *interest_rate* is now referenced.

EXERCISE 2—CIRCULAR REFERENCE

In this exercise, we'll encounter a circular reference.

 **PRACTICE**

To work along, please refer to the Exercise 2 worksheet.

It is time to pay a bonus to an employee. We want the employee to receive a bonus check in the amount of $7,500. We need to withhold taxes, so we decide to compute the gross bonus amount. We begin by entering what we know into some input cells. We enter the tax rate of 25 percent into cell *C14*. We enter the net bonus amount of $7,500 into *C15*.

Now we need to use formulas to compute the tax amount and the gross bonus amount. The tax amount is simply the gross bonus amount times the tax rate. Since the gross bonus amount formula will reside in cell *C17*, and the tax rate is stored in *C14*, we enter the following formula into the tax amount formula cell *C16*:

```
=C17*C14
```

The formula returns zero at this point, but we expect that since the gross bonus cell is still empty. Let's write a formula to compute the gross bonus amount. That formula should be easy, too, since we know the gross bonus amount is equal to the tax amount computed in *C16* plus the net bonus amount stored in *C15*. Thus, we write the following formula into the gross bonus formula cell *C17*:

```
=C15+C16
```

When we hit Enter, we have a problem. We receive an alert saying we have a circular reference. A circular reference occurs when we write a formula that ultimately refers back to itself. That is, it directly or indirectly needs to know its value before it is able to compute its value. We basically created a calculation loop when we wrote these formulas, because the formula in *C16* references *C17* and the formula in *C17* references *C16*. So *C16* has to know the value in *C17* to compute its result, but the formula in *C17* needs to know the value in *C16* to compute its result. As you can see, this loop creates a problem, and the problem is known as a *circular reference*.

We can confirm which cells are involved in a circular reference by viewing the following Ribbon drop-down:

- Formulas > Error Checking > Circular References

As you can see, both of our formula cells are listed. So to clean up the circular reference issue, we delete both of our formulas. If we can't use formulas to compute the gross bonus amount, are we stuck? Not at all. Let's see if Goal Seek can help out in the next exercise.

EXERCISE 3—GOAL SEEK

In this exercise, we'll use Goal Seek to compute the gross bonus amount.

 **PRACTICE**

To work along, please refer to the Exercise 3 worksheet.

We are still trying to compute the gross bonus amount, based on the $7,500 net bonus and 25 percent tax rate. Our formulas in the previous exercise didn't work, what with the circular references and all. So this time we'll use Goal Seek.

With Goal Seek, Excel quickly changes an input cell value in order to find out which value is needed by the formula to satisfy the goal. In our case, we want Excel to cycle through different gross bonus values to find out which one causes our net bonus formula to equal $7,500.

We begin by setting up the input cell that Excel will change, the gross bonus amount cell *C15*. Then we write a formula to compute the tax amount in cell *C16*, which is the gross bonus *C15* times the tax rate *C13*. Next we write a formula that computes the net bonus in *C17*, which is the gross bonus in *C15* minus the tax amount in *C16*.

With the input cell and formulas set up, we use the following Ribbon command:

- Data > What-If Analysis > Goal Seek

In the resulting Goal Seek dialog, we tell Excel to set the net bonus cell *C17* to the value of $7,500, by changing the gross bonus input cell *C15*. We click OK and watch as Excel cycles through various gross bonus values. It stops when the net bonus formula is $7,500, and so we see that the gross bonus amount needs to be $10,000. Yay—we did it!

However, there is an issue with this approach. Even though Goal Seek successfully computed the gross bonus amount, it is a manual step. If this were a one-time project, we could probably live with that. Since we like to eliminate manual steps from recurring-use workbooks, we'd prefer a formula-based approach. But the last time we tried to compute the bonus with formulas, we got stuck in a circular reference. If we prefer to use formulas but can't, what are we supposed to do? Well, let's see if basic algebra can help.

EXERCISE 4—BONUS FORMULA

In this exercise, we'll use a formula to compute the gross bonus amount.

 **PRACTICE**

To work along, please refer to the Exercise 4 worksheet.

We would like to write a formula that computes the gross bonus amount when the tax rate and net bonus amounts are known. The last time we tried this our formulas got tangled up in a circular reference. This time, we'll use some basic principles from algebra class. Fortunately for us, algebra works in Excel.

We know how to conceptually compute the net bonus amount. We just take the gross bonus amount and subtract the tax amount. We know the tax amount is equal to the gross bonus times the tax rate. If we use g for gross bonus, t for tax rate, and n for net bonus, our equation would look like this:

$$g - (g*t) = n$$

Based on the multiplicative identity property, we can rewrite our equation as follows:

$$(g*1)-(g*t) = n$$

We can factor out g and simplify the equation as follows:

$$g*(1-t) = n$$

Based on the equality property, assuming the tax rate is not 100 percent, we can divide both sides by $(1-t)$ and rewrite our equation as follows:

$$g=n/(1-t)$$

Now we know how to write an Excel formula that computes the gross bonus amount given the net bonus amount and tax rate.

Since our net bonus amount is stored in **C16** and our tax rate is stored in **C17**, we can write the following formula in **C19** to compute the gross bonus amount:

```
=C16/(1-C17)
```

We hit Enter and...yes—it worked! We have the expected gross bonus amount of $10,000, and no circular references. The rest is easy. We compute the tax amount by multiplying the gross bonus by the tax rate, and we compute the net bonus by subtracting the tax amount from the gross bonus amount. The net bonus formula shows $7,500 as expected, so we are good to go.

Now we have a formula-based approach that is perfect for recurring-use workbooks.

EXERCISE 5—EVALUATE FORMULA

In this exercise, we'll use the Evaluate Formula command to find a formula error.

 **PRACTICE**

To work along, please refer to the Exercise 5 worksheet.

We are trying to compute inventory turnover. We know that inventory turnover is computed as follows:

Inventory Turnover = Cost of Sales / Average Inventory

We have cost of sales as well as the beginning and ending inventory values. We can compute average inventory based on our beginning and ending inventory balances as follows:

Average Inventory = (Beginning Inventory + Ending Inventory) / 2

We can combine these two formulas into one, as follows:

Inventory Turnover = Cost of Sales / (Beginning Inventory + Ending Inventory) / 2

Since beginning inventory is stored in **C11**, ending inventory is stored in **C12**, and cost of sales is stored in **C13**, we use the following formula to compute inventory turnover in **C20**:

```
=C13/(C11+C12)/2
```

But we aren't 100 percent sure how Excel evaluates the formula. For example, we don't know whether Excel will divide **C13** by the average inventory or by the sum of beginning and ending inventory.

Previously we used a keyboard shortcut to evaluate selected formula text with the F9 key. Now we would like to watch Excel evaluate the entire formula step-by-step.

 XREF

Evaluating selected formula text with F9 is discussed in Volume 2, Chapter 2.

To see how Excel evaluates the formula, we select cell **C20** and then use the following Ribbon command:

- Formulas > Evaluate Formula

This opens the Evaluate Formula dialog. Clicking the Evaluate button causes Excel to show the next step. It uses the same notation we used for our formula evaluation sequences, where it underlines the next step. As we click through the evaluation steps, we notice that Excel actually divides **C13** by the sum of beginning and ending inventory instead of the average inventory as desired. Thus, we want to provide Excel more information about the order of operation and update our formula with some extra parentheses, as follows:

```
=C13/((C11+C12)/2)
```

Now we run the evaluation again, and this time we notice that Excel divides **C13** by average inventory as desired. The Evaluate Formula command helps us confirm that we properly communicated with Excel. That is, what we intended to tell Excel is what we actually communicated in our formula.

EXERCISE 6—TRACE

In this exercise, we'll find a formula mistake with formula auditing commands.

 **PRACTICE**

To work along, please refer to the Exercise 6 worksheet.

Our worksheet computes sales tax. It contains sales by district for the first half of the year. We need to compute how much sales tax to remit. There is one column for each district, and we have entered the tax rate for each district. After computing the tax for each district, we apply the county, state, and local tax rates to total sales and add them all up to determine total sales tax due. Before we write the check, we want to double-check our work.

We select the formula in cell **C36** that computes total sales tax, and click the following Ribbon command:

- Formulas > Trace Precedents

Excel highlights the cells that are referenced by the formula. So far we are looking good. We click the command again and notice Excel highlights the previous step—that is, the cells referenced by those cells. So far, so good. We click the command again and notice something that doesn't look right. We see a diagonal line, which shows that the LA tax rate is used to compute the SF tax amount. When we inspect the SF tax formula, we confirm that indeed the formula applies the wrong tax rate. Before we fix the formula, let's try to find the mistake with a relevant keyboard shortcut.

 KB

Ctrl+[selects direct precedents. Ctrl+] selects direct dependents. Ctrl+Shift+[selects all precedents. Ctrl+Shift+] selects all dependents.

Let's remove the trace arrows by clicking the following Ribbon command:

- Formulas > Remove Arrows

Once again let's select the *Total Sales Tax* cell. We use the Ctrl+[shortcut to select to the precedent cells. We see Excel selects the precedent cells, similar to the Trace Precedents command. We press the keyboard shortcut again and see similar results as before. We hit the shortcut again, and sure enough, the SF tax rate cell is excluded from the selection, indicating it is not used. Before we fix the formula, let's find the mistake yet another way.

Let's view all of the formulas all at once. We click the following Ribbon icon:

- Formulas > Show Formulas

Now we see the formulas instead of their results. As we select various formula cells with our mouse or keyboard, Excel automatically highlights precedent cells. We quickly skim through the district tax formulas, and when we hit the SF formula, we see that the corresponding tax rate cell is not highlighted. We toggle out of this mode by clicking the Show Formula command again.

Now that we've located our formula mistake, we update it to use the correct tax rate.

EXERCISE 7—CELL COMMENTS

In this exercise, we'll use cell comments.

 **PRACTICE**

To work along, please refer to the Exercise 7 worksheet.

Our worksheet computes the payment of a loan using the PMT function. We are familiar with this function; however, the person that will be updating the workbook is not. We want to provide brief documentation for the user, and so we decide to add some helpful cell comments.

We begin with the *Rate* input cell. We want to let the user know to enter the annual interest rate, rather than a periodic interest rate, so we add a cell comment, "Enter the annual interest rate," either by right-clicking and selecting Insert Comment or by using the following command:

- Review > New Comment

 KB

Shift+F2 and Alt+R, C will both add a new comment.

We also want to clarify that the term should be expressed in months, rather than, say, years, so we enter a new comment, "Enter the loan term in months," into the term input cell.

Finally, we want to clarify that the formula provides a monthly payment, rather than an annual or quarterly payment, so we enter a new comment, "This is the monthly payment," into the payment formula cell.

Excel provides several options for displaying and printing cell comments.

For example, we can toggle them on or off with the following command:

- Review > Show All Comments

When we hover our mouse over a comment cell the comment pops up for display. Or we can show or hide them individually by selecting the cell and then using the following command:

- Review > Show/Hide Comment

We can also hide the comment indicators, the little red triangle in the upper-right corner of the cell, using the Excel Options dialog box. In the Advanced category, we see we can hide comments and indicators, show the indicators only, or show the comments and indicators.

We can also control how comments are displayed when printed by selecting the desired choice from the Comments field on the Sheet tab of the Page Setup dialog. For example, we can print them as displayed on the sheet, or we can print them all at the end of the sheet. When we print them at the end of the sheet, they appear as a list with cell references, so it can be helpful when doing this to also print gridlines and row and column headings, which can be turned on using the corresponding checkboxes in the Sheet tab of the Page Setup dialog box or the Page Layout Ribbon tab.

EXERCISE 8—FILL SERIES

In this exercise, we'll play around with a few fill options.

 **PRACTICE**

To work along, please refer to the Exercise 8 worksheet.

Let's experiment with the Fill Series command. First let's see if we can create a column of odd numbers, starting with the number 1. We select the cell that contains the 1 and extend our selection down as desired—in this case, down to the skinny row. Now we need to tell Excel that we want to fill a series down, so we use the following command:

- Home > Fill > Series

In the Series dialog, we confirm the series is in a column and that the type of series is linear. We want to increment each value by 2, so we use 2 for the step value. We click OK and confirm we have a column of odd numbers.

 NOTE

Select the first cell (value 1) and note the effects of dragging the fill handle with and without the Ctrl key.

When the series is simple like this, we can avoid the Series dialog by entering the first two values of the series and asking Excel to guess the pattern. For example, to create a series of even numbers, we enter the first two values in the series, 2 and 4. Then we select both of these cells, click-and-drag the fill handle down, and confirm Excel guessed the correct series of even numbers.

 NOTE

Select the first two cells (values 2 and 4) and note the effects of dragging the fill handle with and without the Ctrl key.

Excel can also fill a series using dates. In the *Month Dates* column, we want to store the first day of every month. We enter the first date into a cell. Then we select the cell and extend our selection down to the skinny row. We open the Series dialog and confirm the series is a date series. We select Month, click OK, and confirm we look good.

 NOTE

Select the first cell (value 1/1/2017) and note the effects of dragging the fill handle with and without the Ctrl key.

Let's do another date series, but this time let's avoid the Series dialog. We want to create a column of weekdays. We enter the first date and select the cell. Instead of dragging the fill handle down with the left mouse button, we drag the fill handle down to the skinny row using the right mouse button. When we release, a shortcut menu pops up with various fill options. We see the one we want, Fill Weekdays, and select it. Yes—it worked!

CHAPTER CONCLUSION

In this chapter we reviewed the Ribbon. We encountered many commands we have used before and met some new friends along the way. Now we have a good idea of where to look for commands when we need them.

Chapter 16: Conditional Formatting Revisited

SET UP

Let's say you have a range of transactions. When you want to identify certain transactions, how do you do it? Do you manually format the cells? For example, you may apply a cell fill to the invoices that are open and need follow-up. Or you may change the font color to red for the accounts that have a large variance and need explanation. Manually formatting cells to identify selected transactions is a common technique. But, depending on your next step, this approach may hinder your productivity, especially in recurring-use workbooks. Here's why. As we've discussed, Excel functions generally operate on stored values rather than displayed values.

 XREF

Stored and displayed values are discussed in Volume 1, Chapter 3.

Functions easily reference cell values, but not cell formatting. For example, if your next step was to try to summarize the highlighted transactions with SUMIFS, you'd be out of luck because the criteria arguments use cell values, not formatting. Many features of Excel use stored values as well. For example, if your next step was to try to summarize the transactions with a PivotTable, you'd once again be out of luck. Although there are some features, such as filtering, that do recognize cell formatting, any formatting inconsistencies can make it difficult to get the results you are after.

XREF

Filtering by color is discussed in Chapter 3.

In practice, an approach that may improve productivity is to use cell values along with conditional formatting. The cell values can be stored values or values calculated with a formula. For example, if we want to identify rows arbitrarily, we can use stored values. We could enter a value such as TRUE or "Yes" into cells in an adjacent column, and then we could apply conditional formatting based on these stored values. When there is a pattern to the transactions we want to highlight, such as all open invoices or all accounts with a variance greater than 10 percent, we can use a formula. There are actually two kinds of formulas we can use here. We could write a formula that we fill down the adjacent column. The formula would return a value, such as TRUE or "Yes," and we'd apply conditional formatting based on the calculated values. Alternately, we could use a formatting formula. Wait, what? Yep—a conditional formatting formula.

It is time to revisit the Conditional Formatting feature and have some real fun. Even though we've discussed this feature several times already, there are more details to uncover, including conditional formatting formulas.

HOW TO

We focus on the following conditional formatting details:

- Formulas
- Manage Rules
- Tables
- PivotTables

Let's walk through each one briefly.

FORMULAS

So far in the series, we have used conditional formatting to format a cell based on the value of the cell. That is, we have formatted a cell based on its own value. But we can also format a cell based on the value of another cell. To do so, we use a conditional formatting formula.

A conditional formatting formula doesn't determine the cell value; rather, it determines the cell formatting. We write our conditional formatting formula to return a Boolean (TRUE/FALSE) value. When the result is TRUE, Excel applies the specified format. We can format one cell based on the value of another by using a simple comparison formula, or our formula can be more complex and apply formatting based on other factors. We can write a crazy-fancy formula and when the formula returns TRUE, the formatting is applied.

 XREF

Comparison formulas are discussed in Volume 2, Chapter 25.

First we select the range to conditionally format. Then we click the following Ribbon command:

- Home > Conditional Formatting > New Rule

The resulting New Formatting Rule dialog has many types of rules. Many of them are available through the Conditional Formatting icon and we discussed them long ago. Since our goal now is to create a conditional formatting formula, we select *Use a formula to determine which cells to format*. Then we define the formula and the formatting to apply when the formula result is TRUE.

When writing the formula, it is important to understand that the active cell matters. You begin by selecting a range of cells to format, and within the selected range, one of the cells is active. Then you open the dialog. Write the formula as if you were writing it into the active cell, and imagine that Excel will fill the formula throughout the selected range. That means you'll want to use appropriate cell reference styles, absolute, relative, or mixed, as needed. The function key F4 cycles through reference styles within the dialog. The F2 key works to switch between Enter and Edit mode. Remember that while in Enter mode, the Arrow keys navigate worksheet cells and while in Edit mode, they move the cursor within in the formula.

 NOTE

When you subsequently edit the conditional formatting formula, it will be based on the upper left of the *Applies to* selection rather than the active cell.

 XREF

Using F4 to cycle cell references is discussed in Volume 1, Chapter 6. Using F2 to toggle between Enter and Edit mode is discussed in Volume 2, Chapter 2.

Now think back to the opening narrative of this chapter. We discussed identifying transactions by using cell values and conditional formatting rather than applying the formatting manually. Conditional formatting formulas allow us to accomplish that because we can format cells based on the results of a formula, which could reference a stored or calculated value in an adjacent column. We have an exercise later in this chapter to practice this technique.

MANAGE RULES

We can use the Conditional Formatting Rules Manager to add, edit, and delete conditional formatting rules. To open the dialog, use the following Ribbon icon:

* Home > Conditional Formatting > Manage Rules

The resulting Conditional Formatting Rules Manager dialog is shown in Figure 11.

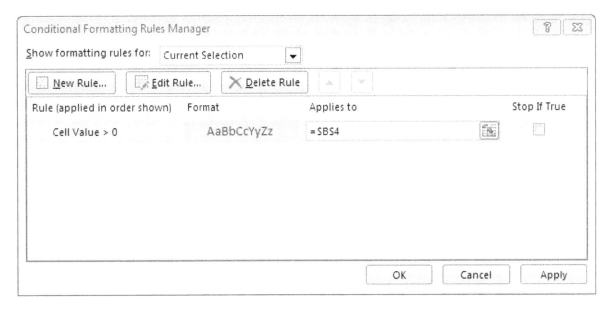

Figure 11

Let's quickly walk through the key dialog controls. We can use the *Show formatting rules for* drop-down to show rules based on where they are applied.

Although you would think that creating a new rule with the New Rule button is straightforward, there is a little surprise for us in there. Actually, it is the same surprise that awaits us in the Edit Rule button. When we use these buttons, we get access to many fun options. For example, let's say we create an icon set by selecting the cells and then using the following Ribbon icon:

- Home > Conditional Formatting > Icon Sets

With this approach, which we've used previously, Excel instantly applies the icon set. But when we use the New Rule button to create an icon set, we have access to a variety of options. The same goes when we use the Edit Rule button to edit an existing icon set rule. We can mix and match icons from different sets, reverse the icon order, show icons only, and change the icon thresholds. By default, icon thresholds are evenly assigned based on the number of icons. For example, when there are three icons in a set, they are displayed based on top, middle, and bottom third of cell values. But we can override the default thresholds and define our own. We will have a chance to practice this in the exercises.

Each rule displays the condition, such as cell value > 0, the defined format, and the applied range. This is the range of cells that is formatted based on the rule. Typically, this is going to be the cell or range that is selected when you define the rule.

The dialog also helps us manage multiple rules. When we set up multiple rules, it is possible that more than one evaluates to TRUE. This is how Excel handles this situation. When two rules format the same attribute, such as fill color, the highest priority rule wins, and you set the priority order by using the Up and Down buttons. When two rules don't have a conflict because they format different elements, such as one formats the fill color and the other formats the font color, they are both applied without issue. You can also tell Excel to stop at a given rule if it is TRUE, by checking the *Stop If True* checkbox. That way, subsequent formatting rules won't be evaluated.

TABLES

There are a couple of things to be aware of when it comes to using conditional formatting with tables, so let's talk about them now. In practice, I think about tables as a way to store data, not as an analysis or report, so I typically avoid applying conditional formatting to a table. But if you do, there are two things to note. First, when you open the Conditional Formatting Rules Manager dialog, you'll notice that you can select the table from the *Show formatting rules for* drop-down, but the *Applies to* range will be displayed as the A1-style reference rather than the table name. If you try to enter the table name, Excel will immediately convert it to the A1-style reference. Second, if you update a recurring-use table by inserting rows, deleting rows, and moving rows around, the rule may become fragmented, meaning, Excel will create a bunch of rules when trying to keep up with the worksheet changes. That means that you'll want to keep an eye on the rules, and you may need to clean them up occasionally by adjusting the *Applies to* range manually and removing any duplicate rules.

The next issue occurs when a conditional formatting formula references a table name. Table names are not supported in conditional formatting directly. If you try to use a structured table reference in a conditional formatting formula, you'll notice that you get an error. Do you remember another time this happened to us? Yes, back in Volume 1 when we tried to reference a table name within a data validation rule. Do you remember our workaround? Yes, we set up a custom name that referred to the table name. Fortunately, the same workaround works here. We can set up a name that refers to the table name and then use the custom name in our formatting formula.

Don't worry. We have exercises to practice this stuff.

PIVOTTABLES

We can apply conditional formatting to PivotTable values. Yay! Just as we applied a number format to value fields, we can apply conditional formatting to value fields as well. By the way, do you remember our strategy for formatting PivotTable values? Recall that we don't format the worksheet cells, we format the value field.

 XREF

Formatting PivotTable values is discussed in Volume 3, Chapter 10.

The same idea holds true when conditionally formatting PivotTable values. We want to conditionally format the value field rather than the worksheet cells. We can apply conditional formatting to a value field by selecting a value cell and then using the New Formatting Rule dialog, which can be opened with the following command:

- Home > Conditional Formatting > New Rule

This dialog enables us to apply conditional formatting to the PivotTable. At the top of the dialog, Excel presents options for where the new conditional formatting rule should be applied—for example, to just the worksheet cells or to the value field. The actual dialog labels depend on the PivotTable field names, but generally, you can choose to include or exclude subtotal and grand total cells.

If you happen to apply conditional formatting to the worksheet cells instead, don't worry. You can tell Excel to apply the rule to the PivotTable by using the Formatting Options icon that pops up next to the formatted cells or the Edit Formatting Rule dialog, which can be opened from within the Conditional Formatting Rules Manager.

We conditionally format the value field, rather than the worksheet cells, so that we don't have to manually update the formatting if the dimensions of the report change. The practice of eliminating or reducing manual steps from recurring-use workbooks is one that we've discussed numerous times throughout the series. Let me share a quick personal story to help reinforce this idea.

Our family loves family game nights, and we play all kinds of board games. One night we decided to play Monopoly. I had built some houses, and as my family members would go around the board, they would frequently land on my houses and pay rent. It was working for a while…until I landed on the Boardwalk hotel. I'm not sure how familiar you are with Monopoly, but the rent there is $2,000. Since I didn't have enough cash to pay rent, I had to sell my houses back to the bank. Frustrated, I exclaimed, "That's bogus, man!" It was bogus because I had to rebuild what I had already built. The same thing applies when working in Excel. Once you build something that is working each period, you don't want to have to rebuild it. You don't want to rewrite formulas or manually update formatting. You want to reduce or eliminate manual steps in recurring-use workbooks.

All right, let's open Excel to get some hands-on practice.

EXAMPLES

We'll work through several conditional formatting exercises.

 **PRACTICE**

To work along, please refer to *Conditional Formatting.xlsx.*

 VIDEO

To watch the solutions video, please visit the Excel University Video Library.

EXERCISE 1—ROW

In this exercise, we'll conditionally format a data row based on the value of a single column.

 **PRACTICE**

To work along, please refer to the Exercise 1 worksheet.

Our worksheet contains a list of orders. We'd like to arbitrarily identify some of the orders so that our support team can call the related customers. There is no pattern, such as all open orders, that we can use for our conditional formatting rule. We want to use our discretion when identifying orders.

One option would be to manually format those orders by, say, changing the fill color. But after we've identified the orders, we'll want to write a formula to summarize the selected orders. Instead of identifying the rows by manually formatting, we use a cell value. We create a column named *Call* that we manually populate to identify the selected orders. We set up a Data Validation drop-down for the *Call* column with TRUE and FALSE options so it is easy to stay consistent. Now we use conditional formatting to highlight the rows where the value is TRUE.

We begin by selecting the entire range of transactions, excluding the *Call* column. We make a mental note of the active cell *C20* and our selected range *C20:H39* so that we write the formatting formula using the correct reference style. We open the New Formatting Rule dialog and select the *Use a formula to determine which cells to format* option. In the *Format values where this formula is true* field, we enter the following formula:

```
=$B20
```

 NOTE

> While entering the conditional formatting formula, be sure to include the equal sign. If you exclude it, Excel may interpret your entry as a text string and yield unexpected results.

We used an absolute column reference and a relative row reference because this formatting formula is essentially filled throughout the selected range. The formatting formula for each cell in the range should reference the *Call* column for its row.

We use the Format button to define the format, and when we apply the rule and return to our worksheet, we see that Excel has formatted the selected orders.

Our final task is to write a formula that summarizes the highlighted rows. We'll use our friend SUMIFS. Since the SUMIFS function works on stored values and ignores cell formatting, we reference the values in the *Call* column. The label is stored in *B11*, so we write the following formula into cell *C11*:

```
=SUMIFS($H$20:$H$39,$B$20:$B$39,B11)
```

Where:

- **$H$20:$H$39** is the sum range

- **$B$20:$B$39** is the criteria range

- **B11** is the criteria value

We fill the formula down and confirm it works as expected.

EXERCISE 2—TABLE

In this exercise, we'll highlight open orders stored in a table.

 **PRACTICE**

To work along, please refer to the Exercise 2 worksheet.

We've stored transactions in a table named **tbl_e2**, and we want to highlight all orders where the status is *Open*. We select all of the data cells in the table and open the New Formatting Rule dialog.

 KB

Ctrl+A selects all table data cells, excluding the header and total rows. Ctrl+* select all table cells, including the header and total rows.

Since the active cell is **B11** and the status is stored in Column **C**, we write the following formatting formula:

```
=$C11="Open"
```

 XREF

Comparison formulas are discussed in Volume 2, Chapter 25.

We define the desired formatting, and when we close the dialog we notice that the table is formatted as expected.

EXERCISE 3—LOOKUP TABLE

In this exercise, we'll highlight open orders.

 **PRACTICE**

To work along, please refer to the Exercise 3 worksheet.

Once again we have transactions in our worksheet, and once again we'd like to highlight the open orders. This time, however, there are three status types that are used to indicate open orders. An order is open, meaning we still have work to perform, when the status is *Pending*, *Processing*, or *Packaging*. If we want to highlight rows where the status is equal to any of these three values, we have multiple options, of course. One option would be to create three separate conditional formatting rules. Another would be to create a single formatting rule but use the OR function to test the three conditions. Both of these approaches, however, would involve storing the status values as text strings inside of the formula. As you know, we prefer to store these types of things in cells and reference the cells instead. That makes the worksheet easier to maintain over time since we can edit the status list without modifying the formula. So what we'll do is store the three status types in a table and then write a conditional formatting rule that references the table. Sound like a plan? All right, let's get to it.

We've stored the three status values in a table named *tbl_e3*. Since table names aren't supported in conditional formatting rules, we've created a custom name *status* that refers to the table name *tbl_e3*. With that done, we are ready to work on the conditional formatting rule.

We are essentially performing a list comparison, where we want to see whether the order status appears in the table. We've done list comparisons before, when we wanted to see whether a value in one list appeared in another list. Remember? Here we want to determine whether the status value in the status column appears in the status table. This is a basic list comparison. As you know, we can perform list comparisons in a variety of ways, including using the exact match logic of lookup functions such as MATCH and VLOOKUP or with a conditional counting function such as COUNTIFS.

 XREF

List comparisons are discussed in Volume 2, Chapters 11 and 13.

Although we could add a calculated column to the worksheet that performs the list comparison, we try to work with the data as it comes and avoid introducing helper columns when possible. So we'll perform the list comparison within the conditional formatting formula instead. We select the transaction range and open the New Formatting Rule dialog. We create the following formatting formula:

```
=COUNTIFS(status,$C12)
```

Where:

- **status** is the criteria range

- **$C12** is the criteria value

This formula works because when the order status exists in the status table, the COUNTIFS function returns 1. Since this is interpreted by Excel as TRUE, the formatting is applied. When the order status does not appear in the status table, the function returns 0. Since this is interpreted as FALSE, the formatting is not applied.

We select the desired formatting and close the dialog. We confirm that the rows for open orders—that is, those with a status appearing in the lookup table—are highlighted.

EXERCISE 4—VARIANCE

In this exercise, we'll use the OR function in our conditional formatting formula.

 **PRACTICE**

To work along, please refer to the Exercise 4 worksheet.

Our worksheet computes the variance between budget and actual values for SG&A expenses. It includes a column for the variance in dollars as well as a variance percent column. We want to highlight the rows where the dollar variance (positive or negative) is greater than $10,000 or where the variance percent (positive or negative) is greater than 10 percent.

We select the data range and then create a new conditional formatting rule based on a formula. Since the dollar variance for the first account is in *F11* and the percentage variance is in *G11*, we use the following formatting formula:

```
=OR(ABS($F11)>10000,ABS($G11)>0.1)
```

Where:

- **ABS($F11)>10000** returns TRUE if the absolute value of the variance is greater than 10,000

- **ABS($G11)>0.1** returns TRUE if the absolute value of the percent variance is greater than 10 percent.

If either or both of the OR arguments are TRUE, then the OR function returns TRUE and the formatting is applied. If neither argument is TRUE, OR returns FALSE and the formatting is not applied.

XREF

OR is discussed in Chapter 10, and ABS is discussed in Chapter 14.

We pick the desired formatting and confirm it is applied as expected.

EXERCISE 5—PIVOTTABLE VALUES

In this exercise, we'll conditionally format PivotTable values.

 **PRACTICE**

To work along, please refer to the Exercise 5 worksheet.

Our worksheet contains a PivotTable that summarizes sales by region by rep.

 XREF

PivotTables are discussed in Volume 3.

We want to sort the report by region, and within each region by rep. We'd like to easily identify reps who have achieved the target sales amount as well as those who have not met the minimum, so we decide to use conditional formatting. To avoid storing the target and minimum values in the conditional formatting rule, we'll store these values in cells named **target** and **min**, respectively.

Let's begin by creating a formatting rule to identify reps who have achieved the target sales amount. We select any value cell in the PivotTable and then open the New Formatting Rule dialog.

The New Formatting Rule dialog seems similar, but not identical, to the ones we've encountered in the past. The dialog now includes the *Apply Rule To* field, along with several related radio buttons at the top. Since we are working with a PivotTable, we don't want to select the first option because it applies the format to the selected worksheet cells. We don't want the second option either, since it formats all of the sales cells, including any subtotals and the grand total. Instead, we'll select the third option because it applies the rule to the sales cells but excludes any subtotals and the grand total.

Next we select the *Format only cells that contain* rule type. We decide to format cells where the cell value is greater than *=target*. We then define the format with a green fill and apply the rule. We confirm that the PivotTable values that exceed the target value are formatted as desired.

NOTE

The preceding equal sign (=target) is important. If excluded, Excel will assume you are referring to the text string "target" instead of the corresponding named reference.

Next we create a red fill for sales cells less than the minimum amount stored in **min**. But this time, let's create the rule a different way. Let's select a PivotTable value cell and then the following Ribbon icon:

- Home > Conditional Formatting > Highlight Cell Values > Less Than

In the resulting Less Than dialog, we ask Excel to format cells that are less than =**min** and use the built-in, light-red fill format. When we click OK, we notice that Excel applies the rule to the selected cell and displays a little Formatting Options button next to it. To tell Excel to apply the new rule to the PivotTable field instead of just the active cell, we can either click the icon and select the desired option or use the Manage Rules command to open the Conditional Formatting Rules Manager dialog.

Now the PivotTable report values are formatted according to our rules, and we can easily change the target and min cell values. Since we applied conditional formatting to the PivotTable, Excel will format the value cells even if the report dimensions change over time.

EXERCISE 6—CASH RECONCILIATION

In this exercise, we'll format a worksheet used to reconcile cash.

**PRACTICE**

To work along, please refer to the Exercise 6 worksheet.

Our worksheet contains a list of checks from our check register. It includes the amount of the check as written in the *Per Book* column and the amount that cleared the bank in the *Per Bank* column. When the check is still outstanding, the Per Bank amount is zero.

We would like to identify any outstanding checks plus any cleared checks where the book amount is different from the bank amount. To accomplish this, we'll use two columns of icon sets.

The formula in the *Cleared* column simply retrieves the bank amount. We want to conditionally format the column to show a green check icon when the check has cleared the bank and a red X icon when it is still outstanding. We select the *Cleared* column and apply the 3 Symbols icon set. Based on the built-in behavior of icons sets, the three icons are applied based on the top, middle, and bottom third of the values. However, that isn't what we want here. Here, we want to identify values greater than zero with a green check icon and values less than or equal to zero with a red X icon. Thus, we head into the Conditional Formatting Rules Manager dialog and edit the icon set rule.

In the Edit Formatting Rule dialog, we can see that each icon is displayed in a drop-down control and that we can pick and choose which icons to display for each threshold, mixing and matching as desired. Let's modify the rules to meet our needs. We use a green check icon when the number is greater than zero. We use a red X icon when the number is greater than or equal to zero. The rule needs to cover all cases, so even though we don't expect a negative amount, we'll use a red X icon if the number is less than zero. We want to display the Alert icons only, and not the underlying cell values, so we check the *Show Icon Only* checkbox. We close the dialog and...yes—it worked!

Now for the *Alert* column. The *Alert* column formula displays the difference between the bank and book amounts for cleared checks. It displays zero for outstanding checks. We want to be notified when there is a problem. There is a problem if the bank and book amounts of a cleared check do not agree. There is no problem if the amounts agree or if the check is outstanding. So we'll conditionally format the column with icon sets. We'll use a red circle icon when there is a problem and something inconspicuous like a white circle icon when there is no problem.

We select the *Alert* column and apply any icon set that has three icons. It technically doesn't matter which set we pick because we are about to customize the icons. We head into the Conditional Formatting Rules Manager dialog and edit the icon set rule. In the Edit Formatting Rule dialog, we update the rules to meet our needs. We select a red circle icon and display it when the number is greater than zero. We select a white circle icon and display it when the number is greater than or equal to zero. We select a red circle icon and display it when the value is less than zero. Since we want to display the Alert icons only, and not the underlying cell values, we check the *Show Icon Only* checkbox, and we are done. We close the dialog and confirm that we are alerted with a red circle icon when we have a potential problem.

 NOTE

We can change the font size of the cells to control the size of the icons.

This is nice because we can easily apply filters as needed to display just the cleared checks, just the outstanding checks, or just the checks where the bank and book amounts differ. Plus these helper columns can be filled down if there are additional checks to reconcile in the future.

EXERCISE 7—REVENUE

In this exercise, we'll conditionally format a single cell with an icon to indicate an increase or decrease from the prior quarter.

 **PRACTICE**

To work along, please refer to the Exercise 7 worksheet.

Our worksheet contains revenue by quarter. We want to display a green up arrow when the change from last quarter is positive and a red down arrow when the change from last quarter is negative.

The percent change is computed in a cell. We select the cell and apply the three-arrow, colored icon set. Since only a single cell was selected, its value is also the max value. Thus, the green up arrow will be displayed even if the value is negative. Since we want to show a red down arrow when the change is negative, we need to customize the formatting rule.

In the Edit Formatting Rule dialog, we set the green up arrow icon to be displayed when the value is greater than the number zero. We set the second yellow icon to be displayed when the value is greater than or equal to the number zero. The red down arrow will be displayed when the value is less than zero. We want to hide the cell value, so we check the *Show Icon Only* checkbox.

We close the dialog and confirm that the expected icon is displayed for positive and negative changes.

 XREF

The worksheet also contains a sparkline and uses built-in cell styles, both of which are discussed in Volume 3, Chapter 26.

CHAPTER CONCLUSION

In this chapter we had fun exploring additional conditional formatting details. As we've seen, this seemingly simple feature that we discussed long ago has a layer of complexity that enables us to apply it in a variety of creative ways.

Chapter 17: Names Revisited

SET UP

Have you ever created or encountered a really long formula—a megaformula? I first heard the term *megaformula* from John Walkenbach, and he describes it as a single formula that does the work of several intermediate formulas. To demonstrate this idea, I grabbed a copy of the biggest formula I think I've developed, which essentially retrieves an account balance:

```
=IFERROR(SUMIFS(INDIRECT(VLOOKUP(B$1,pgr_tbl_a,4,0)&"["&
VLOOKUP(B$2&IF(ISNUMBER(B$3),TEXT(B$3,"yyyymm"),"FY "&
TEXT(RIGHT(B$3,LEN(B$3)-LEN("FY ")),"yyyymm")),
INDIRECT(VLOOKUP(B$1,pgr_tbl_a,4,0)&"DT"),2,0)&"]"),
INDIRECT(VLOOKUP(B$1,pgr_tbl_a,4,0)&"["&
IF(ISERROR(MATCH($A4,
INDIRECT(VLOOKUP(B$1,pgr_tbl_a,4,0)&"[CategoryDesc]"),0)),
IF(ISERROR(MATCH($A4,
INDIRECT(VLOOKUP(B$1,pgr_tbl_a,4,0)&"[Type]"),0)),
IF(ISERROR(MATCH($A4,
INDIRECT(VLOOKUP(B$1,pgr_tbl_a,4,0)&"[ClassDesc]"),0)),
IF(ISERROR(MATCH(TEXT($A4,"general"),
INDIRECT(VLOOKUP(B$1,pgr_tbl_a,4,0)&
"[AcctNumber]"),0)),0,"AcctNumber"),"ClassDesc"),"Type"),
"CategoryDesc")&"]"),$A4),"NA")
```

How do you feel when you see a megaformula like this? Anxious? Me too! I keep my fingers crossed that it continues to work because if it ever broke, I would have no chance of fixing it. It has 37 functions, and I must have been in some type of "Excel zone" when I developed it. Now that I'm out of the zone, it would be difficult to update. Megaformulas like this can be hard to understand and maintain. Since we like to make our recurring-use workbooks easy to maintain, we'll ask an old friend for help.

We began our discussion of names in the first volume and have used this feature in numerous exercises since. Now that we are comfortable with the basics, we'll revisit names and cover additional capabilities and applications. Once we get the hang of the concepts presented in this chapter, we will be able to create modular formulas. A modular formula stores each component in a name. Software developers frequently break complex code into smaller chunks in a process often referred to as *decomposition* or *factoring*. We'll do something similar in Excel, by breaking a megaformula down into the intermediate formulas and storing them as named formulas. In practice, we prefer working with modular formulas because they are easier to understand and maintain over time.

 XREF

Named references are discussed in Volume 1, Chapter 7.

HOW TO

So far our names have referenced an absolute cell or range. Names can reference a variety of other things, such as constants, relative references, and other names. A name that refers to a cell or range is often called a *named range*. A name that does something more sophisticated is often called a *named formula*. Technically, all names are named formulas because of the equal sign that appears before them. Ultimately, named ranges and named formulas are names that reference something. Going forward, it will be helpful to think about names as formulas. I'll call this idea out for reference.

> *A name is a formula.*

As we've done in the past, we use the Name Manager to create names. As a reminder, we can open the Name Manager with the following Ribbon icon:

- Formula > Name Manager

 KB

Ctrl+F3 and Alt+M, N opens the Name Manager.

Once inside, we use the New button to open the New Name dialog, where we define the name, scope, and reference.

From within the Name Manager dialog, Alt+N opens the New Name dialog. When the Name Manager is closed, go directly to the New Name dialog with Ctrl+Alt+F3 or Alt+M, M, D.

We cover the following topics:

- Constants

- Relative references

- Formulas

- Applications

Let's get started.

When using names, be cautious when you copy formula cells or worksheets that contain names. When you paste to another workbook, the name may continue to reference the original workbook. When you paste within the same workbook, Excel may create a duplicate name with a worksheet scope. You may want to paste values instead, and be sure to double-check the Name Manager and delete any duplicate or unnecessary names.

CONSTANTS

Let's say we need to write a formula that uses a constant. For our discussion, a constant will be a fixed value, such as a flat shipping rate of $4.99 or a static commission rate of 4 percent. One option is to use the constant directly in the formula. For example, if you wanted to multiply the value in *A1* by the commission rate of 4 percent, you could use the following formula:

```
=A1*.04
```

As you know, this approach can be difficult to update and maintain over time. Instead, we prefer to place the value in a cell, such as on a Start Here sheet, and then write our formula to reference the cell. For example, if we stored the commission rate in cell *B1*, then the formula could be updated as follows:

```
=A1*B1
```

XREF

Start Here is discussed in Volume 1, Chapter 15.

Yet another option is to store the constant in a name and then write a formula that references the name. For example, we could define a name called *rate* that refers to .04, as shown in Figure 12.

Figure 12

Here our name is a formula that refers to the value .04. We could then make the following update:

```
=A1*rate
```

 NOTE

The F2 and F4 keys operate in the *Refers to* field in the New Name dialog.

With three ways to accomplish the same goal, which one should we use in practice? Here are my thoughts. I try to avoid typing a constant value into a cell formula at all costs. When it comes time to update the value, it can be time-consuming chasing down all the related formulas and updating them. That is bogus, man. When the constant value is unlikely to ever change and I'm not using a Start Here sheet, I may opt to store the constant in a name to keep the workbook clean. But most often I use the Start Here method because it makes it easy for users to change the constant value over time.

Even though I don't frequently use names to reference constants, I wanted to start there to demonstrate that a name can refer to something other than a cell or range. The *Refers to* field in the New Name dialog supports a wide variety of references. Now that you are warmed up, let's take the next step.

RELATIVE REFERENCES

During the series so far, we've written many formulas. We've used absolute, relative, and mixed cell references. An absolute cell reference points to the same cell regardless of the location of the formula. Even as the formula occupies other cells when filled or copied, the absolute reference points to the same cell. This concept applies not only to formulas written in cells but also to named references. I'm not sure whether you've noticed this, but whenever we've used the Name Box to name the active cell, Excel automatically uses an absolute reference. In these cases, our names were formulas that referred to absolute cell references.

Now let's move to relative references. We know a relative cell reference is relative. But relative to what exactly? That depends. When a relative cell reference is used in a cell formula, it is relative to the cell containing the formula. But we can use cell references in other places besides cell formulas. For example, in Chapter 16, we used references in conditional formatting formulas and discovered that the active cell matters. The same applies with names. A relative reference in a name is relative to the active cell—that is, to the cell that is active when we open the New Name dialog. The active cell matters when the reference is relative. I've spent time building to this point, and it is a key point, so I'll call it out for reference.

> *Relative references used in names are relative to the active cell.*

If you'd like, you can test this out right now. Select *A1*, open the Name Manager, and create a new name that refers to cell *B1* (be sure it is a relative reference to *B1*). This name is a formula that refers to a relative cell reference. Close the Name Manager and select *A2*. Open the Name Manager and you'll see that your name now refers to cell *B2*. As you can see, relative references used in names are relative to the active cell.

 NOTE

Excel automatically prepends the sheet name to cell and range references. That is, the name actually refers to say Sheet1!A1 rather than A1. This is important because it means that the sheet will continue to be referenced even if you use the name on a different worksheet.

When you write a formula in a cell, the first thing you do is select the desired cell. In practice, use this same idea when writing named formulas. First select the desired cell, and then use references as if you were writing the formula into the active cell. Now that we understand how references work in names, we can have some fun.

FORMULAS

So far the names we have created were formulas that referred to constants, cells, or ranges. As such, we've really underutilized their power. I mean, come on—names are formulas! That means names have access to the wonderful capabilities and power of Excel formulas, including functions, expressions, and operators. Wow!

For example, we could do a basic math expression and create a name with a formula that computes the average number of work hours in a year by multiplying 40 hours by 52 weeks. Or we could get crazy and use a function. For example, we could create a name that performs a lookup with VLOOKUP, returns the relative position of a list item with MATCH, or computes a monthly payment with PMT. Then we can reference the name inside of a cell formula, just as we've done before.

And while we are here, it is worth pointing out that we already know that a formula written into a cell can refer to a name. Likewise, a formula used in a name can also refer to a name. That is, names can reference other names.

Basically, the formulas we write into cells can also be written into names. When we write a formula into a name, Excel treats the references as if we wrote the formula into the active cell. Remember—a name is a formula. But hang on a sec. Since we can write the same formula in a cell, what is the motivation for writing it in a name? It seems more complicated and takes more effort to write a formula in a name rather than a cell. That brings us to our next discussion where we'll close the loop on our opening dialog about megaformulas.

APPLICATIONS

As you can imagine, all of this opens up some pretty interesting possibilities. Let's talk about three possible applications, creating modular formulas, reducing duplication, and hiding complexity in a safe place. Let's unpack each.

Modular Formulas. We can store a specific task in a name and then use it as needed. This capability enables us to compartmentalize the complexity of a megaformula and break it down into discrete parts, or modules. Remember, a megaformula is a single formula that does the work of several intermediate formulas. We can store each of the intermediate formulas in a name and then combine them as needed in a modular formula. By storing specific tasks in names and using them in a modular formula, we are able to more easily understand, troubleshoot, and maintain the formula over time.

Reduce Duplication. Named formulas also help us reduce duplication in formulas. As you know, we try to reduce duplication within formulas whenever possible. When some part of a formula duplicates—for example, having two identical VLOOKUP functions nested in an IF function—we can push the duplicated part, the VLOOKUP, into a name and then reference the name as needed. That way, if we need to update the VLOOKUP, we can do it in one spot.

 XREF

Reducing duplication within formulas is discussed in Chapter 10.

Hide Complexity in a Safe Place. We can hide or mask complexity from the user and make it harder for a user to change or break our formula. When the formula is written in a cell, it is kind of easy for a user to unintentionally replace or break it. When we store the formula in a name, it is in a pretty safe place.

In practice, most of the time we don't need to go through the effort of using named formulas. When our formulas are pretty simple, involving perhaps only a few functions, it is probably better to keep them in a cell rather than obscure them with names. But when working with a megaformula that has 37 functions, breaking down complexity into bite-size chunks can be quite helpful. By storing the components and complexity in names, we can retrieve the account balance into a cell that contains the following formula instead of the one shown at the beginning of the chapter:

```
=account_balance
```

We've covered a lot, so let's practice what we've learned by jumping into some Excel exercises.

EXAMPLES

Let's work on a few exercises.

 **PRACTICE**

To work along, please refer to *Names.xlsx*.

 VIDEO

To watch the solutions video, please visit the Excel University Video Library.

NOTE

When you create a named formula, please note that Excel will automatically prepend the sheet name to any cell references. For brevity, I note named formulas with their cell references only in this text, but when you are working on the exercises hands-on, if you enter the named formula with the cell reference only, Excel will automatically add the sheet name.

EXERCISE 1—CONSTANT

In this exercise, we'll name a constant.

 **PRACTICE**

To work along, please refer to the Exercise 1 worksheet.

Our worksheet is set up to compute travel expense reimbursement. It enables users to enter the number of miles, and we need to write a formula to apply the standard mileage rate to determine the mileage reimbursement amount. Since this is Excel, we of course have many options. We could store the mileage rate in the formula. As we've discussed, we don't like to store constants in formulas because we'd need to manually update all related formulas whenever we want to change the value. We could instead store the constant in a cell and then reference the cell. In practice, this is often my preferred approach. Yet another option is to store the constant in a name. To do so, we use the Name Manager to create a new name, *mile_rate,* which refers to our mileage rate of $0.58.

 NOTE

You'll want to precede the $0.58 with an equal sign in the dialog box, =0.58, and if you don't, Excel will add it automatically.

Now we can compute the reimbursement amount by multiplying the number of miles stored in *C12* by the name, as follows:

```
=C12*mile_rate
```

We confirm the formula works as expected. Going forward, to update the mileage rate we use the Name Manager to edit the name. When we do, all formulas that reference the name are updated with the new rate.

EXERCISE 2—RELATIVE

In this exercise, we'll wrap our heads around the issue of relative cell references in a name.

 **PRACTICE**

To work along, please refer to the Exercise 2 worksheet.

Our worksheet stores some input cells that contain values we'll use throughout the workbook. The input cells are *Company*, *City*, and *State*.

Let's begin with the *Company* input cell. We select the input cell *C16* and then type the desired name **company** into the Name Box. Since we used the Name Box, this name uses an absolute cell reference. We can confirm this by opening the Name Manager and inspecting the name. As we can see, the name refers to an absolute cell reference as indicated by the dollar signs. So, we just confirmed that when using the Name Box, Excel sets up an absolute reference for the name. That means that the name will refer to this specific cell, regardless of the cell that contains the formula.

Now let's move to the next input cell, the one that stores the city. To create the name, we begin by selecting the input cell *C17*. Rather than name it with the Name Box, this time let's open the Name Manager to add a new name. In the New Name dialog box, we enter the desired name **city** and then confirm that the *Refers to* field is populated with an absolute reference to the active cell. So, we just confirmed that when we add a name using the Name Manager, the default reference style is absolute. Again, this means that regardless of the location of the cell that uses the name, the name will refer to this specific cell.

Let's move to the final input cell, the one that stores the state. To create the name, we begin by selecting the input cell *C18*. Next we open the Name Manager and create a new name. In the New Name dialog, we enter the desired name **state**, but instead of closing the dialog, we head down to the *Refers to* field. We change the reference from fully absolute to fully relative by removing the dollar signs. With the dollar signs gone, we close the dialog.

 NOTE

Removing the dollar signs can be done manually or by using the F4 shortcut. Also, F2 is helpful in order to toggle the field into Edit mode.

Now here is the big deal and the point of the exercise. When we use a relative cell reference in a name, it is relative to the active cell. Our reference happened to refer to the cell that was active at the time we created the name, *C18*. So let's navigate to another cell and see what happens. Let's select cell *A1* so that it is now the active worksheet cell. With *A1* the active cell, we open the Name Manager and now the name *state* refers to *A1*. Spooky.

So we see that the reference is relative to the active cell. When we think about this for a moment, we realize that this behavior makes perfect sense. When we write a formula, references are relative to the formula cell. When we create a name, we create a formula whose references are relative to the active cell. Let's try this idea out in the *Data* section of the worksheet.

We want to create a name and use it in a formula that populates the *Test* column with the values from the *Amount* column. Step one is to select a cell. We select the first cell in the *Test* column, *E23*. We then use the Name Manager to create a new name, *test*, which refers to the first cell in the *Amount* column, *D23*. We use a relative cell reference just as we would if we were writing the formula into the cell. With the name set up, we can now use it in a cell formula. We write the following formula into the first cell of the *Test* column, *E23*:

```
=test
```

Since we used a relative reference in the name, we can fill the formula down and confirm it retrieves the correct value for each cell. So far, so good? Okay, let's take the next step.

EXERCISE 3—FORMULA

In this exercise, we'll create a named formula that uses a relative reference.

 **PRACTICE**

To work along, please refer to the Exercise 3 worksheet.

Our worksheet contains invoice data and we need to compute the sales tax amount. Our goal is to write a formula that multiplies the amount by the tax rate of *8.25 percent* and then fill it down for all of the transactions. Since the first transaction's amount value is stored in *D12*, we could simply write a formula in *E12* to compute the tax as follows:

```
=D12*0.0825
```

That would be just fine. However, we are here to take the next step in named formulas. So we take this simple formula and store it in a name instead of writing it in the cell. We write our named formula using the same references we would if we were writing the formula into the first tax cell, *E12*, so we begin by selecting *E12*. Next we open the Name Manager and add a new name, *tax,* which refers to the same relative reference and formula as before:

```
=D12*0.0825
```

With the named formula set up, we should be able to reference it in our Tax column to compute the sales tax amount. We write the following formula in the first tax cell *E12*:

```
=tax
```

We hit Enter, and it looks good. Now for the big test. We fill the formula down, and…yes—it works! The next step is to use a name within a name, and you are totally ready for this.

EXERCISE 4—OTHER NAMES

In this exercise, we'll use a name within a name.

 **PRACTICE**

> To work along, please refer to the Exercise 4 worksheet.

Similar to the previous exercise, we need to compute the sales tax for each invoice. We need to multiply the amount by the sales tax rate. Rather than store the tax rate constant in a formula, we prefer to store it in a cell. We enter the tax rate into cell *C12* and then use the Name Box to name the cell *rate*. We know that using the Name Box creates an absolute reference to the cell.

Now we need to set up a named formula to compute the sales tax amount. We write our named formula using the same references we would if we were writing the formula into the first sales tax cell, *E18*, so we begin by selecting *E18*. Then we create a new name, *salestax,* which refers to the following formula:

```
=D18*rate
```

With the name established, we write the following formula into the first cell of the *Sales Tax* column:

```
=salestax
```

We fill the formula down and are delighted to see that it works for the entire range.

As you can see, named formulas sort of allow us to push formula logic out of the cell and into the name. Now that you have come this far with me, won't you take another step?

EXERCISE 5—TAX RATES

In this exercise, we'll push a lookup function into a name.

 **PRACTICE**

To work along, please refer to the Exercise 5 worksheet.

In the previous exercise, we assumed that the tax rate was the same for all transactions. As such, we stored the tax rate in an input cell, named the input cell, and then used that name to retrieve the tax rate. In this exercise, the tax rate is not uniform; it depends on the city.

We want to create a name that will retrieve the tax rate. Our named formula will need to look up the city in the tax rates table to determine the correct rate. We'll use VLOOKUP to retrieve the rate, but other lookup functions could be used instead if you prefer.

 XREF

VLOOKUP is discussed in Volume 2, Chapter 5.

Even though we aren't going to write the formula into a cell, we begin by selecting a cell as if we were. We select the first rate cell, *G24*. Since the city for the first transaction is stored in *D24*, and our tax rates table is named *tbl_rates*, we create a new name, *taxrate,* which refers to the following formula:

```
=VLOOKUP(D24,tbl_rates,2,0)
```

Where:

- **D24** is the lookup value, the city

- **tbl_rates** is the lookup range, the tax rates table

- **2** returns the value from the second column, the tax rate

- **0** means exact match

We now enter the following formula into the first rate cell *G24*:

```
=taxrate
```

We fill the formula down and confirm it retrieves the correct sales tax rate for each transaction.

Computing the tax in **H24** is done by applying the tax rate to the amount, as follows:

```
=F24*G24
```

We push the formula down, and we are good to go.

Okay, ready for the last step?

EXERCISE 6—TWO-DIMENSIONAL LOOKUP

In this exercise, we'll write a formula and break it down into modular components with names.

 **PRACTICE**

To work along, please refer to the Exercise 6 worksheet.

Our worksheet allows the user to select an item and a region. We want to write a formula that returns the corresponding price. Since each item has a different price based on the region, our price lookup table **tbl_e6** contains one row for each item and one column for each region.

Let's warm up by writing the formula into cell **C15** without using names. We'll use INDEX and MATCH to perform a two-dimensional lookup on our price table, based on the selected item in **C10** and the selected region in **C11**, as follows:

```
=INDEX(tbl_e6,
MATCH($C$10,tbl_e6[Item],0),
MATCH($C$11,tbl_e6[#Headers],0))
```

Where:

- **tbl_e6** is the price table

- **MATCH($C$10,tbl_e6[Item],0)** returns the row of the selected item

- **MATCH($C$11,tbl_e6[#Headers],0)** returns the column of the selected region

We change the item and region values and confirm that the formula returns the expected price from the table. Now that we are warmed up, let's try it again, but this time let's break the formula down into logical modules.

Let's begin by pushing the first MATCH function into a name. We set up a named formula that computes the row. Since the references are absolute, we don't need to pick a specific cell first. The active cell can be any cell. We create a new name, *item,* which refers to the following formula:

```
=MATCH($C$10,tbl_e6[Item],0)
```

Next we set up a named formula that computes the column. We create a new name, *region,* which refers to the following formula:

```
=MATCH($C$11,tbl_e6[#Headers],0)
```

With these two names established, we can now use them in our INDEX function. We update our original formula in *C15* as follows:

```
=INDEX(tbl_e6,item,region)
```

This version of our formula is easier to read and understand and illustrates the idea of breaking formulas down into modular components.

CHAPTER CONCLUSION

In this chapter we learned how to use names and create modular formulas. This technique hides complexity from the user and helps keep the worksheet clean. This approach also reduces the risk of a user accidentally breaking our formulas because they are editable within the Name Manager rather than the cell. Breaking complex formulas into modular chunks makes them easier to understand and maintain on an ongoing basis.

Chapter 18: Wildcards Revisited

SET UP

Wildcards were briefly mentioned a few times throughout the series. In this chapter we revisit wildcards and examine them in a bit more detail.

 XREF

Wildcards were mentioned in Volume 2, Chapters 13, 20, and 24, and in Volume 3, Chapter 22.

We can use wildcards to represent characters in a variety of places in Excel, including filters, searches, and functions. We examine how this can be helpful and use wildcards with a few of our favorite functions.

HOW TO

A wildcard is a specific character that can stand in to represent an unknown character or characters. The question mark (?) will stand in for a single character. The asterisk (*) will stand in for any number of characters.

We've seen Excel features that use Begins With, Ends With, and Contains logic—for example, the filter controls in tables and PivotTables. The idea behind these options is that we know something, such as a specific character or string, and want to see items that match based on the pattern. Wildcards provide this logic. For example, **a*** will show items that begin with **a**, ***a** will show items that end with **a**, and ***a*** will show items that contain **a**. We can use wildcards in several Excel features and functions.

FEATURES

Have you noticed the search field in various filter controls, such as those in tables and PivotTables? As we type values into the search field, Excel updates the list of choices accordingly, based on Contains logic. Typing **a** into the search field automatically applies Contains logic, so any choice that contains an **a** will be displayed. We can either select our choices from the updated list or hit Enter on our keyboard, and Excel will apply the filter based on the search term we've entered.

We can also use wildcards in the search field to force a different pattern, such as Begins With or Ends With. Entering **a*** will force the Begins With logic, as well as display choices that begin with **a**. Entering ***** will select all items.

Excel's Find and Replace dialog also supports wildcards. Excel automatically applies Contains logic when the *Match entire cell contents* option is unchecked. We can enter wildcards to use a different pattern if desired when the *Match entire cell contents* option is checked.

What do we do if we are looking for an actual question mark or an asterisk stored in a value? We tell Excel that we don't want the wildcard to be a wildcard; rather, we are literally looking for that character, so we precede it with the tilde (~). For example, to have Excel look for an actual question mark, we would use **~?**.

FUNCTIONS

Several functions support the use of wildcards, including some of our favorites: SUMIFS, VLOOKUP, and MATCH. We can use them in various ways. For example, we can use them to simulate the Begins With, Ends With, and Contains logic we see in various Excel features and controls. To enter a wildcard in a function, we enclose it in quotes. If the search term will be typed into the formula, then we can enclose it along with the wildcard. However, since we prefer to store values in cells, rather than in the formula directly, we can use concatenation to join the wildcard with the corresponding cell reference. We can also use a wildcard to help us locate the last data row, which will be a skill helpful in Chapter 19.

 XREF

Concatenation is discussed in Volume 2, Chapter 19.

All right, let's play with some exercises to explore using wildcards.

EXAMPLES

Please work through the following exercises to practice.

 **PRACTICE**

To work along, please refer to **Wildcards.xlsx.**

 VIDEO

To watch the solutions video, please visit the Excel University Video Library.

EXERCISE 1—TABLE FILTER

In this exercise, we'll use a wildcard to filter a table.

 **PRACTICE**

To work along, please refer to the Exercise 1 worksheet.

Our data is stored in a table named **tbl_e1**. We would like to view all of the cash accounts. There are several ways to filter for the cash accounts. Rather than using the checkboxes in the *AcctName* filter control, let's try the wildcard.

When we expand the *AcctName* filter control, we see that Excel detects the column's data type as text and provides a Text Filters option. When we select Text Filters from the drop-down menu, we see several options and select Custom Filter. Selecting this option causes Excel to display the Custom AutoFilter dialog as shown in Figure 13.

Figure 13

We can see that near the bottom of the dialog, Microsoft provides notes to the user about how to use wildcard characters. We set the filter to show rows where *AcctName* is equal to *cash**. When we click OK, the filter is applied and we can see all accounts that begin with *cash*. Since our filter logic is to show all rows that begin with *cash*, we can actually save the step of using a wildcard. Let's clear the filter and try it another way.

We expand the *AcctName* filter control, and in the Text Filters option, we select Begins With. The same Custom AutoFilter dialog opens, but this time the filter condition is automatically set to *begins with* instead of *equals*. We enter cash, without the wildcard, and hit Enter. Bam! The table is filtered as expected. Let's clear the filter and try it one more way.

This time we expand the filter control and type *cash* into the search box. We can see that the list is filtered to display only the labels that contain the word *cash*. We hit Enter and again the table is filtered as expected.

 KB

The corresponding keyboard sequence is as follows: navigate to the AcctName drop-down, use Alt+Down arrow to expand, press e to jump to the search box, type cash, and hit Enter.

 NOTE

The main difference between using the search field and a filter rule is that the filter rule would work for any new accounts entered, whereas the search is a one-time selection.

EXERCISE 2—VLOOKUP WITH WILDCARD

In this exercise, we'll use VLOOKUP with a wildcard.

 **PRACTICE**

To work along, please refer to the Exercise 2 worksheet.

Our worksheet contains actual expenses for each department. We need to retrieve budget values from the *tbl_e2* table, and we decide to use the VLOOKUP function to do so. When we write what should be a straightforward formula, we get an error. As we inspect the department names, we notice that the names in the report do not include any trailing spaces; however, the names stored in the lookup table do. No problem. Instead of matching exact values, we use a wildcard so that VLOOKUP can find a value that begins with our department name. Since our first department name is stored in *B11*, we write the following formula into our first budget cell, *D11*:

```
=VLOOKUP(B11&"*",tbl_e2,2,0)
```

Where:

- **B11&"*"** is the lookup value, a value that begins with our department name
- **tbl_e2** is the lookup range
- **2** returns the value from the second column
- **0** means exact match

We fill the formula down to complete the report. This formula works because we are asking Excel to find a value in the lookup range that begins with our department name. The extra spaces existed in the lookup range, the second function argument. But what if the reverse were true? What if the extra spaces existed in the lookup values, or the first function argument, instead? Well, let's try that in the next exercise.

EXERCISE 3—VLOOKUP WITH TRIM

In this exercise, we'll use VLOOKUP with TRIM.

 **PRACTICE**

To work along, please refer to the Exercise 3 worksheet.

We have the same setup as the previous exercise, but this time the trailing spaces exist in the department names rather than in the lookup table *tbl_e3*. That is, the trailing spaces appear in the lookup values, the first argument, rather than the lookup range, the second argument. We'll simply ask TRIM to remove the spaces for VLOOKUP.

 XREF

TRIM is discussed in Chapter 12.

Since our first department name is stored in *B11*, we write the following formula into our first budget cell, *D11*:

```
=VLOOKUP(TRIM(B11),tbl_e3,2,0)
```

Where:

- **TRIM(B11)** is the lookup value with excess spaces removed

- **tbl_e3** is the lookup range

- **2** returns the value from the second column

- **0** means exact match

We fill the formula down and it works as expected. Hopefully, these two exercises illustrate which technique to use based on the location of the trailing spaces.

EXERCISE 4—MATCH WITH WILDCARD

In this exercise, we'll use MATCH with a wildcard.

 **PRACTICE**

To work along, please refer to the Exercise 4 worksheet.

Our worksheet contains actual expenses for each department. We need to retrieve budget values from the *tbl_e4* table. As we inspect the department names, we notice that the names in the report do not include any trailing spaces; however, the names stored in the lookup table do. Previously, we accomplished this with VLOOKUP. This time we'll use INDEX/MATCH.

The MATCH function supports the use of a wildcard when we are searching for a text string and the third argument is zero. We've used zero for the third argument many times during this series, so we are fairly comfortable writing the formula.

 XREF

MATCH is discussed in Volume 2, Chapter 6.

Since the first department is stored in **B11**, we use the following formula:

```
=INDEX(tbl_e4[Budget],MATCH(B11&"*",tbl_e4[Department],0))
```

Where:

- **tbl_e4[Budget]** returns a value from the budget column
- **MATCH(B11&"*",tbl_e4[Department],0)** returns the row of the department name
- **Where:**
    ○ **B11&"*"** is the lookup value
    ○ **tbl_e4[Department]** is the lookup range
    ○ **0** means exact match

We fill the formula down and confirm we are good to go.

EXERCISE 5—LAST TEXT ROW

In this exercise, we'll locate the last row that contains a text value.

 **PRACTICE**

To work along, please refer to the Exercise 5 worksheet.

In our worksheet we'd like to write a formula that indicates the last data row. Specifically, the formula should return the row number of the last cell in the account name column that contains a text value. We can use the MATCH function to accomplish this. But before we get to the formula, we need to understand the function's third *match_type* argument.

When we first discussed the MATCH function, we set the third argument to zero because we were looking for an exact match. However, the function supports the following values for the third argument:

- **1** or greater finds the largest value in the lookup range that is less than or equal to the lookup value, and it assumes the lookup range is sorted in ascending order.

- **0** finds an exact matching value, and the lookup range does not need to be sorted.

- **-1** or less finds the smallest value in the lookup range that is greater than or equal to the lookup value, and it assumes the lookup range is sorted in descending order.

These official descriptions can be hard to visualize, so here is how I think about them. When I use the MATCH function with 0, I'm trying to find an exact matching value. I imagine Excel starting with the first cell in the lookup range to see if it is a match. If not, then it advances to the next cell, and so on down the list. If it gets to the end of the lookup range without finding a matching value, it returns an error.

When I use MATCH with 1, I imagine simulating the logic of VLOOKUP with the fourth argument set to TRUE. Just like VLOOKUP with TRUE:

- It assumes the sort order is ascending.

- It tries to start at the top of the range, but if the lookup value is smaller than the smallest (first) value in the lookup range, it returns an error.

- If it reaches the end of the range and the lookup value is larger than the largest (last) value in the lookup range, it stays on the last row to return the result.

When I use MATCH with -1, I imagine that the developers wanted it to work when the data was sorted in descending order, so the opposite logic applies:

- It assumes the sort order is descending.

- It tries to start at the top of the range, but if the lookup value is larger than the largest (first) value in the lookup range, it returns an error.

- If it reaches the end of the range and the lookup value is smaller than the smallest (last) value in the lookup range, it stays on the last row to return the result.

Let's see if we can apply this information to our task at hand, finding the last cell in a column that contains text values. Essentially, we'd like to tell Excel to start at the top of the column and work down until it gets to the last cell that contains text—any text. Although we don't know what the text values in the column are, our goal is to find the last text value, whatever it may be.

We know we can use a wildcard with MATCH when searching for a text string and the third argument is 0. When we use the asterisk as the lookup value and set the third argument to 0, the function returns the position of the first text value. This makes sense because it starts at the top of the lookup range and the wildcard matches the first text value encountered. Unfortunately, our goal is to find the last text value, not the first. We don't know what the text values will be, so we need to use the wildcard. We can only use a wildcard when the third argument is 0, but when we do, we don't get the results we need. So, do we give up? No, of course not.

What happens if we change the third argument to 1 while continuing to search for the asterisk? The function returns an error, and here's why. When the third argument is 1, the asterisk isn't being treated as a wildcard; rather, it is being evaluated as the asterisk character. The asterisk happens to fall before letters in Excel's internal sort order. Since it is smaller than the first text string, whatever it may be, the function returns an error.

 NOTE

> To confirm the asterisk falls before letters, enter it along with a few letters into some cells and then sort the cells. According to the Microsoft website, Excel's internal sort order follows: numbers, special characters, letters, Boolean values, errors, blanks. For example: 0...9; !, #, $, %, *; A...Z; FALSE, TRUE; errors; blank cells.

But if we use -1 as the third argument, we get the desired result. Since the asterisk is smaller than the last value in the range, whatever it may be, the function returns the position of the last text value. This works regardless of the sort order of the lookup range. So, we write the following formula:

```
=MATCH("*",B:B,-1)
```

Where:

- **"*"** is the lookup value
- **B:B** is the lookup range
- **-1** is the match type

We confirm that it does indeed return the row number of the last cell in Column **B** that contains a text string. To test it out, we enter additional text values in Column **B** and confirm that the result is updated as expected. We also confirm that it returns the last row number correctly, even when we skip rows and have blank rows in our column.

NOTE

When using this technique, it is important to be sure that the formula cell is not within the column being inspected by the formula, as this will create a circular reference. Also, other special characters falling before the alpha characters in Excel's internal sort order would work with this technique.

Can we do something similar with numbers instead of text strings? We can—and we will—in the next exercise.

EXERCISE 6—LAST NUMBER ROW

In this exercise, we'll perform a similar task as the previous exercise but this time on numeric values.

 **PRACTICE**

To work along, please refer to the Exercise 6 worksheet.

In our worksheet we'd like to write a formula that indicates the last data row. Specifically, the formula should return the row number of the last cell in the account number column that contains a number. If we search for a number that is smaller than the smallest value in the lookup range, and use -1 as the third argument of MATCH, we should get the last data row. Since we don't know what the numbers in the column will be, we'll ask the MIN function to find the smallest value, and we'll then subtract one.

 XREF

MIN is discussed in Chapter 10.

Since our list of account numbers is stored in Column **B**, we can use the following formula:

```
=MATCH(MIN(B:B)-1,B:B,-1)
```

Where:

- **MIN(B:B)-1** returns a number that is one less than the smallest number in the column

- **B:B** is the lookup range

- **-1** is the match type

When we enter this formula into Excel, we are happy to see that the formula returns the last data row. This approach continues to work when you add new data, even if you skip blank rows.

Now that we know how to find the last data row, we apply this technique in the next exercise to retrieve sales for the most recent quarter.

EXERCISE 7—LAST VALUE

In this exercise, we'll use INDEX and MATCH to retrieve the last value.

 **PRACTICE**

To work along, please refer to the Exercise 7 worksheet.

We append sales data to our worksheet each quarter, and we want to write a formula that retrieves the most recent (last) sales amount from this data range. To accomplish this, we use a pair of functions we have used together numerous times: INDEX and MATCH. We use INDEX to return the cell value and MATCH to determine the proper row. Since our quarter labels are text strings, we use MATCH with the asterisk.

 NOTE

If we wanted to determine the last row based on the numeric *Sales* column, we know we could use MATCH with MIN instead.

Since the quarter labels are stored in Column *B* and the sales amounts in Column *C*, we write the following formula:

```
=INDEX(C:C,MATCH("*",B:B,-1))
```

Where:

- **C:C** is the sales column

- **MATCH("*",B:B,-1)** returns the row of the last text string in the period column

We confirm the formula returns the last sales value. To test it out for future periods, we add a quarter label and the corresponding sales amount, and…yes—it worked!

CHAPTER CONCLUSION

In this chapter we revisited wildcards and explored using them in features and functions.

Chapter 19: Tables Revisited

SET UP

I hope that this far into the series you are using tables to store data all the time. We love storing data in tables because they auto-expand. We have used tables in numerous exercises in every volume so far. Could there be more to say about tables? Believe it or not, yes. It is time to revisit tables and discuss a few additional details.

HOW TO

We'll examine the following items:

- Header row
- Total row
- Table alternatives

Let's begin.

HEADER ROW

The values in a table's header row are text strings. When you convert an ordinary range into a table, any other data types stored in the header row are converted to text strings. This is usually not a big deal because our column headers are often text strings, such as "Account Name." But a table doesn't support numbers, dates, or formulas in the header row, and they will thus be converted to text values.

For example, Excel would convert a number that represents a year into the corresponding text string, breaking lookup functions such as VLOOKUP that rely on matching data types. Fortunately, we solved a similar issue long ago with the TEXT function, which can once again help here.

 XREF

TEXT is discussed in Volume 2, Chapter 7.

We can nest the TEXT function into our lookup functions to convert the stored data type into a text string that can be found in the table's header row. We can set the second argument of the TEXT function to match the formatting found in the header row.

The header row includes built-in drop-downs to filter and sort. When we apply a filter, it updates the total row formula. Well, it does unless you customize the total row formula. Let's talk about the total row next.

TOTAL ROW

Let's begin by reviewing a few things we already know about the total row. We can turn it on or off anytime by using the Total Row checkbox in the Ribbon. We can pick the type of math for each column. The total row automatically uses the SUBTOTAL function, which excludes any table rows hidden with a filter. Since the total row can be customized, we can update the formulas if needed. For example, if we needed the total row to include any rows hidden by a filter, we could change the formula's SUBTOTAL function to a SUM function. We have the full arsenal of Excel functions at our fingertips, and we can customize the total row to fit our needs. Any customizations are retained when we turn off the total row. But we don't need to turn off a total row to add data. Check it out.

We can add data to a table when it has a total row. We can select the last cell in the last data row, and then use the Tab key to insert a new blank table row. We can resize the table by clicking and dragging the Resize control displayed in the lower right corner of the total row, or we can resize with the following command:

- Table Tools > Design > Resize Table

When we copy multiple transactions, we can paste-append them to the table by selecting the first cell in the total row and then doing a paste. This causes Excel to insert the data above the total row, pushing the total row down. It is important to note that this works when you copy and paste more than one row of data. If you only copy one row, Excel actually pastes it into the total row and replaces the values in the total row. It is also important to note that this works when you copy the data range only, but not when you copy the worksheet rows that contain the data.

TABLE ALTERNATIVES

If you are like me, you use tables all the time. In practice, we can use tables for just about all of our data-storing needs. But there are a few situations where we need to do something that isn't supported in tables, such as using dates, numbers, or formulas in the header row. In these rare circumstances when we are precluded from using a table, we can simulate the benefits of a table such as the total row, header row filters, selecting data, structured references, and auto-expansion. Let's simulate each of these key properties of tables.

 NOTE

Custom views and shared workbooks are features that are unavailable when a workbook contains a table.

Total Row

We can simulate the total row by inserting a skinny row under the data and then using a SUBTOTAL function to compute the total.

 XREF

SUBTOTAL is discussed in Volume 1, Chapter 11, and skinny rows are discussed in Volume 1, Chapter 12.

Header Row Filters

We can simulate the header row filters with the Filter feature.

 XREF

The Filter feature is discussed in Chapter 3.

Selecting Data

We can select a table column by clicking the top edge of a column header. When the mouse is positioned over the top cell border of the header cell, the pointer changes to a Down Selection arrow. A single click selects the data cells in that column; a second click includes the header and total cells if displayed. This works for selecting the cells within the worksheet, as well as within formulas to use the corresponding structured reference as a function argument. You can do this for an ordinary range by using one of the first shortcuts we discussed, Ctrl+Shift+Down, or by selecting the header cell and holding down Shift while double-clicking the selected cell's bottom border.

We can select a table row by clicking the left border of the table row. Positioning the mouse over the left cell border, the pointer changes to a Right Selection arrow. We can do this for an ordinary range by using the Ctrl+Shift+Right shortcut or by selecting the desired cell in the left column and holding down Shift while double-clicking the selected cell's right border.

We can select all data by clicking the upper-left corner of the table. When we position our mouse over the top-left cell corner, the mouse pointer changes into a Diagonal Selection arrow. We can do this in an ordinary data range, with Ctrl+A or Ctrl+*, or by selecting the top-left cell and then holding down Shift while double-clicking the selected cell's bottom border and then the selection's right border.

We can reposition a column in an active table by clicking the bottom cell border of the desired column header and dragging it left or right as desired. We can do this in an ordinary range by selecting the data column and dragging left or right as desired while holding down the Shift key.

Structured References

We can simulate structured table references by assigning a name to the data range and then referencing specified columns or rows within the name using the INDEX function.

 XREF

INDEX is discussed in Volume 2, Chapter 8.

Auto-Expansion

We can simulate auto-expansion by using a dynamic named range. Dynamic named ranges were more common in the old days, you know, before we had tables. A dynamic named range is essentially a named formula that returns a range reference based on function arguments. We can create a dynamic named range using our old friend INDEX.

In Chapter 18, we used INDEX and MATCH to return a value from the last data row. We can do something similar here and return a cell reference to the last data row. As we've discussed, the INDEX function has two forms: the array form, which returns a cell value, and the reference form, which returns a reference. The reference form enables us to create a named formula that returns a range that begins with a specified cell and ends with the last data cell. For example, we could create a dynamic named range from *A1* to the last cell in Column *B* containing a text value with the following named formula:

```
=A1:INDEX(B:B,MATCH("*",B:B,-1))
```

Once created, the dynamic named range simulates table auto-expansion because it automatically includes new values we type or paste under the existing range. As a result, any formulas that reference the name will automatically include those new values.

 NOTE

When creating dynamic named ranges, it is helpful to test them with the Go To (F5) dialog. The name won't be displayed, but you can type it in and Excel will select the range.

The table alternatives presented are essentially a collection of the various methods Excel users had to implement prior to the rollout of the table feature. As you can see, the table feature is wonderful and absolutely makes our lives easier than the old days.

EXAMPLES

Please work through the following exercises to practice.

 **PRACTICE**

To work along, please refer to *Tables.xlsx*.

 VIDEO

To watch the solutions video, please visit the Excel University Video Library.

EXERCISE 1—DATE HEADERS

In this exercise, we'll examine date column headers.

 **PRACTICE**

To work along, please refer to the Exercise 1 worksheet.

Our worksheet stores account balances in monthly columns. The header for each column is the last day of the month, stored as a date value and right-aligned in the cell. The user will enter an account and a date into corresponding input cells, and we'd like Excel to retrieve the related amount. Fortunately, we know how to perform two-dimensional lookups with INDEX and MATCH. Since the data is stored in **B19:H30**, the account in **C13**, and the date in **C14**, we write the following formula:

```
=INDEX(B19:H30,MATCH(C13,B19:B30,0),MATCH(C14,B19:H19,0))
```

Where:

- **B19:H30** is the data range

- **MATCH(C13,B19:B30,0)** returns the row of the selected account

- **MATCH(C14,B19:H19,0)** returns the column of the entered date

We confirm our formula retrieves the correct value from the range. And life is good—until next period when we realize that each time we add new data, we need to update our formulas. So we decide to convert this ordinary range into a table. We select any cell in the range and insert a table. Argh! Our formula is broken. Now our beautiful two-dimensional lookup formula returns #N/A. Drat—we were so close!

After the frustration subsides, we inspect the worksheet more closely. We notice that the date values stored in the header row are now left-aligned, like a text string. Indeed, they are text strings. Since tables do not support date headers, Excel converted them into text strings. Fortunately, we know that the TEXT function converts a numeric value into a text string, so we decide to update our formula to work with the text headers.

We begin by naming the table *tbl_e1.* Then we update our formula to use structured references and convert the date into a text string, as follows:

```
=INDEX(tbl_e1,MATCH(C13,tbl_e1[Account],0),
MATCH(TEXT(C14,"m/d/yyyy"),tbl_e1[#Headers],0))
```

Where:

- **tbl_e1** is the data range

- **MATCH(C13,tbl_e1[Account],0)** returns the row of the selected account

- **MATCH(TEXT(C14,"m/d/yyyy"),tbl_e1[#Headers],0)** returns the column of the entered date

Yes—it worked! The TEXT function converted the date stored in the Date input cell to a text string so that the MATCH function was able to match it to the table's header row.

EXERCISE 2—FILTER AND APPEND

In this exercise, we'll see how the total row works with filters and we'll paste-append new transactions into the table while the total row is active.

 **PRACTICE**

To work along, please refer to the Exercise 2 worksheet.

We have stored a bunch of transactions in a table. We'd like to see the total, so we turn on the table's total row. We want to see which function Excel uses to compute the total, so we select the total amount cell and inspect the formula bar and confirm that it is computed with the SUBTOTAL function.

Now we'd like to see the total of the January transactions only, so we simply use the filter control at the top of the *Date* column and select January. As expected, the SUBTOTAL function includes only the visible rows. We clear the filter to see all transactions again and confirm the total is updated accordingly.

We want to paste-append some new transactions while the total row is still active. We head to the *E2 Data* worksheet and copy the data range. We flip back to the table and select the first cell in the total row. We paste it in and are happy to see that the transactions are inserted into the table and that the total row was pushed down as needed. Perfect.

EXERCISE 3—CUSTOMIZE TOTALS

In this exercise, we'll see how to customize total row formulas.

 **PRACTICE**

To work along, please refer to the Exercise 3 worksheet.

Our worksheet contains invoice data in a table named *tbl_e3*. We would like to create a formula-based report that summarizes the amount by class. Since the first class is stored in *B14*, we populate the report using our dear friend SUMIFS, as follows:

```
=SUMIFS(tbl_e3[Amount],tbl_e3[Class],B14)
```

Where:

- **tbl_e3[Amount]** is the sum range

- **tbl_e3[Class]** is the criteria range

- **B14** is the criteria value

We fill the formula down and our report is done.

Since we really like to set up error checking, we decide to create a little test that compares the report total with the table total. That way, if a new class is pasted into the table in the future, our error check will indicate that not all table data flowed into the report.

To build our error check, we retrieve the totals from the desired cells by entering "=" and then clicking the corresponding total cell. To grab the report total, our formula uses a direct cell reference to the report total cell:

```
=C17
```

To grab the table total, our formula uses the structured table reference for the total row cell:

```
=tbl_e3[[#Totals],[Amount]]
```

We confirm the difference between the report total and the table total is zero, so we move on with our life. And life is good—until we decide to filter the table. When we filter the table to show the transactions where *Class* is equal to *Remodel*, our error check indicates an error. This is because the table's total row uses the SUBTOTAL function and thus only includes the visible rows. But we can change the function used in the total row, so we select the total row amount cell and replace the default formula with the following:

```
=SUM([Amount])
```

Now the table's total row reflects the total of the column, regardless of any filter applied, and we can see that the error check is now showing a difference of zero. Excellent.

 NOTE

> In practice, an alternative approach is to retrieve the table total using a SUM function rather than a reference to the total row cell. For example, SUM(tbl_e3[Amount]) would continue working regardless of the filter and even if the total row was turned off.

EXERCISE 4—TOTAL ROW

In this exercise, we'll simulate a table's total row.

 **PRACTICE**

To work along, please refer to the Exercise 4 worksheet.

Our sheet stores the data in an ordinary range, not a table. We would really like to have a total row under the data range, and we'd like to ensure that if we insert new transactions above the total row that they are included in the total. If we enable filters, we want to ensure that the total row includes just the visible rows. This functionality is built in to tables, but since our data is stored in an ordinary range, we have to simulate it using a skinny row, the SUBTOTAL function, and the AutoFilter feature.

We begin by creating a skinny row under the data range. We use the SUBTOTAL function to add up the *Amount* column and we include the skinny row in the formula. Then we turn on filtering for the range. Now let's test it out.

First let's see what happens if we add some new transactions. We look at the data on the *E2 Data* sheet that we will paste-append to our range. We note it has 11 rows, so we insert at least 11 new worksheet rows above our skinny row. We then copy the data from the *E2 Data* sheet and paste it into our newly inserted rows. We confirm the total includes the new data as expected.

Next let's see what happens if we apply a filter. We use a filter to show only the July transactions, and we note that the total includes the visible rows only. That is exactly what we wanted. So, in essence, we have simulated a table's total row with the help of a few friends.

EXERCISE 5—REPORT

In this exercise, we'll use an ordinary range as a data source for a formula-based report.

 **PRACTICE**

To work along, please refer to the Exercise 5 worksheet.

We'd like to create a formula-based report that summarizes data stored in the little simulated table on the *E5 Data* sheet. We populate our report's *Amount* column with SUMIFS, and we ensure that the formula includes the data's skinny row. So far, so good.

Now we want to confirm that if we add new data to our simulated table, our report will include the new rows. The data we copy is stored on the *E2 Data* sheet, and we note that it has 11 rows. We insert at least 11 new rows above the data's skinny row on the *E5 Data* sheet. We copy the data from the *E2 Data* sheet and paste it into the new rows on the *E5 Data* sheet. We flip back to our report and note that it includes the new data rows as expected.

EXERCISE 6—STRUCTURED REFERENCES

In this exercise, we'll simulate structured table references.

 **PRACTICE**

To work along, please refer to the Exercise 6 worksheet.

Our sheet stores data in a little pretend table, complete with a skinny row, a total row, and filters. Now we'd like to see if we can simulate structured table references. So we define a new name, *tbl_e6,* which refers to the data range, including the skinny row and excluding the total row. Since the name includes the skinny row, we know that any future transactions inserted above the skinny row will be included in the name, so we feel good so far.

Now we need to write a formula to populate our report. We will simulate structured table references by referring to the data range by name, *tbl_e6,* rather than A1-style range references. After all, structured table references use the table's name, not A1-style references.

For the report formula, we'll use SUMIFS. The first argument is the *Amount* column. The Amount column is the third column in the name. So we can use the INDEX function to reference the third column in the name. Similarly, we can use the INDEX function to reference the *Account* column. Since the first account label is stored in *B14*, we write the following formula to populate the report's *Amount* column:

```
=SUMIFS(INDEX(tbl_e6,0,3),INDEX(tbl_e6,0,1),B14)
```

Where:

- **INDEX(tbl_e6,0,3)** is the sum range, the amount column

- **INDEX(tbl_e6,0,1)** is the criteria range, the account column

- **B14** is the criteria value

We fill the formula down and confirm it works as expected.

This is how we can simulate structured table references even when we can't store the data in a table. That is nice, but let's go for the gold. Our favorite capability of tables is auto-expansion. Let's simulate this in the next exercise.

EXERCISE 7—AUTO-EXPANSION

In this exercise, we'll simulate a table's auto-expansion capability.

 **PRACTICE**

To work along, please refer to the Exercise 7 worksheet.

We would like to create a formula-based report that summarizes the data stored in an ordinary range on the *E7 Data* sheet. We are going to want to paste-append new data each month, and we would like our report to automatically include these new rows. We don't want to rewrite our formulas because that is obviously bogus.

We don't want to use a skinny row and a total row because then we have to manually insert new worksheet rows, which slows us down. Our objective is to be able to paste and go, without inserting new worksheet rows. Fortunately, we have all of the tools we need; we just need to put them together.

First let's head over to the *E7 Data* sheet. We need to create a name that refers to the data range. This dynamic name needs to automatically update to include new data. Fortunately, in Chapter 18 we learned how to use MATCH to determine the last data row. We also used MATCH with INDEX to return the last cell value. As we recall, the INDEX function can return a cell value or a reference, and so we'll use the reference form to build our dynamic name. Specifically, we will define the range by specifying the upper-left and lower-right cells.

Before we define our new name, let's figure out how to specify the upper-left and lower-right cells of the range. The upper-left cell will be the header cell of the *Account* column, **B12**. This won't change as we add new data, so we'll simply refer to the cell with an absolute cell reference. The lower-right cell will change as we add new data, so we need to use INDEX and MATCH to create a reference to the last cell in the *Amount* column that contains a number. Thus, we create a new name, *tbl_e7,* which refers to the following:

```
=$B$12:INDEX($D:$D,MATCH(MIN($D:$D)-1,$D:$D,-1))
```

Where:

- **$B$12** is the upper-left cell of the dynamic named range

- **INDEX($D:$D,MATCH(MIN($D:$D)-1,$D:$D,-1))** is the lower-right cell

- **Where:**

    o **$D:$D** is the amount column

    o **MATCH(MIN($D:$D)-1,$D:$D,-1)** returns the last row containing a number

Now let's test the name to confirm it refers to our data range. We use F5 to open the Go To dialog, manually type in the new name, *tbl_e7*, and click OK. We see that Excel selects our data range, which means our name seems to be working so far. Yay! But we need to ensure the named range expands as new data is added. So we head over to the *E2 Data* sheet, copy the data, and then paste it under our data range. Now for the big test. We hit the F5 key, type in our name, and Excel selects the entire data range, including the new cells. Wow—it worked! It is truly a dynamic named range.

With the dynamic name set up, the hard part is done. We flip back to our report and use SUMIFS to compute the report values. As in the previous exercise, we simulate structured references with the INDEX function. Since the first report label is stored in *B13*, we use the following formula to populate our report:

    =SUMIFS(INDEX(tbl_e7,0,3),INDEX(tbl_e7,0,1),B13)

Where:

- **INDEX(tbl_e7,0,3)** is the sum range, the amount column

- **INDEX(tbl_e7,0,1)** is the criteria range, the account column

- **B13** is the criteria value

We fill the formula down, and…yes—it worked!

 NOTE

Other functions can be used to create dynamic named ranges, including OFFSET and COUNTA. If you use COUNTA instead of MATCH, be sure that when you paste new data you don't skip any blank rows. If there are empty cells in the data range, the formula may return an unexpected result.

CHAPTER CONCLUSION

In this chapter we played with tables a bit. We love storing data in tables when we can, but when we can't, it is at least good to know that we can simulate their capabilities.

Chapter 20: Start Here Revisited

SET UP

Early on in the series, we discussed the idea of centrally storing input cells on a single worksheet. This provides an organized place for users to enter values used throughout the workbook. It is time to revisit and improve the Start Here sheet.

 XREF

Start Here is discussed in Volume 1, Chapter 15.

HOW TO

The Start Here sheet is essentially a collection of input cells. In this chapter we discuss techniques that can improve our input cells. By improving input cells stored on the Start Here sheet, or anywhere else for that matter, we make our workbook faster and easier to maintain over time.

But hang on a sec. How can we improve input cells? I mean, they just store a value entered by the user. In the exercises that follow, we simulate a disabled input cell using conditional formatting, use worksheet protection to limit access only to input cells, allow a user to override a data validation rule, identify input cells that are invalid, set up dependent drop-down cells, use slicers as input cells, and create a drop-down of unique choices from a table column full of duplicate values.

Since we are already familiar with all of the Excel features and functions needed for this chapter, we won't rehash the details of each. Instead, we will learn how to configure them to work in harmony together.

EXAMPLES

Please open Excel and work along.

 **PRACTICE**

To work along, please refer to **Start Here.xlsx**.

 VIDEO

To watch the solutions video, please visit the Excel University Video Library.

EXERCISE 1—EMPLOYEE COST

In this exercise, we'll use conditional formatting to dim an input cell to simulate it being disabled.

 **PRACTICE**

To work along, please refer to the Exercise 1 worksheet.

In our worksheet, we compute the annual employee cost by adding the annual wage, overhead, and employer taxes. We want to make it easy for our user to enter the pay rate based on the employee type. That is, if an employee is salaried, we want the user to express the pay rate as an annual salary. If an employee is hourly, we want the user to express the pay rate as an hourly rate. Let's dial in the related input cells.

The employee type input cell provides a drop-down menu that allows the user to select *Salary* or *Hourly*. We use two additional input cells: one for the hourly rate and one for the annual salary. When the user selects *Salary* from the drop-down, our formulas use the value from the annual salary input cell. Likewise, when the user selects *Hourly*, our formulas use the value from the hourly rate input cell. We'd like to make it clear to the user which rate cell to use based on the selected employee type. Both rate input cells are formatted with the Input cell style. When the formulas use an input cell, we won't change its formatting. We'll use conditional formatting to dim the unused input cell.

Our employee type input cell is *C11*. We select the hourly rate input cell, *C12*, and create a new conditional formatting rule based on the following formula:

```
=$C$11="Salary"
```

When this formula returns TRUE, we want to dim the hourly rate input cell. We define the conditional format to include a light-gray fill and a dark-gray font.

Now we need to do something similar for the annual salary input cell. We select the salary input cell, *C13*, and create a new conditional formatting rule based on the following formula:

```
=$C$11="Hourly"
```

When this formula returns TRUE, we want to dim out the annual salary input cell, so we change the format to a light-gray fill and a dark-gray font.

Now we test it out. We select *Salary* from the Type drop-down and confirm that the hourly rate input cell is dimmed. We select *Hourly* and confirm that the salary input cell is dimmed. Even though the user can still enter values into the dimmed input cells, we have communicated that they are being ignored by the formulas.

EXERCISE 2—PROTECTION

In this exercise, we'll limit the user to selecting only input cells.

 **PRACTICE**

To work along, please refer to the Exercise 2 worksheet.

Our worksheet has a couple of input cells and many formulas. Our objective is to allow the user to change the input cell values but not the formulas. We know we can accomplish this by unlocking the input cells and applying worksheet protection. But in addition to that, we want to limit the user to selecting only the input cells—that is, only the unlocked cells.

The Input cell style has been modified to unlock cells and was applied to the input cells. We turn on worksheet protection and in the Protect Sheet dialog box we clear the *Select locked cells* checkbox and leave the *Select unlocked cells* option checked.

 XREF

Using worksheet protection and cell styles is discussed in Chapter 7.

We confirm that we can select the input cells but not any others.

EXERCISE 3—HOURS WORKED

In this exercise, we'll allow the user to bypass our data validation rule.

 **PRACTICE**

To work along, please refer to the Exercise 3 worksheet.

Our worksheet allows the user to enter hours worked for each employee. Typically, employees work between four and eight hours per day. We will use data validation to allow the user to enter a decimal value within this range. However, we would like to allow the user to override this restriction when needed. For example, the user should be able to enter 0 or 9. Can we do this? Yes, no problem.

To begin, we store our range endpoints 4 and 8 on an admin sheet. We name the cells *hours_from* and *hours_to* accordingly. This approach makes it is easy to modify the range by changing cell values rather than the data validation rule. We could optionally hide the admin sheet if desired.

 XREF

Hidden admin sheets are discussed in Volume 1, Chapter 13.

Next we select the range of input cells that will store the hours and use data validation to allow a decimal value between *hours_from* and *hours_to*. Let's test it out. We enter a decimal value between 4 and 8 and Excel allows the entry. However, when we enter a value outside of the range, such as 0, Excel, as expected, prevents the entry. No problem. We can make a minor modification to the data validation rule to allow the user to override the rule and enter invalid data.

We select the input cell range and open the Data Validation dialog box. On the Error Alert tab, we change the Alert Style from Stop (the default) to Information. We can optionally set the title to "Confirm" and the error message to "Are you sure?" To test it, we enter an invalid value such as 0. This time, we confirm that Excel will accept the entry even though it violates the data validation rule.

 NOTE

The main difference between the Information and Warning error alert styles is the default button in the Alert dialog. When Information is selected, the default button is OK, so hitting Enter submits the invalid entry. With Warning, the default button is No, so hitting Enter does not submit the invalid entry.

At this point, many of the entries in our worksheet fall within the data validation range. But we have also entered values that fall outside of the data validation range. At a glance, it is difficult to tell which values are valid and which are invalid. So, can we ask Excel to identify invalid data? We can—and we will—in the next exercise.

EXERCISE 4—CIRCLE INVALID DATA

In this exercise, we'll have Excel identify invalid input values.

 **PRACTICE**

To work along, please refer to the Exercise 4 worksheet.

We use the same basic idea from the previous exercise. Data validation allows a decimal between 4 and 8 and the alert style is Information so that a user can bypass the rule. As a result, our worksheet contains valid and invalid entries. Fortunately, we can ask Excel to put a big red circle around invalid entries. We use the following Ribbon command:

- Data > Data Validation > Circle Invalid Data

Now it is easy to see the invalid entries.

To remove these circles, we use:

- Data > Data Validation > Clear Validation Circles

That was fun!

EXERCISE 5—DEPENDENT DROP-DOWNS

In this exercise, we'll create dependent drop-downs, where the selection in the primary drop-down determines the choices that appear in the secondary drop-down. This idea is commonly known as dependent drop-downs, conditional drop-downs, cascading drop-downs, and dynamic drop-downs.

 **PRACTICE**

To work along, please refer to the Exercise 5 worksheet.

Our worksheet contains a table used for data entry. The user needs to complete it to obtain an expense reimbursement for a business conference. The table contains three columns: *Type*, *Expense*, and *Amount*. Our objective is to make it easy for the user to enter consistent data by selecting the type and expense values from drop-downs. The choices in the Type drop-down will be the same for each table row—namely, Travel, Fees, and Other. The choices in the Expense drop-down depend on the value selected in the Type column. For example, when Type is Travel, the choices in the Expense drop-down should be Air, Room, Taxi, Rental Car, and so on. However, when Type is Fees, then the choices in the Expense drop-down should be Registration, Materials, and so on. Since this is Excel, there are several ways to accomplish this.

In the technique we use for this exercise, we store the primary choices in a table. We store each set of secondary choices in separate tables. The name for each secondary table will match the primary choice. For example, since one of the primary choices is Travel, the table that stores the related secondary choices will be named *Travel*. We have another primary choice, Fees, so we store the related secondary choices in a table named *Fees*, and so on.

We create the drop-downs using data validation. The primary drop-down list source will be a name that refers to the primary choice table. The secondary drop-down list source will use the INDIRECT function to create a reference to the related secondary table based on the primary choice.

Before we create the drop-downs, let's check out the tables on the **E5 Admin** worksheet. The primary choices are stored in a table named **Type**, and the choices are Travel, Fees, and Other. The secondary choices are stored in separate tables named **Travel**, **Fees**, and **Other**.

Let's create the drop-downs on the **Exercise 5** worksheet. We start by selecting the *Type* column. Since the Data Validation feature doesn't support the use of table names directly, we use the name **dd_type,** which refers to the table name **Type**. We use data validation to allow a list equal to **dd_type**. We test the resulting drop-down and confirm it contains the expected choices. We select one of the choices and are ready for the next step.

Now for the secondary drop-downs. The idea is to reference the table that has the same name as the selected Type value. We select the *Expense* column and note the active cell is **C14**. Since the first Type cell is **B14**, we use data validation to allow a list equal to the following formula:

```
=INDIRECT(B14)
```

Where:

- **B14** is a relative reference to the primary input cell

NOTE

If you receive an alert stating that the Source currently evaluates to an error, this is most likely because **B14** is blank. Click Yes to continue, make a selection in **B14**, and then see whether the secondary drop-down works as expected.

The INDIRECT function converts the value stored in **B14** into a valid table reference. We test it out by confirming that the secondary choices change depending on the primary input cell value. Yay—we did it!

 NOTE

This technique works in simple applications but can be cumbersome to maintain. Changing a primary choice label requires you to change the corresponding secondary table name to match. Plus, the primary choices must be valid table names. For more sophisticated techniques, feel free to explore the Extra Credit exercises.

EXERCISE 6—SLICERS

In this exercise, we'll use slicers as an alternative to dependent drop-downs.

 **PRACTICE**

To work along, please refer to the Exercise 6 worksheet.

We would like to allow our user to select a department and an employee. Rather than use Data Validation drop-downs, we'll have the user make selections with slicers.

Using slicers instead of data validation lists has several benefits. Slicers automatically create a unique list even when there are duplicates in the source field. They don't require the use of names or formulas. Plus, they are intuitive and offer many design options.

The underlying data is stored in a table on the **E6 Data** sheet. This data is summarized in a PivotTable on the **E6 PT** sheet. Now it is time to create the slicers. On the **E6 PT** sheet, we create Department and Employee slicers. The Department slicer contains a unique list of departments. Since we want the employee slicer to display only the employees in the selected department, we check *Hide items with no data* in the Slicer Setting dialog. As we select different departments, we see the PivotTable and the Employee slicer are updated accordingly. This relationship between the two slicers is inherited from the PivotTable automatically, and it offers an alternative to dependent drop-downs. When we select an employee, we see the PivotTable is filtered down to one row with the employee data.

With the slicers created and working well, we move them to the *Exercise 6* sheet with a standard cut and paste. All that remains is writing a formula to retrieve the related employee data.

Since a slicer can have multiple items selected at once, we need a way to tell our formula only to retrieve values when a single employee is selected. As with anything in Excel, there are different ways to approach this. We'll use the PivotTable's grand total, which is a count of the number of employees displayed. When the grand total is 1, we know only a single employee is selected.

We remember that the GETPIVOTDATA function is designed to retrieve values from PivotTables. So we write a formula that retrieves the grand total from the PivotTable. If it is 1, we go ahead and retrieve the related employee data. If it is not equal to 1, it means that either multiple or no employees are selected, and thus we won't retrieve any values.

Since our first report label is stored in *B26*, we write the following formula in *C26* to retrieve the values from the PivotTable:

```
=IF(GETPIVOTDATA("Employee",'E6 PT'!$B$12)=1,
HLOOKUP(B26,'E6 PT'!$B$12:$M$13,2,0),
"-")
```

Where:

- **GETPIVOTDATA("Employee",'E6 PT'!$B$12)=1** retrieves the grand total and returns TRUE if equal to 1

- **HLOOKUP(B26,'E6 PT'!$B$12:$M$13,2,0)** retrieves the first report value based on the column header

- **"-"** returns a dash if the grand total is not equal to 1

We fill the formula down and test it out. We select an employee from the slicer, and…yes—it works! When we select multiple employees, we notice that a dash is returned instead, which is exactly what we wanted. Next period when we update the table, we just refresh the PivotTable and the slicers are updated accordingly.

 XREF

PivotTables, slicers, and GETPIVOTDATA are discussed in Volume 3. Learning about unfamiliar functions such as HLOOKUP is discussed in Chapter 14.

NOTE

The GETPIVOTDATA function retrieves value fields, not row fields, from a PivotTable.

EXERCISE 7—PIVOTTABLE UNIQUE

In this exercise, we'll create a Data Validation drop-down that is based on a transaction table.

 **PRACTICE**

To work along, please refer to the Exercise 7 worksheet.

We exported a bunch of sales transactions from our accounting system and stored them in a table on the **E7 Data** sheet. One of the columns in the table stores the sales rep. Since there are numerous transactions for each rep, each rep name is repeated many times in the *Rep* column.

On the **Exercise 7** worksheet, we'd like to allow a user to select a rep name from a drop-down. Based on the selected rep, our formulas will provide summary values such as total and average sales.

Let's take a moment and consider the *Rep* drop-down. We want it to display a unique list of choices—that is, one choice for each rep. The problem is that our transaction export contains numerous transactions for each rep, and as a result, the table's *Rep* column contains duplicated labels. This prevents us from using the table column as the data validation list source. Let's think about our options.

One option would be to copy and paste the *Rep* column into a new worksheet. We could then remove the duplicate entries and use the resulting list for our drop-down. We could save, close, and move on with our life. And life is good—until next period. When we paste in a bunch of new transactions and discover that there are new reps, we see that our drop-down excludes them. To get the new reps to appear in the drop-down, we would need to manually update the unique rep list. That doesn't sound fun, so let's figure out another way.

We would like to create a unique list of labels from a data source, and we'd like to be able to easily update the list when new items are added. Does this remind you of anything? Yes—PivotTables! We could easily set up a PivotTable that contains a unique list of reps. When new transactions are added, we could simply refresh the report to update the list. But can we use a PivotTable as a data validation list source? Yes, we can. And the good news is you already have the Excel skills needed. Ready? Me too.

The PivotTable on the **E7 PT** worksheet summarizes the data on the **E7 Data** sheet. It includes a single row field and doesn't display grand totals. All we need to do is figure out how to use it as a data validation list source. We need the data validation source range to automatically expand if new reps are added. Fortunately, we know how to build a dynamic named range with INDEX and MATCH.

 XREF

Using INDEX and MATCH to create a dynamic named range is discussed in Chapters 18 and 19.

We'll create a new name that dynamically adapts to the PivotTable's dimensions. That way the name will automatically include any new reps in the PivotTable. Since the first data cell in the PivotTable is *B14*, we create a new name, *dd_reps,* which refers to the following formula:

```
=$B$14:INDEX($B:$B,MATCH("*",$B:$B,-1))
```

Where:

- **$B$14** is the first data cell in the report

- **INDEX($B:$B,MATCH("*", $B:$B,-1))** returns the last data cell

- **Where:**

    o **$B:$B** is the report column

    o **MATCH("*",$B:$B,-1)** returns the row of the last cell with text

We test the name by using F5 to select it. With the name set up and working, we can now create the drop-down on the *Exercise 7* worksheet. We select our input cell and use data validation to allow a list equal to our name *dd_reps.* We test it out and…yes—it works!

 NOTE

If a data validation list source is a named range that includes blank cells, Excel will allow a user-override even when the alert style is set to Error.

This is awesome because whenever we add transactions to the data table, we simply refresh the PivotTable, and the reps will appear in the drop-down.

With the hard work complete, we just need to write a few summary formulas. To compute the total sales for the selected rep stored in *C11*, we use the SUMIFS function as follows:

```
=SUMIFS(tbl_e7[Amount],tbl_e7[Rep],C11)
```

We do something similar to compute the average, as follows:

```
=AVERAGEIFS(tbl_e7[Amount],tbl_e7[Rep],C11)
```

We also do something similar to compute the number of transactions, as follows:

```
=COUNTIFS(tbl_e7[Rep],C11)
```

We test it out by changing the reps, and—yep—we look good!

CHAPTER CONCLUSION

In this chapter we revisited the Start Here sheet. We applied several techniques that improve the efficiency of our workbooks.

.

APPLICATIONS

Let's see what we can accomplish by applying our Excel skills.

Chapter 21: JE Preparation

SET UP

In this part we depart from our traditional format a bit. The chapters in the series thus far were primarily designed to teach a specific Excel skill, some type of feature, function, or technique. It is time to make a critical transition. We begin with a real-world task and figure out how to accomplish it with Excel. We are going to have fun applying what we've learned to classic accounting and finance projects.

In this chapter our task is to prepare journal entries for our monthly close. Since this is a monthly process, we want to carefully build the recurring-use workbook. We are going to apply our Excel skills to make this workbook easy to maintain each month.

 NOTE

> Even if you aren't personally responsible for preparing journal entries, I would encourage you to work through this chapter because there are some interesting ideas that can be applied to other workbooks as well.

HOW TO

The goal of the workbook is to help us efficiently prepare our monthly journal entries. To achieve this goal, our workbook needs to help us stay organized during the closing process, ensure that each entry is in balance, provide the accounts and amounts for each entry, document our calculations, and summarize the impact to the general ledger.

To help us stay organized, we create a log that displays a list of all the journal entries. To ensure each entry is in balance, our log will also contain an alert that compares debits and credits for each entry. To provide the accounts and amounts, each journal entry gets a cover sheet. To document the calculations, each entry will have one or more supporting worksheets. To summarize the impact to the general ledger, we include a worksheet that shows beginning account balances, the total of each journal entry, and the adjusted balances.

There are no new mechanics to discuss since we already have the Excel skills we need. Let's go ahead and apply what we know to build the workbook.

EXAMPLES

Crack open Excel and work along.

 **PRACTICE**

To work along, please refer to *JE Prep.xlsx*.

 VIDEO

To watch the solutions video, please visit the Excel University Video Library.

EXERCISE 1—JE LOG

In this exercise, we'll set up our JE log worksheet.

 **PRACTICE**

To work along, please refer to the Exercise 1 worksheet.

This worksheet contains one row for each journal entry and essentially combines the functionality of a Start Here sheet with input cells, an Index sheet with hyperlinks, and an Error Check sheet with alerts. The input cells include the closing period, named *period*, and status cells for each entry with Data Validation drop-downs. Hyperlinks in the JE column provide quick access to the journal entries. Now we need to use Conditional Formatting icon sets to create the alerts that indicate whether the retrieved debit and credit amounts agree.

Our goal is to use a green circle icon for good (in balance) and a red circle icon for bad (out of balance). We select the formula cells in the *Alert* column and open the New Formatting Rule dialog. We opt to format all cells based on their values and to use an icon set for the format style. We'll use the three traffic lights icon set. We set the rules so that Excel displays the red circle when the number value is greater than 0, the green circle icon when the number value is greater than or equal to 0, and the red circle icon when the value is less than 0. We also want to prevent Excel from showing the cell value, so we opt to show the alert icons only. We test out the conditional formatting and confirm that a green circle is displayed for entries that are in balance, and a red circle is displayed when an entry is out of balance.

In addition to the *Exercise 1* worksheet, the workbook contains an *E1 Support* worksheet. For the most part, each exercise sheet contains a support sheet that provides a place to store data or perform related calculations. In this case, the support sheet contains an input cell named *start* that allows us to control the starting period for schedules used throughout the workbook, as well as the department table and the chart of accounts.

With our journal entry log worksheet looking good, it is time to move on to our first journal entry computation.

EXERCISE 2—SUBSCRIPTION REVENUE

This journal entry helps us recognize subscription revenue. Since we collect payment at the time of purchase but provide the content over the subscription term, we need to defer the income and recognize it over time. This journal entry tracks each subscription and term and helps us record income in the correct accounting period.

 **PRACTICE**

To work along, please refer to the Exercise 2 worksheet.

The *Exercise 2* worksheet contains our journal entry cover sheet, which basically stores the accounts and departments and retrieves the debit and credit amounts from the *E2 Support* worksheet. Let's head to the support sheet to check it out.

The *E2 Support* sheet is where the hard work happens. Our job is to compute monthly revenue based on the subscription terms. The worksheet includes monthly columns computed with formulas that return dynamic date values.

XREF

Dynamic headers are discussed in Volume 2, Chapter 21.

We need to write a formula that computes the amount of revenue to recognize in each of the monthly columns. We'll use consistent formulas. Before we get to the mechanics of the formula, let's understand what it needs to accomplish. The formula needs to see if the date in the column header falls between the subscription start and end dates. If it does, then it needs to return the monthly amount; otherwise, it needs to return zero. Since this is Excel, there are numerous ways to accomplish this. We'll use the AND function as an IF alternative.

 XREF

Using AND as an alternative to IF is discussed in Chapter 10.

Since the first monthly column header date is in *G13*, the start date for the first subscription is in *E14*, the end date is in *F14*, and the monthly amount is in *C14*, we write the following formula:

```
=AND(G$13>=$E14,G$13<=$F14)*$C14
```

Where:

- **G$13>=$E14** returns TRUE if the column header date is greater than or equal to the start date

- **G$13<=$F14** returns TRUE if the column header date is less than or equal to the end date

- **$C14** the monthly amount, which is multiplied by the result of the AND function, 1 (TRUE) or 0 (FALSE)

When the monthly column header falls within the subscription start and end dates, the AND function returns TRUE and Excel multiplies the monthly amount by 1. Otherwise, the AND function returns FALSE and Excel multiplies the monthly amount by 0. The net effect is that the formula returns the monthly amount for all columns within the subscription term. We fill the formula down and right and confirm it returns the monthly amount for columns within the subscription term as expected.

With the formula complete, let's turn our attention to getting the correct column total back to the journal entry cover sheet. We want to return the total from the column corresponding to the closing period. To make the data easier to retrieve, we name the subscription revenue range on the *E2 Support* sheet. We are precluded from using a table because of the dynamic date headers, so we simply select the entire data range, including the header and total rows, and name it *sub_data*.

Before we flip back to the cover sheet to write the formula to retrieve the amount, let's think about what our formula needs to accomplish. It needs to grab the value from the total row for the column that corresponds to the closing period. When thinking about lookup functions, there are many that come to mind, including VLOOKUP, HLOOKUP, INDEX, and MATCH. Since this is Excel, there are numerous ways we could go about this task. For the purposes of this exercise, we'll use the familiar INDEX/ MATCH combination along with our new friend ROWS to determine the last row within the range.

 XREF

Using ROWS to return the last row in a range is discussed in Chapter 11.

Back on the cover sheet, *Exercise 2*, we want to retrieve the correct total amount from the support sheet. Specifically, our formula should retrieve the value from the last row in the *sub_data* range for the column that corresponds to the closing period stored in the cell on the *Exercise 1* sheet named *period*. Thus, we write the following formula:

```
=INDEX(sub_data,
ROWS(sub_data),
MATCH(period,INDEX(sub_data,1,0),0))
```

Where:

- **sub_data** is the subscription data range

- **ROWS(sub_data)** returns the last row by computing the number of rows

- **MATCH(period,INDEX(sub_data,1,0),0)** returns the column by matching the closing period in the column headers row

Yes—it works! Let's see what will happen next period. We head back to the JE log worksheet and change the closing period. We flip back to our cover sheet and confirm that the expected amount is returned. This is excellent because once we update the closing date, the correct amount automatically flows to the cover sheet.

Want to automate another journal entry? Me too!

EXERCISE 3—DEFERRED RENT

This journal entry helps us compute and record deferred rent. We have a three-year lease term that includes escalating payment amounts each year. We want to record the rent expense in equal monthly amounts over the lease term. This journal entry adjusts the rent expense to a straight-line amount.

 **PRACTICE**

To work along, please refer to the Exercise 3 worksheet.

The *Exercise 3* worksheet is the journal entry cover sheet, and we simply retrieve the journal entry amount from the supporting sheet *E3 Support*.

The *E3 Support* sheet does all the hard work for us. The *Payments* section of the worksheet allows us to enter the monthly payment by year per the lease agreement. Formulas compute the total rent over the lease term.

The *Straight Line* section of the worksheet computes the monthly straight-line amount by dividing the total lease amount by the number of months in the term.

The *Deferred Rent* section of the worksheet computes the monthly journal entry amount. We need to write four formulas and fill them down. One formula computes the actual payment based on the lease agreement. One computes the straight-line amount. One computes the difference, or the deferred rent adjustment. And one computes the total unamortized amount just to ensure our math is accurate. Let's begin with the first formula.

For the *Payment* column, we can simply retrieve the monthly payment amount from the *Payments* section with a VLOOKUP function. Since our first monthly date is stored in *B31* and our payments are stored in *B14:E17*, we can use the following formula in *C31* to retrieve the payment amount:

```
=VLOOKUP(B31,$B$14:$E$17,2,TRUE)
```

Where:

- **B31** is the lookup value, the date

- **$B$14:$E$17** is the lookup range

- **2** returns the value from the second column, the monthly payment

- **TRUE** indicates we are doing a range lookup

We fill the formula down and confirm that the monthly payment amounts look good.

Next up is the *Straight Line* column. We can simply retrieve the straight-line amount from the *Straight Line* section of the worksheet. Since the monthly straight-line amount was computed in *C25*, we can use the following formula:

```
=$C$25
```

We fill the formula down, and we are looking good.

The next column is the deferred rent amount, which is simply the difference between the straight-line amount and the payment amount. We write the following formula into our first deferred rent cell *E31*:

```
=D31-C31
```

We fill the formula down and note that the first 12 months show a positive amount. This is when the straight-line amount is greater than the payment amount per the lease agreement. This reverses beginning with the second year. The straight-line amount is less than the payment amount, and we confirm that the deferred rent amount is a negative number as expected. Our calculations look good, so we move on to the final column.

The last column is the total unamortized amount. We essentially want to compute the running total of the deferred rent column. If all our math is correct, this total should be equal to zero in the final month. We use a SUM function to add up the current month amount in *E31* and the amount from the row above *F30* as follows:

```
=SUM(E31,F30)
```

We fill the formula down and confirm that, as expected, the amount for the final period is indeed zero.

 NOTE

> If we tried to use the addition operator to add *E31* and *F30* instead of the SUM function, our formula for the first row would return an error because the column label is a text value.

We want to make it easy to retrieve values from this range, so we name it ***def_rent***. We are sure to include the skinny row in the name so that any new worksheet rows added down the road will be included in our formulas. Feeling good about our deferred rent schedule, it is now time to head back to the cover sheet.

On the ***Exercise 3*** worksheet, let's write a formula that retrieves the amount from the supporting scheduled based on the closing period. The basic formula is easy, but we need to address the fact that the deferred rent amount changes from a positive to negative number. Let's get our basic lookup formula working first. Since the closing period is stored in a cell named *period* and the deferred rent calculations are stored in a range named *def_rent*, we can use the following formula in *F17* to retrieve the rental expense debit amount:

```
=VLOOKUP(period,def_rent,4,0)
```

Where:

- **period** is the lookup value

- **def_rent** is the lookup range

- **4** returns the value from the fourth column, the deferred rent column

- **0** means exact match

This works well for the first 12 months of the lease, when the deferred rent amount is a positive number. This is because we record a debit to the expense account, which essentially increases the rental expense. However, beginning with the second year, the sign changes, and we actually need to record the amount as a credit. Since this is Excel, there are a variety of ways to approach this. In this exercise we use the MAX and MIN functions as IF alternatives.

When the deferred rent amount is a positive number, we want it. But when it is a negative number, we want zero. Thus, we update our existing VLOOKUP function in *F17* by wrapping a MAX function around it, as follows:

```
=MAX(VLOOKUP(period,def_rent,4,0),0)
```

Where:

- **VLOOKUP(period,def_rent,4,0)** returns the deferred rent amount

- **0** returns zero when the deferred rent is a negative number

We test it out by changing the closing period to a month where the deferred rent is negative, and we confirm that our debit amount changes to zero as expected.

With our debit formula working well, we write a formula that basically does the reverse for the credit amount. We want it to return an amount when the deferred rent is a negative number; otherwise, it should return zero. We use the MIN function to accomplish that in *G17* as follows:

```
=MIN(VLOOKUP(period,def_rent,4,0),0)
```

Where:

- **VLOOKUP(period,def_rent,4,0)** returns the deferred rent amount

- **0** returns zero when the deferred rent amount is a positive number

We look good except for the fact that the amount retrieved is a negative value. We convert this negative value into a positive one by wrapping the absolute value ABS function around it, as shown below:

```
=ABS(MIN(VLOOKUP(period,def_rent,4,0),0))
```

Yes—now it works!

ABS is discussed in Chapter 14.

We test it out by updating the closing period and confirm that our cover sheet is recording the amounts correctly.

If you prefer to have the debit account listed first in the cover sheet for all periods, you could use formulas to populate the account column accordingly. There is an Extra Credit exercise for practice.

EXERCISE 4—ALLOCATION

This journal entry helps us allocate corporate expenses. When we pay certain supplier invoices, we book the expense to the corporate department even though they relate to multiple departments. We use this journal entry to allocate the expenses from the corporate department to various departments.

To work along, please refer to the Exercise 4 worksheet.

Our company has created departments around the type of product each team of employees manages and sells. The departments are hardware, software, online, and service. Our department managers have had lengthy and sometimes heated discussions about the fairest way to allocate expenses. The reality is that none of the managers want these corporate expenses hitting their P&L. The profitability of their department is very important.

There has been much debate about the allocation methods. One option is that all departments share the expenses evenly. Another option is to base the allocation on department revenue. Yet another idea is to base the allocation on headcount. The managers ultimately agreed that the fairest allocation method depends on the nature of the expense. Because postage is such a small amount, they've agreed to allocate it evenly. Office supplies and Internet expense should be allocated based on headcount, while marketing expense should be based on revenue.

Our goal is to create a worksheet that allocates expenses based on the selected methods. We suspect that the allocation method debate isn't over, and may change from time to time. So we want to ensure that it is easy to change the allocation method used for any account at any time.

The *Exercise 4* sheet is our journal entry cover sheet, and we'll retrieve values from the support sheet in a bit.

The *E4 Support* sheet performs the hard work. It essentially allows us to select an allocation method for each account from a Data Validation drop-down, including *Headcount*, *Revenue*, or *Even*. Based on the method selected, we need to write a formula that multiplies the expense amount by the proper department percentage. Before we write the formula, let's have a quick look at the percentages stored on the *E4 Data* sheet.

The *E4 Data* worksheet helps us compute the percentage for each department for each allocation method. The *Methods* section of the worksheet simply contains a list of allocation methods, which is ultimately used to create the Data Validation drop-down on the *E4 Support* worksheet. The *Department Stats* section computes the percentages for each department for each allocation method and stores the results in a table named *tbl_alloc*. For example, the revenue allocation method column divides the department revenue by the total revenue to determine the allocation percentage for each department. Now that we have a visual on how the allocation percentages are stored, let's head back to the support sheet to write the allocation formulas.

In the *E4 Support* sheet, we need to write the allocation formulas. Let's take it in two steps. First we retrieve the percentage from the *E4 Data* sheet. Once we confirm this is working, we simply multiply the amount by the percentage.

To retrieve the percentage, we essentially need to perform a two-dimensional lookup based on the allocation method and the department. Since this is Excel, there are many ways to perform this type of lookup. For this exercise we use INDEX and MATCH. We want to retrieve the percentage from the *tbl_alloc* table. We want Excel to look down the department column to find the matching department and right through the header row to find the matching allocation method. The intersection of this row and column stores the percentage we want to return. Since the first department is stored in *F11* and the first method in *E12*, we write the following formula:

```
=INDEX(tbl_alloc,
MATCH(F$11,tbl_alloc[Dept],0),
MATCH($E12,tbl_alloc[#Headers],0))
```

Where:

- **tbl_alloc** is the lookup range

- **MATCH(F$11,tbl_alloc[Dept],0)** returns the row for the department

- **MATCH($E12,tbl_alloc[#Headers],0)** returns the column for the method

We fill the formula down and right and confirm that it retrieves the correct allocation percentage for each cell. Excellent! We are almost there. Now we update the formula to multiply the amount by the retrieved percentage, as shown below:

```
=$D12*INDEX(tbl_alloc,
MATCH(F$11,tbl_alloc[Dept],0),
MATCH($E12,tbl_alloc[#Headers],0))
```

We fill the updated formula down and right and confirm it works as expected. This is excellent because if the management team changes its mind about which allocation method to use for any given account, we can simply update the drop-down, and we are done. No need to update or rewrite formulas—which is exactly how we like it. To make it easy to pull these allocations up to the cover sheet, the range is named *allocations*.

On the *Exercise 4* sheet, we need to write formulas to pull in the correct amounts from the *E4 Support* sheet. We'll use a VLOOKUP to find the correct account and then use the MATCH function to find the department column. Since the account number for our first account is stored in *B16*, and the department is stored in *E16*, we write the following formula to retrieve the debit amount:

```
=VLOOKUP($B16,allocations,
MATCH($E16,INDEX(allocations,1,0),0))
```

Where:

- **$B16** is the lookup value, the account number

- **allocations** is the lookup range

- **MATCH($E16,INDEX(allocations,1,0))** returns the department column

- **0** means exact match

We fill the formula down for all debit amounts and copy it to retrieve the credit amounts for the corporate department. We are happy because recording this journal entry has never been easier.

EXERCISE 5—ACCRUED PAYROLL

This journal entry helps us record accrued payroll.

 **PRACTICE**

To work along, please refer to the Exercise 5 worksheet.

We know that there are often days between the final payroll period and the last day of the month for which we are obligated to pay our employees. This means that we want to record a liability and related expense for the workdays that fall between the date of our final pay period and the last day of the month.

The *Exercise 5* sheet is our journal entry cover sheet, and we'll pull the values from the support sheet in a bit.

The *E5 Support* sheet does all of the hard work. The *Settings* section enables the user to enter the average daily wages and salary, as well as the overhead rate. The *Accrual* section contains our calculations. We compute the number of workdays that fall between the pay period end date and the last day of the month. We multiply the number of workdays by the average daily wage and salary, and then we apply the overhead rate. To compute the number of workdays, we first need to determine the last day of the pay period. This brings us to the *E5 Data* sheet.

The *E5 Data* sheet computes the last date of each pay period. The input cell stores the last day of the first pay period of the year. Then 14 days are added to that to compute the last day of the next pay period, and so on. We name the pay periods range **ppe**. Now that we see how the pay period end range is set up, let's turn back to the *E5 Support* sheet.

The *E5 Support* sheet includes one row for each month so that we can easily retrieve the accrued payroll for the closing period. Let's work through each of the columns.

The *Period* column simply contains the first day of each month.

The *Month End* column contains the last day of each month. We know that we can compute the last day of the month with the EOMONTH function.

XREF

EOMONTH is discussed in Volume 2, Chapter 16.

The *Pay Period End* column needs to retrieve the last day of the pay period from the **ppe** range. Since the last day of the month for the first month is stored in **C19**, we can use the following formula:

```
=VLOOKUP(C19,ppe,1,TRUE)
```

Where:

- **C19** is the lookup value, the last day of the month
- **ppe** is the lookup range
- **1** returns the value from the first column
- **TRUE** means we are performing a range lookup

We fill the formula down and we look good. It returns the pay period end date, which is the date through which employees are paid.

The *Workdays* column is where we compute the number of workdays between the pay period end date and the last day of the month. Since the pay period end date is stored in **D19** and the last day of the month is stored in **C19**, we can use the following formula:

```
=NETWORKDAYS(D19,C19)
```

Where:

- **D19** is the pay period end date for the last pay period in the month
- **C19** is the last day of the month

We fill the formula down and confirm it is working as expected.

The *Wages* and *Salary* columns multiply the number of workdays by the average daily wages and salary rates, respectively.

The *Overhead* column multiplies the overhead rate by the sum of the accrued wages and salary.

After filling all formulas down, we look good. To make it easy to retrieve the values based on the closing period, the range is named **pr_accrual**, which brings us back to our cover sheet.

The *Exercise 5* worksheet needs to retrieve the accrual amounts based on the pay period. Since this is Excel, there are numerous ways to tackle this. We'll use VLOOKUP to retrieve the amount based on the closing period as follows:

```
=VLOOKUP(period,pr_accrual,
MATCH(C17,INDEX(pr_accrual,1,0),0),0)
```

Where:

- **period** is the lookup value, the closing period

- **pr_accrual** is the lookup range

- **MATCH(C17,INDEX(pr_accrual,1,0),0)** returns the column number based on the account

- **0** means exact match

We fill the formula down for the debit amounts and then sum them to compute the credit amount. And there you have it—another automated journal entry!

Now, here's a question for you. What if we wanted an easy way to preview the impact of all these journal entries? Can we do that? We can—and we will—in the final exercise of the chapter.

EXERCISE 6—JE SUMMARY

In this exercise, we'll create a summary sheet that allows us to preview the impact of all our journal entries.

 **PRACTICE**

To work along, please refer to the Exercise 6 worksheet.

The worksheet contains a basic trial balance that includes the current account balances. We have one column for each journal entry, and our goal is to retrieve amounts from the cover sheets.

As you know, we like to write consistent formulas, and this sheet is no exception. If we can pull this off, it means that when we add a new journal entry, we simply fill the formula right instead of writing a new custom formula. Since we are trying to add up the values from the cover sheets based on accounts and departments, our instinct is to use a SUMIFS function. We'd like to store the sheet name as a text string in a cell and then use the cell reference in the SUMIFS function. That will enable us to write a consistent formula that pulls values from different sheets.

Can you think of a function that can create a valid reference based on a text string? If you said INDIRECT, good for you! We can use the INDIRECT function to create the correct references based on the worksheet names stored in the column headers.

The first account is stored in **B12**, the first department in **D12**, and the worksheet name in **G10**. The cover sheets are all set up with the same basic structure. The accounts are stored in Column **B**, the departments in Column **D**, debits in Column **F**, and credits in Column **G**. Thus, we can use the following formula to retrieve the debit amount for the first account:

```
=SUMIFS(
INDIRECT("'"&G$10&"'!F:F"),
INDIRECT("'"&G$10&"'!B:B"),$B12,
INDIRECT("'"&G$10&"'!D:D"),$D12)
```

Where:

- **INDIRECT(""&G$10&"'!F:F")** returns a reference to the debit column

- **INDIRECT(""&G$10&"'!B:B")** returns a reference to the account column

- **$B12** means the account

- **INDIRECT(""&G$10&"'!D:D")** returns a reference to the department column

- **$D12** means the department

We can fill the formula down and right and confirm that it retrieves the correct amount from the cover sheets as expected. Now all we need to do is subtract the credit amount from the debit amount computed above. To do this, we simply write a similar SUMIFS function and subtract it from the debit amount above. The final formula, with duplicate arguments omitted for simplicity, is shown below for reference:

```
=SUMIFS(INDIRECT("'"&G$10&"'!F:F"),…)-
SUMIFS(INDIRECT("'"&G$10&"'!G:G"),…)
```

Where:

- **SUMIFS(INDIRECT(""&G$10&"'!F:F"),…)** returns the debit amount

- **SUMIFS(INDIRECT(""&G$10&"'!G:G"),…)** returns the credit amount

We push the updated formula down and right and are pleased that we now have a summary sheet that shows us the impact of all the journal entries. Outstanding!

NOTE

When using the INDIRECT function to specify function arguments, remember that Excel won't automatically update the references when new rows or columns are inserted or when the worksheet name is changed because these values are text strings.

CHAPTER CONCLUSION

In this chapter we got a chance to streamline the real-world task of preparing journal entries for the monthly close. We looked at how to apply numerous features, functions, and techniques to help us build recurring-use workbooks that are easier and faster to maintain than ever before.

Chapter 22: Budget Ideas

SET UP

In this chapter our task is budgeting. How do you feel about budgets? Do you like them? It seems as if people don't really like budgets. If I had to guess the reason, I'd say it was probably because humans generally don't like constraints. We don't like budgets telling us "no." If an initiative or great idea isn't in the budget, it may not get approved or implemented. Budgets often feel like they prevent us from getting where we want to go.

Living within a budget is bad enough, but there is also the matter of preparing it. We don't really like that either. It feels as if we are being asked to predict the future, and who can really do that? Ridiculous. Business circumstances can change, making our initial assumptions invalid, and the budget can rapidly lose its accuracy and relevance. It can feel as though all our budget work was for nothing. Plus there is the looming accountability that comes when we compare budget with actuals. We don't really like variance reports or the related consequences. Let's face it; nothing about budgeting is fun.

It may seem as if budgets hinder or stop us. But here's the thing: budgets do help organizations plan, stay on track, and get where they want to go. Even though Excel probably won't make living on a budget easier, it can certainly help us prepare and maintain budgets.

HOW TO

Our company has many departments. We'll create one budget workbook for each department. Our goal is to make it easy for department managers to prepare their Selling, General & Administrative (SG&A)

expense budgets. As such, our workbooks will display prior year actual amounts for each account and provide an easy way to enter assumptions for budget year values.

The majority of our SG&A expenses are payroll-related. So we provide a headcount worksheet that makes it easy to document staffing assumptions. For other accounts we make the process easy by allowing managers to select a budget method for each account. The budget methods are an important feature of the workbook, so let's unpack this idea a bit.

For each account we want to make it as fast and easy as possible for the manager to define the budget amounts. To accomplish this we ask the manager to apply a budget method to each account by selecting it from the drop-down menu. There are several budget methods to choose from, as follows:

- Spread PY—spread prior year actuals evenly for budget year

- Match PY—match prior year actuals

- Headcount—apply based on budgeted headcount

- Manual—manually budget this account

- Decrease—apply the defined decrease percentage

- Zero—make budget year amounts zero

For example, a manager may want to budget office supplies by spreading prior year actual amounts because the expenditures are typically made evenly throughout the year. The manager may want to budget the trade shows account by matching prior year amounts because the trade show occurs in Q3 each year. Based on the selected budget method, our snazzy Excel formulas will compute the budget year amounts.

The good news is that we have all the Excel skills we need to build such a budget workbook. Now let's see if we can make budgeting fun.

EXAMPLES

Let's budget.

 **PRACTICE**

To work along, please refer to *Budget Ideas.xlsx*.

VIDEO

To watch the solutions video, please visit the Excel University Video Library.

EXERCISE 1—ADMIN SETTINGS

In this exercise, we'll set up a few assumptions.

 **PRACTICE**

To work along, please refer to the Exercise 1 worksheet.

This worksheet stores settings used throughout the workbook. For example, the overhead rate input cell, named *oh_rate*, will be used to estimate the overhead based on the wages.

The budget methods table, named ***bud_methods***, contains a list of budget methods that we want to provide as drop-down choices to the manager. We have created enough drop-downs during the series that we know we need to create a name that refers to the table name. However, this table has two columns, the *Method* and the *Index_num* column. We'll talk about the purpose of these two columns and then the name for the drop-downs.

First let's address the reason for having two columns instead of one. The end game is that we'll allow the user to pick a budget method from a drop-down menu, and based on the selection, our formula will perform the related calculations. We'll use the CHOOSE function, which, as you recall, expects an integer for its first argument. If we stored the drop-down choices in a table with one column, we could use the MATCH function to return the relative position as an integer as we've done in the past.

 XREF

Using MATCH with CHOOSE is discussed in Chapter 10.

But if we used the MATCH function, what would happen if we changed the order of the drop-down choices? For example, let's say that instead of the *Spread PY* method being the first choice, we wanted *Headcount* to be the first choice. If we changed the order of the choices for presentation purposes, then we would also have to modify the formulas by changing the order of the CHOOSE arguments accordingly. This is problematic. If we ever changed the choice order, we would have to hunt down each and every CHOOSE function to perform the manual update. Manually updating formulas is bogus. This brings us to the reason for having two columns in the *Budget Methods* table.

Having two columns allows the choice order to be independent of the function argument order. That is, we can change the order of the choices without needing to rewrite the formulas. We can use VLOOKUP instead of MATCH as the first CHOOSE argument. VLOOKUP will return the assigned index number value from the *Budget Methods* table. This also enables us to add a new budget method anytime and position it in the desired order.

Now let's close the loop with the name for the drop-downs. The name can't simply refer to the table name as we've done in the past because that would include all cells in the table. Instead, we need the name to refer to the structured reference for the *Method* column. We create a new name, **dd_methods**, which refers to the *Method* column of the **bud_methods** table, as follows:

```
=bud_methods[Method]
```

With our custom name in place, we are ready to move on to the next exercise.

EXERCISE 2—HEADCOUNT

This worksheet is where our managers can document their anticipated staffing for the upcoming year.

 **PRACTICE**

To work along, please refer to the Exercise 2 worksheet.

The *Hourly Wages* section of the sheet is where the manager can plan for hourly staff. For existing staff, the employee name is listed and a 1 notes each quarter they were employed during the prior year. If the manager intends to keep this staff member, the manager will simply enter a 1 into each of the quarterly columns for the budget year. Any new hires can be budgeted by entering the title, the number of corresponding staff by quarter, and the corresponding pay rate. For example, if the manager expects to hire a receptionist in Q3, then the manger will enter the title, a 1 in the *Q3* and *Q4* columns, and the pay rate.

The formulas to compute the wages based on the headcount are straightforward. For budget purposes, we compute the quarterly wage by multiplying the hourly rate by the number of hours per year divided by four. Since the Q1 headcount for the first employee is stored in *G13* and the hourly rate is stored in *K13*, we use the following formula to compute the budgeted wage amount for Q1:

```
=G13*($K13*hrs_year)/4
```

This formula is filled down and right and computes the budgeted wages for each quarter.

NOTE

> If we wanted more precision for quarterly wages, we could compute the wages based on workdays with NETWORKDAYS instead of dividing the annual amount by four.

The Salary section of the worksheet performs the same function for salaried employees. Since the headcount for Q1 is stored in *G26*, and the annual salary is stored in *K26*, we use the following formula to compute the budgeted salary amount for Q1:

```
=G26*($K26/4)
```

We fill the formula down and right, and we are looking good.

With the headcount budgeted, it is time to move to the next exercise.

EXERCISE 3—MANUAL

This worksheet provides a place for manual budget amounts.

 **PRACTICE**

> To work along, please refer to the Exercise 3 worksheet.

One of the budget methods is *Manual*. When the manager wishes to manually budget an account, we need to provide input cells accordingly. This worksheet provides a place to enter amounts for any manually budgeted accounts. Since the payroll values essentially are manually budgeted on the headcount worksheet, we retrieve those values. Then for the remaining accounts, we provide empty input cells that can be used as needed.

To retrieve the hourly wages and salary values from the **Exercise 2** headcount worksheet, we use direct cell references. For the *Overhead* account, we multiply the sum of the *Wages* and *Salary* accounts by the overhead assumption stored in the cell named **oh_rate**. To help retrieve manually budgeted values, the range is named **bud_manual**.

All right, now that the manager has a place to enter manually budgeted accounts, we are ready for the budget summary sheet. This is where all the magic happens.

EXERCISE 4—BUDGET

This worksheet enables the budget manager to select a budget method for each account. Our job is to write formulas that compute the budget year amounts based on the selected budget method.

 **PRACTICE**

To work along, please refer to the Exercise 4 worksheet.

The first several columns of the worksheet store the accounts, as well as the prior year actuals for each quarter.

The *Method* column is where we want to allow the user to select a budget method. We create a drop-down using the name *dd_methods,* which we set up previously. For now let's set the budget method to Spread PY for all accounts.

The next set of columns is where we compute the budget year amounts based on the selected budget method. We use the CHOOSE function to apply the selected budget method. For example, if the user selects Spread PY, then we need to divide prior year actual by four. If the user selects Match PY, then we need to use the actual amount from the corresponding prior year quarter. We build the CHOOSE function one argument at a time.

The first argument of the CHOOSE function is the index_num argument. We use VLOOKUP to retrieve the **index_num** from the budget methods table. We use VLOOKUP to retrieve the **index_num** integer value from a table so that going forward, if we want to change the order of the choices or add new budget methods, we won't need to reorder the CHOOSE function arguments. Since the first budget method selection is stored in *I20*, we write the following formula to retrieve the correct **index_num** from the budget methods table:

```
=VLOOKUP($I20,bud_methods,2,0)
```

Where:

- **$I20** is the lookup value

- **bud_methods** is the lookup range

- **2** returns the value in the second column

- **0** means exact match

We can fill the formula down and right and confirm it works to convert the budget method into an **index_num**. Let's use this VLOOKUP function as the first argument of the CHOOSE function, and we'll update our formula as follows:

```
=CHOOSE(VLOOKUP($I20,bud_methods,2,0),1,2,3,4,5,6)
```

Now all that remains is to replace the temporary argument values with expressions that compute the correct budget amount.

When the budget method is 1, the manager has selected Spread PY, so computing the budget year amount is pretty easy. We simply need to divide the prior year total by four. Since the prior year total is stored in *H20*, we can change the second argument from a 1 to the following:

```
$H20/4
```

When the budget method is 2, the manager has selected Match PY, so computing the budget amount is pretty easy. We simply need to pull the prior year actual for the corresponding quarter. Since the prior year actual for the first quarter for the first account is stored in *D20*, we can change the next argument from a 2 to the following:

```
D20
```

When the budget method is 3, the manager has selected the Headcount budget method. For each quarter, we need to divide prior year actual by prior year headcount, and then we apply the rate to the budgeted headcount. Since the prior year actual is stored in *D20*, the prior headcount is stored on the *Exercise 2* worksheet in cell *C37*, and the budgeted headcount is stored on the *Exercise 2* sheet in cell *G37*, we can change the next argument from 3 to the following:

```
(D20/'Exercise 2'!C$37)*'Exercise 2'!G$37
```

When the budget method is 4, the manager has selected Decrease as the budget method. That means we need to take prior year actual and decrease it by the percentage stored in the input cell named *dec_rate*. Since prior year actual for the first quarter is stored in *D20*, we change the next argument from 4 to the following:

```
D20*(1-dec_rate)
```

When the budget method is 5, the manager has selected Manual as the budget method. That means we need to pull in the values from the manual input worksheet. Since the account number is in *B20* and the quarter label in *J19*, we can use familiar lookup functions and change the next argument from 5 to the following:

```
VLOOKUP($B20,bud_manual,
MATCH(J$19,INDEX(bud_manual,1,0),0),0)
```

Where:

- **$B20** is the lookup value, the account number

- **bud_manual** is the lookup range

- **MATCH(J$19,INDEX(bud_manual,1,0),0)** returns the column based on the quarter

- **0** means exact match

When the budget method is 6, the manager has selected Zero as the budget method. That means we just need to place 0 into the cell. So we change the final argument from 6 to the following:

```
0
```

Now that we have replaced the temporary integer arguments with their actual expressions, here is the final formula for reference:

```
=CHOOSE(VLOOKUP($I20,bud_methods,2,0),
$H20/4,
D20,
(D20/'Exercise 2'!C$37)*'Exercise 2'!G$37,
D20*(1-dec_rate),
VLOOKUP($B20,bud_manual,MATCH(J$19,INDEX(bud_manual,1,0),0),0),
0)
```

We fill it down and right and confirm it is working as expected. Yes—it works!

But that formula is pretty long and hard to understand. So what do you say we create a named formula for each argument? Can we do that? We can—and we will—in the next exercise.

EXERCISE 5—MODULAR FORMULAS

In this exercise, we'll redo the formula from the previous exercise, but this time it will look clean and organized.

 **PRACTICE**

To work along, please refer to the Exercise 5 worksheet.

We are going to use the same budget methods and logic as the previous exercise. The only difference will be that our CHOOSE function will contain named formulas for each of its arguments. When we are done, the updated formula will look like this:

```
=CHOOSE(Method,Spread_PY,Match_PY,Headcount,Decrease,Manual,
Zero)
```

Since the underlying logic is the same as the previous exercise, we stay focused on converting the arguments into names. Remember from our previous discussion that when creating named formulas, the references are relative to the active cell. Keeping this in mind, let's begin.

 XREF

Relative references in names is discussed in Chapter 17.

We start with the first CHOOSE argument. We need to create a new name *Method* that will use the VLOOKUP function to return the index_num from the table. Thus, we begin by selecting the first formula cell, in this case *J20*. After selecting *J20*, and noting that *J20* is the active cell, we open the New Name dialog box and create a new name *Method* that refers to the following:

```
=VLOOKUP($I20,bud_methods,2,0)
```

We create a new name *Spread_PY* that refers to the following formula:

```
=$H20/4
```

We create a new name *Match_PY* that refers to the following formula:

```
=D20
```

We create a new name *Headcount* that refers to the following formula:

```
=(D20/'Exercise 2'!C$37)*'Exercise 2'!G$37
```

We create a new name *Decrease* that refers to the following formula:

```
=D20*(1-dec_rate)
```

We create a new name *Manual* that refers to the following formula:

```
=VLOOKUP($B20,bud_manual,
MATCH(J$19,INDEX(bud_manual,1,0),0),0)
```

Finally, we create a new name *Zero* that refers to the following formula:

```
=0
```

With all of our named formulas set up, we write the following formula into the worksheet:

```
=CHOOSE(Method,Spread_PY,Match_PY,Headcount,Decrease,Manual,
Zero)
```

We fill the formula down and right and confirm it works as expected. Way back in Volume 1, I mentioned that Excel formulas can be beautiful, and this formula is indeed beautiful!

CHAPTER CONCLUSION

In this chapter we were able to apply numerous features, functions, and techniques to streamline the mechanics of our budget process. Preparing the budget is now easier than ever. The only hard part is getting the department managers to stick to it!

Chapter 23: Common Workpapers

SET UP

Although accountants work on many different things in practice, we share some fairly common tasks. These tasks often result in specific documents. For example, when we need to figure out how each payment of a loan is allocated between interest and principal, we create a loan amortization schedule. When we need to determine when to recognize the cost of an asset over its useful life, we prepare a depreciation schedule.

For our final chapter, I have created a game to practice what you've learned. I'm going to throw a bunch of common tasks at you, and you'll have to apply what you know to build the related document in Excel. Ready to play?

HOW TO

Each task is a mission worth 10 points. Your goal is to complete each mission on your own. Here are the missions:

1. Depreciation

2. AR aging with formulas

3. AR aging with a PivotTable

4. AR aging with a PivotChart

5. Loan comparison

6. Loan amortization

7. Ratio analysis

You'll be working on seven missions, for a total of 70 possible points. Let's talk about scoring, penalties, and bonus points.

SCORING

The goal is to complete each mission on your own, without referring to the narrative in this book or any other external resource. You have successfully completed the mission when your workpaper provides accurate results. Your formulas don't have to be the same as the formulas provided; they just have to return the same results. You start each mission with 10 points, and you deduct penalty points and add bonus points as you go along.

PENALTIES

You lose points for incorrect results and using external resources. If your formulas don't provide the same result as the solution provided, deduct one point and try again. Revise the formulas, check again, and continue until they do work. If you decide to abandon the mission before getting accurate results, you receive zero points for the mission.

Deduct one point each time you refer to an external resource. Remember, the goal is to complete each mission on your own, without referring to the narrative in this book, the answers version of the workbook, the solutions video, or any other external resource. An external resource is anything outside of Excel. You can use the Excel Help system to look up a function or research its arguments, but you cannot use anything outside of Excel. This means no Google. I know you are clever, so I bet you are thinking about Excel's built-in web browser. Technically, you could use Excel's web browser to do a Google search and stay within Excel. Although I'd love to award you a bonus point for creativity, you are still accessing an external resource. Sorry, but it was a nice try.

BONUSES

Some missions have bonus points. Although the steps for accomplishing the bonuses aren't provided in the narrative below, they are available in the solutions videos.

I hope you have fun with this game, and I hope that you feel comfortable using Excel to complete your accounting tasks. Good luck, and the missions…start…now!

MISSIONS

Complete each mission below and keep track of your score on the Start Here sheet as you proceed.

 **PRACTICE**

To work along, please refer to *Common Workpapers.xlsx*.

 VIDEO

To watch the solutions video, please visit the Excel University Video Library.

MISSION 1—DEPRECIATION

In this mission, we'll create a basic deprecation schedule.

 **PRACTICE**

To work along, please refer to the Mission 1 worksheet.

Mission Briefing

Let's walk through the worksheet sections. The *Settings* section of the worksheet contains a single input cell, which represents the date that the depreciation schedule should begin. The columns use dynamic headers that are based on the start date. The *Deprecation* section contains the relevant asset information and is where you will write your formulas.

The mission objective is to compute straight-line depreciation. Consistent formulas are required, so you should write a formula and fill it down and right through the depreciation schedule. You will want to ensure that your formulas fully depreciate each asset by viewing the *Alert* column.

Once you have completed the mission, check your results against the *M1 Solution* worksheet.

Bonus: Award one bonus point if you display the *Alert* column as a Conditional Formatting icon set. Use a green circle icon for good (fully depreciated) and a red circle icon for bad.

Penalties: Deduct one point each time you reference an external resource. Remember—using the Excel Help system to research functions and arguments is okay and can be done without a penalty. If you check your formula against the solution worksheet and it returns a different result, deduct one point and try again. Continue until your formula returns the same result.

Begin your mission now. Good luck, I know you can do it!

Mission Debrief

After you have tried to accomplish this mission on your own, feel free to continue reading to learn more. The solution provided below is but one possible solution. Since this is Excel, there are several ways to write the formula. Your formula doesn't have to be the same as the one below, but it does need to return the same result.

The formula needs to compute the straight-line depreciation amount in each column that falls between the in-service date and the end of the estimated useful life. Let's take it one step at a time. We'll start by figuring out whether the month header falls within the depreciation period. We want Excel to return TRUE if the column header date falls between the in-service date and the end of the estimated useful life. We can use the AND function. Since the first dynamic header is stored in *G13*, the in-service date is stored in *E14*, and the life is stored in *D14*, we can use the following formula:

```
=AND(G$13>=$E14,G$13<=EOMONTH($E14,$D14-1))
```

Where:

- **G$13>=$E14** determines if the date header is greater than or equal to the in-service date

- **G$13<=EOMONTH($E14,$D14-1)** determines if the date header is less than or equal to the last day of the month of the useful life

We fill the formula down and right and confirm that it returns TRUE and FALSE as expected.

With that working, all we need to do is multiply that result by the amount we want to be displayed in the cell, which is the monthly deprecation amount. For this, we'll simply use the SLN function.

We update our formula as follows:

```
=SLN($C14,0,$D14)*
AND(G$13>=$E14,G$13<=EOMONTH($E14,$D14-1))
```

Where:

- **SLN($C14,0,$D14)** is the straight-line depreciation amount

- **AND(G$13>=$E14,G$13<=EOMONTH($E14,$D14-1))** returns TRUE for columns that fall within the deprecation period

We fill our updated formula down and right and spot-check several cells to ensure it is working as expected. We confirm our *Alert* column shows that the assets have been fully depreciated, so we are good to go.

MISSION 2—AR AGING

In this mission, we'll create an AR aging.

 **PRACTICE**

To work along, please refer to the Mission 2 worksheet.

Mission Briefing

The worksheet has four sections, so let's walk through them. The *Settings* section contains an aging date input cell. The *Aging Buckets* section defines the days for each *AR Aging* column. These cells will be useful in your upcoming formula. The *AR Aging* section will contain the completed AR aging schedule. The *Aging Chart* section will contain the chart you create.

The mission objective is to build the AR aging schedule and related chart. You'll need to write a formula that places each invoice amount into the correct column based on the number of days. Once complete, you'll need to build a column chart that visually displays the AR aging totals.

Once you have completed the mission, check your results against the *M2 Solution* worksheet.

Bonuses: Award one point if you make it easy to show/hide the *Settings* and *Aging Buckets* sections. Give yourself one point for converting the *AR Aging* section title from a text string to a formula that reflects the current aging date—for example, "AR Aging as of June 30, 2017." You get one point for creating a dynamic chart title that retrieves the *AR Aging* section label stored in *B22* and one point for changing the AR Aging Bucket headers in *G24:K24* from static text to consistent formulas that return the same exact labels, 0-30, 31-60, 61-90, 91-120, 121+.

Penalties: Deduct one point each time you reference an external resource. If you check your formula against the solution worksheet and it returns a different result, deduct one point and try again. Continue until your formula returns the same result.

Begin your mission now. Good luck!

Mission Debrief

After you have tried to accomplish this mission on your own, feel free to continue reading to learn more. The solution provided below is but one possible solution. Your formula doesn't have to be the same as the one below, but it does need to return the same result.

We need to write a formula that places the invoice amount into one of several columns, based on the number of days. We'll use the AND function to return TRUE or FALSE if the value falls within the aging range, and then we'll multiply this result by the invoice amount. Since the amount for the first invoice is stored in **E25**, the days for the first invoice in **F25**, the first day in the aging range in **G18**, and the last day of the aging range in **G19**, we can use the following formula:

```
=$E25*AND(($F25>=G$18),($F25<=G$19))
```

Where:

- **$E25** is the invoice amount

- **$F25>=G$18** compares the number of days with the start day

- **$F25<=G$19** compares the number of days with the end day

We fill the formula down and right and—bam!—the AR aging is complete. Now let's add a little chart.

 NOTE

The above formula works for the final column, 121+, because Excel sorts numbers before special characters such as +. The comparison is TRUE for any number of days because any number is less than +.

In the *Aging Chart* section, let's create a column chart. We first need to select the chart data. We can do this by selecting two distinct ranges at the same time. Do you remember how to group-select two nonadjacent ranges? Yes, we do it by holding down the Ctrl key.

So, we first select the aging header cells **G24:K24**, hold down the Ctrl key, and then select the aging totals in **G36:K36**. With these two ranges selected at the same time, we insert a new column chart by clicking the following Ribbon icon:

- Insert > Column Chart

We pick any chart style, size it, and move it into place.

We just built a formula-based AR aging report. As you know, we can often reproduce formula-based reports with PivotTables. Can we create an AR aging report with a PivotTable? Yes, of course we can. Want to give it a try? I hope so, because that is your next mission.

MISSION 3—AR AGING PIVOTTABLE

In this mission, we'll build an AR aging PivotTable report.

 **PRACTICE**

To work along, please refer to the Mission 3 worksheet.

Mission Briefing

The AR aging report will be built on the *Mission 3* worksheet, and the corresponding data is stored on the *M3 Data* sheet. No modifications to the data or data table are allowed.

The mission objective is to build an AR aging report with a PivotTable. Specifically, it should age the open invoices by customer in 30-day buckets, such as 1-30, 31-60, and so on, up through >121. Hide the field headers and change the remaining label to *AR Aging*.

Once you have completed the mission, check your results against the *M3 Solution* worksheet.

Bonus: Award one point if you display a 91–120 column.

Penalties: Deduct one point each time you reference an external resource. If you check your report against the solution worksheet and it displays different numbers, deduct one point and try again. Continue until your report returns the same values.

Begin your mission now. You can do this!

Mission Debrief

After you have tried to accomplish this mission on your own, feel free to continue reading to learn more.

We will create a PivotTable based on the *tbl_e3* data, as follows:

- PT ROWS: Cust; COLUMNS: Days; VALUES: Sum(Amount); FILTERS: Status

Once the basic PivotTable is done, we just have a few tweaks. First let's filter the report to show only open invoices—that is, rows where the status is equal to open. Easy. Next let's group the Days field. Do you remember how? Yes, by using the Group command. In the Grouping dialog, we update the options so that the grouping starts at day 1, ends at day 120, and increments by 30 days. For cosmetic purposes, we'll apply a number format to the value field, showing commas and no decimals. We'll turn off field headers and change the name of the remaining report label to *AR Aging*. We pick a style we like, and I think we've got it!

In the previous mission, we also built an aging chart. Can you build an aging chart from a PivotTable? Well, I hope you can, because that is your next mission.

MISSION 4—AR AGING PIVOTCHART

In this mission, we'll build an AR aging chart with a PivotChart.

 **PRACTICE**

To work along, please refer to the Mission 4 worksheet.

Mission Briefing

The AR aging chart will be built on the *Mission 4* worksheet, and the corresponding data is stored on the *M3 Data* sheet. No modifications to the data or data table are allowed.

The mission objective is to build an AR aging chart with a PivotChart. Specifically, it should include open invoices only and display the total of each 30-day aging bucket in a column chart. You'll want to build the corresponding PivotTable first and then plot those values in a PivotChart.

Once you have completed the mission, check your results against the *M4 Solution* worksheet.

Bonus: Award one point if you display a 91–120 bucket.

Penalties: Deduct one point each time you reference an external resource. If you check your chart against the solution worksheet and it displays different values, deduct one point and try again. Continue until your chart displays the same values.

Begin your mission now. Stay focused. You can do it!

Mission Debrief

After you have tried to accomplish this mission on your own, feel free to continue reading to learn more.

Begin by inserting a new PivotTable, as follows:

- PT ROWS: Days; VALUES: Sum(Amount); FILTERS: Status

Update the filter to include rows where *Status* is equal to *Open*. Group the Days field into 30-day buckets from 1 to 120. Then insert a column PivotChart by selecting the PivotTable and using the following Ribbon command:

- PivotTable Tools > Analyze > PivotChart

Pick a style, and size and position the chart as desired.

MISSION 5—LOAN COMPARISON

In this mission, we'll compare loans with different terms.

 **PRACTICE**

To work along, please refer to the Mission 5 worksheet.

Mission Briefing

The worksheet has three sections. The *Settings* section stores the loan amount. The *Analysis* section is designed to compare three different loans. The *Chart* section is designed to display the loan comparison as a stacked column chart.

The mission objective is to complete the analysis and create the chart. Complete the analysis by writing four unique formulas that return positive values for the monthly payment, total principal, total interest, and total payments during the life of the loan. Once you've written them for Loan 1, fill the formulas right for the remaining two loans. Next insert a stacked column chart that plots the total interest and total principal.

Once you have completed the mission, check your results against the *M5 Solution* worksheet.

Bonus: Award one point if you show a data table at the bottom of the chart. Add one point for plotting the monthly payment in the chart on the secondary axis.

Penalties: Deduct one point each time you reference an external resource. If you check your worksheet against the solution worksheet and it displays different values, deduct one point and try again. Continue until your worksheet displays the same values.

Begin your mission now. You have trained and prepared for this. You can do it.

Mission Debrief

After you have tried to accomplish this mission on your own, feel free to continue reading to learn more.

We've previously discussed each of the functions needed, so let's just jump right into the monthly payment formula. Since the annual interest rate for the first loan is stored in *C19*, the number of months in *C20*, and the principal amount in *C14*, we can use the following formula to compute the monthly payment and return it as a positive value:

```
=ABS(PMT(C19/12,C20,$C$14))
```

To compute the total principal and return it as a positive number, we write the following formula:

```
=ABS(CUMPRINC(C19/12,C20,$C$14,1,C20,1))
```

To compute the total interest and return it as a positive number, we write the following formula:

```
=ABS(CUMIPMT(C19/12,C20,$C$14,1,C20,1))
```

To compute the total payments, we simply add up the total principal and total interest amounts as follows:

```
=SUM(C22:C23)
```

We fill the formulas right, and our analysis is looking good. With that done, let's display our data graphically. We want to show the total payments in a stacked column chart that combines total interest and total principal. We first select the header cells *C18:E18*, hold down the Ctrl key, and then select the data range *C22:E23,* which contains the principal and interest payments. We insert the stacked column chart with the following Ribbon command:

- Insert > Column Chart > Stacked Column

Now that we are done, we can enter various principal, rate, and month assumptions and the analysis and chart update accordingly.

But in addition to the summary values, we would like to see a full amortization schedule. That sounds like a great idea for your next mission.

MISSION 6—LOAN AMORTIZATION

In this mission, we'll create a loan amortization schedule.

 **PRACTICE**

To work along, please refer to the Mission 6 worksheet.

Mission Briefing

The worksheet has two sections. The *Loan Values* section contains four input cells and four calculated summary values. The *Amortization Schedule* section will display specific values for each period of the loan.

The mission objective is to complete the amortization schedule. Specifically, you'll need to write seven formulas, one for each column. The formula details are provided in the worksheet. Be sure that you have filled the seven formulas down to the skinny row and that none of the formulas return an error. Set the print titles to repeat the amortization schedule column headers, just in case multiple pages are printed. Finally, conditionally format the amortization schedule formula cells so that nothing is displayed for rows beyond the loan term.

Once you have completed the mission, check your results against the **M6 Solution** worksheet.

Bonus: Award one point if you set a Print Area and then change the corresponding name to refer to a formula that returns a range that starts with the Loan Values section header and ends with the last period in the loan term. This will prevent any excess or blank pages from being printed. Give yourself one point for allowing the user to enter only positive decimals for the principal and rate input cells, positive whole numbers for months, and a date that is the first day of the month for the loan date. You get one point for allowing the user to select and change the four input cells only.

Penalties: Deduct one point each time you reference an external resource. If you check your worksheet against the solution worksheet and it displays different values, deduct one point and try again. Continue until your worksheet displays the same values.

Begin your mission now. Take your time, apply your skills, and good luck.

Mission Debrief

After you have tried to accomplish this mission on your own, feel free to continue reading to learn more. Your formulas don't have to be the same as the formulas below, but they do need to return the same results.

Period. The period formula needs to start at 1 and increase by 1 for each row. We know we need to fill the formula down, so we'll add 1 to the value in the row above. Since the row above the first period is a text column header, we'll need to use a SUM function instead of the addition operator, which returns an error if you try to add a text string. Since the column header cell is **B30**, we use the following formula to populate the first period cell in **B31**:

```
=SUM(B30,1)
```

This has the effect of adding one to the value in the cell above and works for all periods, including the first. We fill the formula down to the skinny row and confirm we are looking good.

Date. The *Date* column needs to store the first day of the month for each period starting with the loan date input cell value. We need to fill the formula down. We want to use the EOMONTH function to compute the last day of the month for the previous period and then add one day. If we used this function for the first period, we would get an error because the cell above the first period is the column label and the EOMONTH function returns an error if we use a text string. So we'll simply use IFERROR to return the loan date input cell value for the first period. Since the header cell is **C30** and the loan date input cell is named *date*, we write the following formula:

```
=IFERROR(EOMONTH(C30,0)+1,date)
```

We push the formula down and confirm it shows the first day of the month for all periods.

Beginning Balance. Next is the *Beginning Balance* column. The beginning balance is the loan amount for the first period and the prior ending balance for subsequent periods. We'll leverage the fact that the addition operator returns an error when you try to add a text string. Since the principal input cell is named **prin** and the ending balance for the prior row is **H30**, we write the following formula into **D3:**

```
=IFERROR(H30+0,prin)
```

We push the formula down, and since the ending balance isn't computed yet, the results are not accurate. But we feel pretty confident it will work, so for now let's push ahead to the next formula.

Payment. The *Payment* column needs to be the monthly payment amount. This is the same for all periods, so we'll simply refer to the monthly payment cell. Since the monthly payment is computed in **H22**, we write the following formula in cell **E31**:

```
=$H$22
```

We push the formula down and—hey, that one was easy.

Principal. The *Principal* column needs to display the portion of the monthly payment that is applied to the principal balance. Although we haven't specifically examined the function that computes this, we have discussed how to find and implement functions. So we open the Insert Function dialog and do a search or browse the financial functions. We discover the PPMT function that computes the principal payment amount of a loan for a given period.

We know these types of finance functions return a negative value because of the cash flow model, so we wrap an ABS function around it. Additionally, we want to substitute 0 instead of any error that the function may generate for periods that are outside of the loan term, so we wrap an IFERROR function around it. Since the interest rate is stored in the input cell named *rate*, the first period in **B31**, the number of periods in an input cell named **months**, and the loan amount in an input cell named **prin**, we write the following formula:

```
=IFERROR(ABS(PPMT(rate/12,B31,months,prin)),0)
```

We push the formula down, and we notice that the value returned increases during the loan term as expected.

Interest. The *Interest* column needs to compute the portion of the monthly payment that is applied to interest. Again we'll use the Insert Function dialog box to locate the IPMT function, which returns the interest payment for any given period. Again we wrap the ABS function around it to ensure a positive number is returned and an IFERROR function around that to replace any errors generated for formulas beyond the loan term with a zero. The resulting formula is shown below:

```
=IFERROR(ABS(IPMT(rate/12,B31,months,prin)),0)
```

We fill the formula down and note that the amount decreases over time as expected.

Just to double-check, we know that the sum of the principal and interest column for any row should be equal to the monthly payment amount. We spot-check a couple of rows by selecting the principal and interest amounts and looking at the status bar in the lower right of the Excel window, and we confirm that the sum is indeed equal to the monthly payment amount. That makes us, as accountants, all warm and fuzzy inside.

Ending Balance. The *Ending Balance* column represents the ending principal balance after the payment, so we simply need to subtract the principal amount from the beginning balance. Since the beginning balance is stored in *D31* and the principal portion of the payment in *F31*, we can use the following formula:

```
=D31-F31
```

We fill the formula down, and now the amortization schedule is complete. To spot-check it, we verify that the ending balance amount for the loan term row is equal to zero. Yes—it worked!

With our formulas working, the hard part is done. All that remains now is a couple of cosmetic items. First we want to ensure that if the user prints the amortization schedule, the column headers appear on each printed page. So we set the Print Titles to repeat the amortization schedule header row by using the following Ribbon icon:

- Page Layout > Print Titles

We pick row *30* by selecting the entire row. We confirm that Excel places the absolute row reference *$30:$30* into the dialog field and we close the dialog box.

Finally, let's hide formula results for rows beyond the loan term. To do this, we'll use a feature we've used numerous times during our time together—conditional formatting. We'll use the custom number format ;;; to hide the formula results. We select the amortization formulas all the way down to the skinny row. Then we insert a new conditional formatting rule that uses a formula to determine which cells to format. Our formula needs to return TRUE for any periods beyond our loan term. So we'll use a simple comparison formula. Since the first period is calculated in **B31** and the number of periods of the loan term is stored in an input cell named ***months***, we write the following conditional formatting formula:

```
=$B31>months
```

We apply the custom number format ;;; and apply the rule. Bam! All the values in the rows beyond the loan term disappear. Just to make sure this is working, we change the months input cell value and confirm that only the values within the loan term are displayed. It feels good to use Excel like a boss.

MISSION 7—RATIO ANALYSIS

In this mission, we'll perform some basic ratio analysis.

 **PRACTICE**

To work along, please refer to the Mission 7 worksheet.

Mission Briefing

This mission has three worksheets. The ***Mission 7*** worksheet will contain our ratio analysis. The ***M7 Analysis*** sheet computes the ratios by retrieving values from the exported accounting data. The exported accounting data is stored in a table on the ***M7 Data*** sheet.

The mission objective is to complete the ratio analysis. You'll need to begin on the ***M7 Analysis*** sheet. Here, you'll write a formula that retrieves the amounts from the ***tbl_e7*** table. You should be able to fill the formula right, and then copy it down to retrieve all values.

Next you'll need to work on the **Mission 7** worksheet. For the current column values, write a formula that retrieves the corresponding value from the last column of the *M7 Analysis* data range named ***ratios***. For the *Year* column, insert sparklines to show the trend of the ratio over the year, and be sure set a red marker for the final data point, which represents the current value. In the *Variance* column, write a formula that computes the percentage difference between the current value and the target value. Be sure to use a positive percentage to represent a favorable variance and a negative percentage to represent an unfavorable variance. To know if the variance is favorable or unfavorable, you'll need to consider the target value, and whether having a current value larger than the target is good or bad. Use conditional formatting data bars to show green for good and red for bad, and set the conditional formatting range from -1 to 1. Finally, remove gridlines. And that's it.

Once you have completed the mission, check your results against the *M7 Solution* worksheet.

Bonus: No bonus points for this mission.

Penalties: Deduct one point each time you reference an external resource. If you check your worksheet against the solution worksheet and it displays different values, deduct one point and try again. Continue until your worksheet displays the same values.

Begin your mission now. May the force be with you.

Mission Debrief

After you have tried to accomplish this mission on your own, feel free to continue reading to learn more. Your formulas don't have to be the same as the formulas below, but they do need to return the same results.

The *M7 Data* sheet simply stores the exported accounting system data. We exported the data and converted the ordinary range into a table. When we did, we noticed that the date values stored in the table header row were converted from dates to text strings.

The *M7 Analysis* is where our work begins. We need to write a formula that retrieves the monthly balances from the data table. Of course, we need to be able to copy this formula down. We've performed similar two-dimensional lookups before with INDEX and MATCH. The only complexity is that the date headers here are stored as dates, whereas they are stored as text strings in the table. No problem—we know how to convert a date into a text string with the TEXT function. Since the first label is stored in *B18* and the first date header is stored in *C15*, we write the following formula in *C18* to retrieve the value from the *tbl_e7* table:

```
=INDEX(tbl_e7,
MATCH($B18,tbl_e7[Item],0),
MATCH(TEXT(C$15,"m/d/yyyy"),tbl_e7[#Headers],0))
```

Where:

- **tbl_e7** is the data table

- **MATCH($B17,tbl_e7[Item],0)** provides the row number

- **MATCH(TEXT(C$15,"m/d/yyyy"),tbl_e7[#Headers],0)** provides the column number

We hit the Enter key, and…yes—it works! We fill the formula right and confirm it retrieves the correct monthly balances. We copy the formulas down to retrieve the remaining amounts. To make it easy to retrieve values from this range, it has been named *ratios*. Now we turn our attention to the summary.

The *Mission 7* worksheet is our summary. We need to address the year, current, and variance columns. Let's take them one at a time.

The *Current* column will display the ratio values for the final month of the analysis. Since the analysis data is stored in a range named *ratios*, and the first ratio name is stored in cell *B15*, we write the following formula to retrieve the value from the last column in the range:

```
=VLOOKUP(B15,ratios,COLUMNS(ratios),0)
```

Where:

- **B15** is the lookup value

- **ratios** is the lookup range

- **COLUMNS(ratios)** returns the number of columns in the lookup range

- **0** means exact match

We copy this formula down to retrieve the amounts for all ratios in the worksheet.

The *Year* column will allow management to see the ratio trend over the past year. Since we don't have much space to work with, we use a sparkline. To create the current ratio sparkline, we select cell *C15* and then use the following Ribbon command:

- Insert > Line Sparkline

In the Create Sparklines dialog box, we select the data range by selecting the range of cells on the *M7 Analysis* sheet that computes the monthly current ratio, *C20:N20*. When we close the dialog, we see the sparkline in the cell. We want to add a marker that represents the current ratio amount. Since the current value is the last month in the analysis, we add a marker point by checking the following checkbox:

- Sparkline Tools > Design > Last Point

Now it is easy for management to see which data element is represented in the *Current* column.

Finally, we tackle the *Variance* column. The *Variance* column has two components, the variance amount expressed as a percentage and the conditional formatting data bars. We begin with the calculation of the variance percentage.

The variance percentage is the difference between the current and the target amounts divided by the target amount. Management wants us to display each variance as favorable or unfavorable. For some ratios, the variance is favorable when the current value exceeds the target—for example, when the profit margin is greater than the target. For other ratios, the variance is unfavorable when the current value exceeds the target—for example, when the debt ratio is greater than the target. To accommodate this request, we include a comparison operator next to each target value. This makes it clear to everyone whether our goal is to be above or below the target value—for example, the quick ratio target is > 4 and the debt ratio target is < 1. To compute the variance and communicate whether the variance is good or bad, our formula needs to consider the comparison operator and its logic. The math that computes the percentage is the same for all ratios, current minus target divided by target. We just need to adjust the sign so that a positive value represents a favorable variance and a negative value indicates an unfavorable variance. Since the current is stored in *D15,* the target is in *F15*, and the comparison operator in *E15*, we write the following formula:

```
=((D15-F15)/F15)*IF(E15=">",1,-1)
```

We can copy this formula down for all ratios and confirm the variance is being expressed correctly. Now that we have computed the variance percentage, we would like to quickly communicate whether each ratio is favorable or unfavorable, as well as provide a sense of how favorable or unfavorable. To accomplish this, we use a conditional formatting data bar.

The second variance column simply retrieves the value from the first variance column. To apply a data bar, we select the second variance column cells and use the following Ribbon command:

- Home > Conditional Formatting > Data Bars > Green Data Bar

So far, so good, but let's dial it in. We want to make a couple of cosmetic changes, so we open the Edit Formatting Rule dialog box. Since we want to hide the percentage in the data bar cells, we check the *Show Bar Only* checkbox. Since we want to give the reader an indication of how the variance compares on a scale of -100 percent to 100 percent, we update the minimum and maximum values from the default (Automatic) to a minimum number of -1 and a maximum number of 1. We apply these changes, and our data bars are looking good.

The last step is to remove the worksheet's gridlines, which we do with the following checkbox:

- View > Gridlines

Now our summary looks clean and ready to deliver. At a glance, management can quickly determine the current ratio value, its trend over time, how it compares with the target, and how far off target we are. But, of course, our favorite part is that our worksheet is easy to update and maintain over time.

CHAPTER CONCLUSION

I hope you had fun working on the missions! As we reflect on these worksheets, we are reminded of the workbook design principles discussed in Volume 1. Automation is delegating tasks to Excel, such as the dynamic section title in Mission 2. Bulletproof workbooks anticipate and address potential errors, such as the data validation and worksheet protection used in Mission 6. Checking for errors is detecting and reporting potential errors, such as the alert column in Mission 1. Design ensures that data flows through the workbook in an organized and structured manner, such as the data in Mission 7. Efficiency is making the workbook easy to maintain and update each cycle, such as the PivotTable used in Mission 3. These principles helped us figure out which features, functions, and techniques to use, and I hope they can serve as a guide in your own workbooks as well.

My goal is that you are able to apply all of your Excel skills and knowledge to your accounting tasks and build efficient workbooks—efficient not only for the current period but for all future periods. I want your recurring-use workbooks to be dialed in so that you can get your work done fast.

Conclusion

The primary objective of this volume was to discuss the features, functions, and techniques that enable you to prepare efficient workpapers.

I'm proud of you for working through these four Excel University volumes, and if I can leave you with any inspirational words of wisdom, it would be these: be lazy. Wait, what? Yep, be lazy. You see, when you are lazy, you look for as many opportunities as possible to delegate your manual tasks to Excel. You figure out clever ways to have Excel do your work for you, and you devise workbooks that require as little human effort as possible to update. That's what I'm talking about. Get Excel to do your work so that you can get your work done faster and more efficiently.

And remember—Excel rules!

Shortcut Reference

The following list reflects the shortcuts presented through this volume.

Shortcut	Action	Volume	Chapter
Arrow Keys	Navigate within worksheet and cell values	1	6
Shift+Arrow Keys	Extend selection	1	6
Ctrl+Arrow Keys	Jump to edge of region or word	1	6
Ctrl+A	Select all cells in region	1	6
F2	Edit mode	1	6
F4	Cycle through cell reference styles (absolute, relative, mixed)	1	6
Double-click fill handle	Fill formula down	1	6
Ctrl+PageUp Ctrl+PageDown	Activate previous/next sheet	1	6
Alt+=	Insert SUM function	1	6
F5	Go To	1	7
Ctrl+T and Alt+N, T	Insert table	1	8
Alt+N, T	Insert table	1	8
Alt+D, L	Data validation	1	9
Alt+A, V, V	Data validation	1	9
Alt+Down Arrow	Expand drop-down	1	9
F3	Paste name	1	9
Alt+I, N, D	Insert name	1	9
Alt+M, N	Insert name	1	9
Ctrl+F3	Insert name	1	9
Alt+O, R, E	Format row height	1	12
Alt+I, R	Insert row	1	12
Alt+H, I, R	Insert row	1	12
Alt+O, C, W	Format column width	1	12
Alt+O, H, H	Hide sheet	1	13
Alt+O, H, U	Unhide sheet	1	13

Shortcut	Action	Volume	Chapter
Alt+O, H, R	Rename sheet	1	15
Alt+E, L	Delete active sheet	1	15
Alt+I, W	Insert worksheet	1	15
Ctrl+Enter	Enter formula and fill it down	1	18
Shift+Ctrl+PageUp Shift+Ctrl+PageDown	Group select adjacent sheets	1	18
F9	Convert formula text to evaluated result	2	2
Alt+E, I, D	Fill down	2	2
Ctrl+D	Fill down	2	2
Alt+E, I, R	Fill right	2	2
Ctrl+R	Fill right	2	2
Ctrl+C	Copy	2	2
Ctrl+V	Paste	2	2
Alt+E, S	Paste special	2	2
Ctrl+Alt+V	Paste special	2	2
Ctrl+Home	Jump to A1	2	2
Shift+Space	Select entire row	2	2
Alt+E, D	Delete selected row or column	2	2
Ctrl+-	Delete selected row or column	2	2
Alt+I, C	Insert column	2	2
Alt+H, I, C	Insert column	2	2
Ctrl+Space	Select entire column	2	2
Ctrl+Shift+Space	Select all cells	2	2
Alt+H, 6	Increase indent	2	14
Alt+H, 5	Decrease indent	2	14
Alt+O, D	Conditional formatting	2	25
Ctrl+PageUp Ctrl+PageDown	Dialog Box tab control navigation	3	2
Alt+Underlined Letter	Activate dialog box control with underlined letter	3	2
Tab	Navigate through dialog box controls and fields	3	2
Shift+Tab	Navigate through dialog box controls in reverse order	3	2

Shortcut	Action	Volume	Chapter
Arrows	Select values in certain dialog controls, such as a combo box	3	2
Letters	Jump to items within certain dialog box controls, such as list boxes	3	2
Space	Toggle selection in certain dialog box controls, such as a checkbox	3	2
Enter	Activate OK button in dialog box to accept changes	3	2
Esc	Activate Cancel button to close dialog without saving changes	3	2
Ctrl+1	Open Format Cells dialog box	3	2
Alt+O, E	Open Format Cells dialog box	3	2
Alt+D, R	Refresh PivotTable data while active	3	8
Alt+D, P	Legacy PivotTable Wizard	3	8
Ctrl+;	Insert current date	4	2
Ctrl+:	Insert current time	4	2
Ctrl+'	Copy value/formula	4	2
Ctrl+"	Copy value	4	2
Alt+PageDown	Page right	4	2
Alt+PageUp	Page left	4	2
Ctrl+Tab	Next workbook	4	2
Ctrl+Shift+Tab	Previous workbook	4	2
Alt+W, W	Switch windows	4	2
Ctrl+.	Move active cell to corners of selected range	4	3
Tab	Move active cell through selected range	4	3
Shift+Tab	Move active cell through selected range	4	3
Alt+H, S, U	Sort dialog	4	3
Alt+A, T	Filter controls	4	3
Ctrl+Shift+L	Filter controls	4	3

Shortcut	Action	Volume	Chapter
Alt+=	Insert SUBTOTAL under filtered range	4	3
Shift+Alt+Right	Group	4	4
Shift+Alt+Left	Ungroup	4	4
Alt+A, H	Hide Outline group	4	4
Alt+A, J	Show Outline group	4	4
Ctrl+9	Toggle Outline buttons	4	4
Alt+H, K	Accounting format without symbol	4	5
Ctrl+$	Currency format	4	5
Ctrl+%	Percentage format	4	5
Ctrl+Mouse Wheel	Zoom	4	6
Alt+P, SP	Page Setup dialog	4	6
Ctrl+P	Print preview	4	6
Ctrl+F2	Print preview	4	6
Alt+R, P, S	Worksheet protection	4	7
Alt+R, P, W	Workbook protection	4	7
Ctrl+K	Hyperlink dialog	4	8
Ctrl+G	Go To	4	8
F9	Calculate now	4	11
Shift+F9	Calculate worksheet	4	11
Shift+F3	Insert function	4	14
Alt+M, F	Insert function	4	14
Ctrl+F1	Ribbon tab display	4	15
Ctrl+[	Direct precedents	4	15
Ctrl+]	Direct dependents	4	15
Ctrl+Shift+{	All precedents	4	15
Ctrl+Shift+}	All dependents	4	15
Ctrl+A	Select all data cells in table	4	16
Ctrl+*	Select all	4	16
Ctrl+Alt+F3	New name	4	17
Alt+M, M, D	New name	4	17

Function Reference

The following list reflects the functions presented through the series.

Function	Returns	Volume	Chapter
PMT	The payment of a loan	1	3
SUM	The sum of a range	1	3
SUBTOTAL	The subtotal of the range excluding other SUBTOTAL functions	1	11
ROUND	The value rounded to the specified number of decimals	1	17
SUMIFS	The sum of a range based on specified conditions	2	3
VLOOKUP	The related value from lookup range	2	5
MATCH	The relative position of a list item	2	6
VALUE	The numeric value of a text string that represents a number	2	7
TEXT	The text string of a value in the specified format	2	7
INDEX	A cell value from a range at a given position	2	8
IFERROR	A specified value when its first argument is an error	2	9
IF	The specified value based on its first argument	2	10
COUNTIFS	The count of a range based on specified conditions	2	13
EOMONTH	The last day of the month	2	16
MONTH	The month number of the date	2	17
YEAR	The year of the date	2	17
DAY	The day of the date	2	17
DATE	A date based on its arguments	2	18
CONCATENATE	A text string that combines its arguments	2	19
AND	TRUE when all arguments are TRUE; otherwise FALSE	2	25
GETPIVOTDATA	Values from a PivotTable	3	20

Function	Returns	Volume	Chapter
LEFT	A given number of characters from the beginning of a text string	3	24
RIGHT	A given number of characters from the end of a text string	3	24
MID	A given number of characters from the middle of a text string	3	24
FIND	The position of the matching character in a text string	3	24
LEN	The length of a text string	3	24
REPT	A text string that repeats a given character a specified number of times	3	26
HYPERLINK	A hyperlink to the specified destination	4	9
MAX	The largest number from its arguments	4	10
MIN	The smallest number from its arguments	4	10
OR	TRUE if one or more arguments are TRUE	4	10
NOT	Reverses a Boolean value	4	10
CHOOSE	The value based on the specified argument	4	10
OFFSET	A range reference based on its arguments	4	11
ROW	The row number of the reference	4	11
ROWS	The number of rows in the reference	4	11
COLUMN	The column number of the reference	4	11
COLUMNS	The number of columns in the reference	4	11
INDIRECT	An Excel reference based on a text string	4	11
ADDRESS	A cell reference based on its arguments	4	11
TRIM	A text string with excess spaces removed	4	12
SUBSTITUTE	A text string after replacing specified characters	4	12
DOLLAR	A text string formatted as a currency	4	12
UPPER	A text string with all upper case text	4	12
LOWER	A text string with all lower case text	4	12
PROPER	A text string with proper case text	4	12
DATEVALUE	A date from a text string that represents a date	4	13
EDATE	A date a given number of months before or after the specified date	4	13

Function	Returns	Volume	Chapter
WEEKDAY	The day of the week	4	13
TODAY	Today's date	4	13
NOW	Current time	4	13
NETWORKDAYS	The number of workdays between two dates	4	13
WORKDAY	The end date given a start date and the number of workdays	4	13
CUMPRINC	The cumulative principal paid on a loan between two periods	4	14
CUMIPMT	The cumulative interest paid between two periods	4	14
PV	The present value	4	14
SLN	The straight-line depreciation of an asset	4	14
SYD	The sum-of-years' digits depreciation of an asset	4	14
DB	The depreciation using the fixed-declining balance method	4	14
DDB	The depreciation using the double-declining balance method	4	14
VDB	The depreciation using the double-declining method or some other method you specify	4	14
ROUNDUP	The number rounded up, away from zero	4	14
ABS	The absolute value of a number	4	14

Index

www.ingramcontent.com/pod-product-compliance
Lightning Source LLC
Chambersburg PA
CBHW080153060326
40689CB00018B/3959